REVIVAL ON BROADWAY!

Messages to God's Church
From the Heart of
Times Square

Times Square Church Pulpit Series
The Ministry of David Wilkerson

A Wilkerson Trust Publication

Introduction

It has been my joy and privilege to share my messages preached at Times Square Church with a great host of readers throughout the United States and around the world.

This book is a compilation of messages selected as being the most effective, measured by the many testimonies we have received from our readers.

The most common response to these messages has been: "We anxiously await every message....It seems they nearly always confirm what God is saying to me....Where I live, there is a famine of the true Word of God. Your messages are the only meat we receive...."

I trust these messages will prove to be spiritual meat to every hungry reader. I do not recommend reading more than one or two chapters a day. The reader needs time to prayerfully digest a little at a time, and should ask the Holy Spirit to illuminate it and apply it to the heart and mind.

Keep this book close at hand, especially for difficult and trying times. Included are a number of encouraging messages for times of crisis. You can go back and read certain chapters over again, each time gaining new strength and spiritual encouragement.

May the Holy Spirit open your eyes and deliver to you God's Word in season.

DAVID WILKERSON
Times Square, New York City

Contents

1

The Zadok Priesthood

Being Fearless Against Sin

The book of First Samuel tells us that an unnamed prophet came to Eli with an awful message. This unknown man delivered an amazing prophecy — one that has everything to do with what we see going on in the church today. It is a word that reveals much about dead, dry, ungodly ministers and churches in operation right now!

This prophecy tells of two priesthoods that would develop and continue, from that day forward until the very end of time. Both of these priesthoods would be ministering in the church. One would be a cursed, abominable shame. But the other would be a ministry after God's own heart.

The unnamed prophet told Eli: "Behold, the days come, that I will cut off thine arm, and the arm of thy father's house, that there shall not be an old man in thine house" (1 Samuel 2:31). He was describing a curse upon the ministry of Eli!

But then he continued: "And I will raise me up a faithful priest, that shall do according to that which is in mine heart and in my mind: and I will build him a sure house; and he shall walk before mine anointed for ever" (verse 35).

This prophecy of two priesthoods is being fulfilled today — right before our eyes. Indeed, both ministries are operating simultaneously, in nations all around the world!

First, the prophet spoke of the ongoing ministry of a self-centered, backslidden, compromising priesthood. He described those priests who are of the spirit of Eli, mentioning two things:

1. Such priests are people-pleasers more than pleasers of God. "Wherefore kick ye at my sacrifice and at mine offering...and honourest thy sons above me..." (verse 29).

Eli was soft on sin! He never made any decisions that would offend his two sons. Only once, in over fifty years of ministry, did Eli correct them.

They had been committing adultery, raping women, performing the most vile acts. Yet even then, all Eli could say to them was, "Why do you do this?" This man had no righteous indignation! He never shared God's wrath and hatred toward sin. Eli represents a priesthood of ministers who are afraid to reprove God's family, the congregation.

There are churches today that you can attend for up to a year and yet never hear one word of reproof. A church can be totally corrupted — half of the congregation divorcing, adultery rampant, teenagers sleeping around, children unruly. The whole congregation can be given over to pleasure, sports, entertainment — but there is never a word of correction from the pulpit. Instead, the pastor caters to the people's weaknesses and cravings. He is afraid to offend anyone — fearful that the offerings will go down and he'll lose his income.

This is the first characteristic of the evil ministry developing in Eli's soul. And it is the mark of every ongoing, compromising priesthood today!

2. They cater to their own needs and comfort rather than give themselves toward the needs of the flock. They "…make (themselves) fat with the chiefest of all the offerings of Israel my people" *(verse 29)*.

When the people brought the meat offering to the priest, it was supposed to go into the seething pot to be boiled. Afterward, the priest dipped a three-pronged hook into the pot, and whatever came out on the hook went onto his table.

But Eli's two sons didn't want the boiled, sodden meat. They wanted the red, raw filet mignon! So they brought their father the prime cuts. There was no sodden flesh on his table. That's how Eli got fat, lazy and careless. If he would have dealt with his sons, he might have lost his filet mignon.

Eli was concerned with his own interests, his own table. And that is what is happening in many dying churches today: Preachers are interested only in their own comfort, in caring for themselves — instead of spending time on their knees for the sake of the people! The prophet here was saying, "You are self-absorbed, Eli — feathering your own nest! To you, the ministry means nothing more than food on the table, security for you and your family. You don't really care about the flock. You're more interested in what goes onto your table than in what goes into the people's hearts. Yet you never once think about how your compromise and selfishness bring reproach to God's name. You never consider the people who watch as your sons steal the prime meat. You are soft on sin, afraid to

8

reprove — because you're consumed with things that make you comfortable!"

The Prophet Pronounced Three Terrible
Judgments on This Priesthood!

Every so-called minister who is of the seed of Eli — compromising, soft on sin, concerned only for himself — will face three judgments:

1. They will experience loss of all spiritual power and authority. "...they that despise me shall be lightly esteemed. Behold, the days come, that I will cut off thine arm [strength], and the arm of thy father's house..." *(1 Samuel 2 30-31)*.

To be "lightly esteemed" by the Lord meant a loss of God's favor and blessing. It meant having no impact against Satan's kingdom. Such a minister may be esteemed by others — but in God's eyes he is a lightweight, someone in whom the Lord puts no trust.

God said, "You despise Me by not preaching My whole counsel. You're not a man of prayer. You're not concerned about My people, but only about your success and reputation. You just want to make sure there's a crowd. You have lightly esteemed My Word — and now I am going to lightly esteem you! Go your way — do your own works. You are lightly esteemed in My eyes!"

This cutting off of God's anointing leaves the Eli priesthood to busy, helter-skelter programs — works of the flesh that merely look good. It all sounds like important kingdom work. But God refuses to touch it! It is simply busy activity — lightly esteemed ministries undertaken by lightly esteemed ministers!

2. They will be bypassed by the true anointing and blessing of God in the last days. "And you will see the distress of My dwelling, in spite of all that I do good for Israel..." *(verse 32, NAS)*.

In other words: "When I choose the time to pour out My Spirit, you'll be standing in ruins!" And that's exactly what is happening in America today: Preachers are standing in churches that are dead, dry and ruined! God has said to them, "I will pass you by!"

This priesthood will be standing among the ruins as God blesses and anoints another priesthood — men of God who have paid the price! Right now, in these last days, His anointing is falling on those who have given their lives completely to Him. The Spirit is laying hold of these praying, fearless men. But those of Eli's seed are being bypassed — left to play their church games!

God is saying, in essence, "In spite of all I do, you will not see the good! You will not be part of My last-day, holy remnant. You are lightly esteemed — and you will go about your ministry with no real spiritual authority!"

3. They will lose God's touch in the very prime of their life. "...all the increase of your house will die in the prime of life" *(verse 33, NAS).*

This verse is taken two ways. First, it was fulfilled literally when Saul sent Doeg up to Nob to slay eighty-five priests who were of the seed of Eli.

But the verse also has a spiritual application: It is saying that this priesthood will look good up to a certain point. The ministers will be very active and busy. But just at the time when they ought to be at their best — full of energy, power, wisdom and holiness, ready to be used the most — a spiritual death will take place. God is going to leave them! They'll be left standing before the people as dead men — while in the very prime of their lives!

Yet perhaps the most tragic of all the prophecies given by this unnamed man of God is that this backslidden, compromised priesthood would never be cut off from God's altars! The evil ministry would continue to the very end: "Yet I will not cut off every man of yours from My altar that your eyes may fail from weeping and your soul grieve..." *(verse 33, NAS).*

God will not cut them off! Compromising, spiritless, dead men are going to exist till the last day, when the Lord returns. But, God says, "What a grief they're going to be. They will be a cause for weeping!"

Yet Now I Want to Show You Another Kind of Priesthood.

This is the other ministry that the prophet said God was raising up:

"But I will raise up for Myself a faithful priest who will do according to what is in My heart and in My soul; and I will build him an enduring house, and he will walk before My anointed always" *(verse 35, NAS).*

This holy ministry is the Zadok priesthood! It is made up of faithful, holy ministers of God who walk and live according to His desire. And such a priesthood remains to this very day!

Everything that this unnamed prophet prophesied is fully illustrated in David's kingdom. David is a type of Christ, and Israel is a type of the church. David had two priests who fulfilled these two prophetic priesthoods to the letter: Abiathar and Zadok. "And hast thou not there with thee Zadok and Abiathar the priests?" *(2 Samuel 15:35).*

1. Let Us First Consider Zadok.

Zadok's name means "one who's proved righteous." "Now these are they that came to David to Ziklag.... And Zadok, a young man mighty of valour, and of his father's house twenty and two captains" *(1 Chronicles 12:1, 28)*. Zadok was the first young priest to recognize God's anointing on David.

Men were fleeing to David, coming from all over to join his forces. Zadok recognized that the Spirit had left Saul; his ministry now was all hype, flesh, with no call or touch of heaven. Zadok said, "I don't want any part of that kind of ministry. It's dead — and God has departed from it. I'm going with David, who has the Spirit's anointing!"

So Zadok went to David at Ziklag — never to leave him for the rest of his life! Through every rebellion, Zadok stood with him, a man proved righteous. David had captured the priest's heart — and Zadok never looked back.

Thank God, there are men of God like this in many pulpits today. These are men of prayer who are committed to Jesus, having walked away from all flesh, entertainment and worldliness. And you know it when you hear them preach — because something registers in your soul!

When others forsook David, Zadok remained faithful. David was running from his son Absalom, who had rebelled. And when David came to the brook Kidron, Scripture says, "Now behold, Zadok also came . . . and Abiathar went up..." *(2 Samuel 15:24, NAS)*.

Notice here that both Zadok and Abiathar were with David. Both were at the brook Kidron with him, and both went back to Jerusalem at David's order. So, while Absalom defiled David's concubines in full public view, and Israel went berserk with wickedness and revelry, two holy men stood in God's house — Zadok and Abiathar.

And so it is today! While the whole world is going to hell amid unheard-of wickedness, God still has His holy men serving at His altar. He still has a Zadok priesthood, faithful in all God's Word.

2. Consider Now the Abiathar Priesthood.

Abiathar's name means "at peace with God." He was with Zadok as they took the ark back to Jerusalem. At this point, Abiathar appears to be holy, dedicated, devoted, loyal to David. He would have nothing to do with Absalom's rebellion. He went about his ministry looking as pure and uncompromising as Zadok.

But why is he never mentioned in the Word after this? Why is he not named among the prophets? Why does his name die out? Something happened. Suddenly, Abiathar was "lightly esteemed" — and Zadok was made the example of the holy, remnant priesthood. Why? It was because Abiathar had the spirit of Eli in him! All those awful prophecies spoken by the unnamed prophet fell upon him — and it all happened quickly!

The unnamed prophet had said that not all such kind would be cut off. Abiathar's father and eighty-three other priests who wore an ephod were slain by Doeg. Only Abiathar escaped. He ran to David — and the ministry he represented survived, which was according to prophecy.

Yet just as the prophet had spoken, Abiathar — the seed of Eli — in the prime of his life and at the peak of his blessings, was seduced by the call of success. He lost his place with God's anointed!

You see, David had another son, Adonijah. His name means "success and prosperity." This young man pretended to introduce a "new move" in the land by naming himself king. Yet it was only another rebellion — not a move of God, but a snare of Satan. This was the very ministry the prophet had warned of: self-exaltation and success! "Then Adonijah... exalted himself..." *(1 Kings 1:5)*. It was all self-centeredness, pride. Adonijah said, "I will set myself up as king!"

This young man had been raised under a ministry of "no reproof": "And his father had not displeased him at any time in saying, Why hast thou done so?" *(verse 6)*.

Notice here: Everything the prophet had prophesied of this kind of ministry had come to pass. All of the elements he had said would happen under this kind of priesthood were in this man, Adonijah!

"And he conferred with Joab, the son of Zeruiah..." *(verse 7)*. Adonijah surrounded himself with ungodly men! There was not a holy man among them — not Zadok, not Nathan, not any faithful men of David *(see verse 8)*. And, Scripture says, this group met at "the stone of Zoheleth" — which means "place of the serpent."

This was a group of self-serving, success-driven, ego-stroking rebels. They cried, "Here is something new, something that works! Away with David's old, worn-out ways. God is doing a new thing in the land!"

Up to that point, Abiathar had been loyal to David. But now the word was out: "There's a new move taking place — some great, new thing happening in the land. And it's very exciting!" It grabbed the heart of Abiathar — because it looked like a ticket to success and prosperity. Now he could make it! He had found a new man and a new message.

I meet many people who come to this country from places in Europe, Africa and Asia where churches are dying. They hear about some new work happening in the churches here, and they become hungry to see it happen in their church — a new move of God!

Once, when I was overseas, I told one pastor friend, "You and your wife used to be on your faces continually, weeping before God. That's why your church was so blessed. But you've gotten so busy, you don't know God anymore!" This couple began to weep, confessing, "You're right!" But instead of repenting, they came to America — looking for some new program that would make their ministry work.

That is the ministry of Abiathar! He got caught up in a fleshly, ungodly work of Satan. And he gathered with the others at the stone of Satan, eating, drinking and shouting, "Long live King Adonijah!"

When David was told about it, he cried, "Get me Nathan!" You see, when God wants to do something that really counts for His eternal purposes, He calls on those who have been shut in with Him. David is a type of Christ here. And he cried, "Forget Abiathar. Go get Nathan! I lightly esteem Abiathar. Tell Nathan to get the trumpet and the oil, and to go anoint Solomon!"

So Solomon was anointed king. And the first thing he did was to kill Shimei, who cursed David. Then he began dealing with all of David's enemies — and he called forth Abiathar.

Now, I remind you that the unnamed prophet said this Eli-Abiathar ministry would never be cut off. And Solomon knew all about this prophecy. Abiathar should have been executed for treason. But instead, Solomon told him:

"You cast your lot in with my brother Adonijah. You tried to bring down this kingdom. And because of that, you deserve to die. But I'm not going to kill you. You carried the ark of God for my father, David, and you were afflicted with him. Because of those things, I will not put you to death at this time. Now, go to Anathoth, to your own field, to do your own thing. You are lightly esteemed!"

"So Solomon thrust out Abiathar from being priest unto the Lord; that he might fulfill the word of the Lord, which he spake concerning the house of Eli in Shiloh" *(2:27)*.

The Eli priesthood is still here today. But God says to their kind, "Go, do your own thing. I lightly esteem you!"

3. Ezekiel Understood the Prophetic
Importance of These Two Priesthoods!

Both the Zadok and Abiathar priesthoods were operating in Ezekiel's day. And, like the unnamed prophet, Ezekiel prophesied they both would flow as two streams of ministry to the very end:

"...mark well the entering in of the house, with every going forth of the sanctuary" *(Ezekiel 44:5)*. God was telling Ezekiel, "Stand at My house and see all the people coming and going. Discern all the activities going on here. It's all an abomination! They're bringing strangers and foreigners into My house to defile it!"

Likewise today, the abominations going on in churches are so horrible, God is saying, "Enough — I've had it!" Ungodly ministers have brought into the holy sanctuary rock-and-roll, entertainment, utter foolishness, singers who use drugs and alcohol and don't even know God. These people stand ministering in the pulpit, and the people don't even know the difference!

"And ye have not kept the charge of mine holy things: but ye have set keepers of my charge in my sanctuary for yourselves" *(verse 8)*. He was saying, in other words: "You've brought in foreigners, people who do not know Me, to keep charge of My sanctuary!" These were foreign elements — wicked, unholy, unseparated, still of the world. God's house was being profaned!

So God appointed an Abiathar priesthood to minister to a people whose hearts were set on idols. The shepherds had strayed far from God. They were filled with the spirit of Eli, chasing fame and success — and the people loved to have it so! Thus, God appointed idolatrous priests to give the people what they wanted. He said, "Like people, like priest!"

"Yet I will appoint them to keep charge of the house, of all its service, and of all that shall be done in it" *(verse 14, NAS)*.

How blind such ministers are! God says of them, "And they shall not come near unto me . . ." *(verse 13)*. They stand in the pulpit lightly esteemed by God, full of self and idolatry, nowhere near to the Lord. Yet they go through all the motions: preaching, teaching, counseling, all the ministerial duties. But they don't know the difference! They have no discernment, no witness of the Spirit.

Beloved, if you do not repent and surrender all to Jesus — if you hold onto an idol in your heart — you will end up listening to a minister who preaches to your idolatry!

God Made a Promise in His Word That If His People Would Repent and Return to Him With All Their Hearts, He Would Raise Up for Them Zadok Shepherds!

"Turn, O backsliding children, saith the Lord...and I will bring you to Zion: And I will give you pastors according to mine heart, which shall feed you with knowledge and understanding" *(Jeremiah 3:14-15)*.

Ezekiel prophesied that a Zadok priesthood would be very much alive and well in the last days: "But...the sons of Zadok, that kept the charge of my sanctuary when the children of Israel went astray from me, they shall come near to me to minister unto me, and they shall stand before me to offer unto me the fat and the blood, said the Lord God: They shall enter into my sanctuary, and they shall come near to my table, to minister unto me, and they shall keep my charge" *(Ezekiel 44:15-16)*.

There will be no mixture in this priesthood: "...they shall be clothed with linen garments; and no wool shall come upon them, while they minister..." *(verse 17)*. Wool mixed with linen represents mixture — a little bit of God and a little bit of flesh. But God says, "My priesthood is made of pure linen. There is no mixture!"

This Zadok priesthood will be fearless against sin — and will have the power to lead people into righteousness and holiness. "And they shall teach my people the difference between the holy and the profane, and cause them to discern between the unclean and the clean" *(verse 23)*.

These are the marks of the Zadok priesthood:

• They are not afraid to reprove with the power and authority of the Holy Ghost;

• They make clear to you what wrong and right are, until you gain the knowledge and wisdom to make right choices;

• These men know the voice of the Lord. They know what God speaks, because they sit and wait on Him! They don't pray, "Bless me, bless my programs, give me money...." Rather, they cry, "Oh, Jesus, I love You. I want to know Your mind and Your heart!"

You may be saying, "It's good to know all this about preachers." But God is saying to you right now: "What about you?"

Dear Saint, Did You Know This Message Is All About You?

Scripture says, "(He) hath made us kings and priests unto God and his

Father; to him be the glory and dominion for ever and ever..." *(Revelation 1:6)*. Beloved, this verse is true for the whole body. Everyone who calls himself or herself by God's name is to be a priest unto the Lord.

So, I ask you: Which priesthood describes your walk with God? Are you of Zadok? Or Abiathar? Do you receive reproof with joy, knowing that God wants to cut the cancer of sin out of you in order to heal you? Or are you self-centered — running around to conventions and seminars looking for comforting answers? Are you learning to discern God's voice for yourself, by giving quality time to Him in the secret closet? Or do you buy tape after tape of some evangelist, to try to get a word from heaven?

Everyone who lives by the name of Jesus should be learning to hear God's voice. He wants you to hear His word in your own heart. If you learn that, you can go to any church anywhere and know within five minutes if the Spirit of the Lord is there. If it's really Zadok, your hands will go up in the air. You'll say, "I'm hearing something good. Something is registering in my soul. This is God!"

Or — you will discern what is of Abiathar. And it will make you sick to your stomach! You will flee, because you cannot stand the stench of flesh.

Oh, God — give us the spirit of the Zadok Priesthood!

2   Bringing Christ Into Your Crisis

Three Faithful Commitments

Go with me to the plain of Dura near Babylon, where King Nebuchadnezzar had summoned every leader — governors, princes and sheriffs — from his far-flung empire. Imagine the sight — multitudes of people dressed in their various native garb, speaking many languages. And they all had gathered for one purpose — to honor the gods of the king!

Nebuchadnezzar had erected a huge, golden image ninety feet tall. And now these leaders, having made their way to the great plain of Dura, were to bow in worship as soon as the royal orchestra began playing. It was that or death!

But three Hebrew men — Shadrach, Meshach and Abednego — refused to bow. These men had been taken captive from Jerusalem by the Chaldeans and brought to the palace of Shushan. Here they had been trained in the language of the Chaldeans and, along with Daniel, had been appointed as leaders in the government. Now, all around them, men from other nations were bowing to the golden image, conforming to the king's decree. But they would not!

Jealous leaders reported this to Nebuchadnezzar — and when he heard of it, he flew into a rage. He thought, "How dare any member of my own government stand against me in disobedience!"

It was not unusual in those days to punish violators of the king's decrees by casting them into a burning oven. Jeremiah speaks of "... Zedekiah and...Ahab, whom the king of Babylon roasted in the fire" *(Jeremiah 29:22)*. No doubt, Nebuchadnezzar was used to seeing bodies thrown into an open furnace — seeing the instant flash of the burning bodies and smelling the stench of burning flesh. Now he was in such a rage, he ordered his soldiers to stoke the furnace seven times hotter than usual.

When the guards brought the three Hebrew men before the king, Nebuchadnezzar bellowed, "So — you refused to bow before my god when the music sounded. Well, I'm going to let you try it again. You should know the fiery furnace is burning seven times hotter right now. And if you don't bow this time, you'll be thrown in and roasted!"

You can be sure these three men could feel the heat of the white-hot furnace from where they stood. And they probably saw the strong soldiers falling exhausted as they stoked the furnace, overcome by the intense heat. These Hebrew men didn't want to die. They were human beings, like you and me. Anyone would be crazy to want to die roasting in a fire! Yet these men had an incredible faith placed in their hearts by the Holy Spirit. And so they replied to the king, "O king, we don't even have to think about our answer to you. We will not bow! Our God is able to deliver us. But even if He doesn't, we will not worship the image."

You know the rest of the story. Word probably spread about the great burning, and curious multitudes gathered the way crowds did for Old West hangings. People strained just to get a glimpse of these men who had dared to disobey the royal decree — and who would be roasted alive!

Soon the royal party arrived. The king took his seat — a safe distance from the heat, but close enough to witness the actual burning of the bodies. "Will these rebellious fools never learn?" he probably thought to himself. "Shortly, three more rebels will be nothing but ashes."

Then the three Hebrew men were brought in, bound hand and foot. The mightiest soldiers in the king's army had picked them up and were carrying them to the mouth of the furnace to cast them in. But the flames were so hot, the soldiers themselves began to fall, one after another — slain from the heat!

Somehow, the three Hebrews were finally cast into the oven. But the king was puzzled. There had been no sudden flash of roasting bodies, no smell of burning flesh. He peered into the fire — and he was astonished at what he saw. The three Hebrew men were walking about on top of the coals — as if they were walking on rose petals! The fire had only burned their bonds — and now their hands were raised in praise to God.

Nebuchadnezzar turned to one of his associates and said, "How many men did we throw in there?"

"Three, O King," came the answer.

"But I see four!" the king replied. "And none of them is burning. None is even hurt. One of them has the appearance of the Son of God!" *(see Daniel 3:24-25)*.

Now, how could a heathen king recognize the Son of God? It was because Christ's glory cannot be hidden. Whenever angels appear in Scripture, they are dressed in white and shine with a heavenly brightness. Yet this bright One was no seraphim; it was not Gabriel, nor Moses nor Elijah raised from the dead. This was Jesus Himself — and He was brighter than that seven-times-hotter flame!

Beloved, this testimony came from heathen lips: Christ appeared with the Hebrews in their crisis! And talk about a life-or-death situation. This was the crisis of a lifetime — a hopeless circumstance according to the flesh, one that demanded a miracle. But Christ walked in beside these men, comforting them. He came into it with them to rescue and deliver them.

This Message Is All About How You, I and Every Believer Are to Bring Christ Into Our Crisis!

Jesus did not come into the Hebrews' crisis to impress the heathen king. He had already done that in a previous chapter. When Daniel interpreted Nebuchadnezzar's dream, the king had declared, "...Of a truth it is, that your God is a God of gods, and a Lord of kings..." *(Daniel 2:47)*. But how soon he forgot this!

No, this was not an evangelistic visitation. God knew the heart of the vacillating king — and He knew that miracles impress heathen minds only for about three days. Rather, Jesus came into these men's crisis for one reason — for their sake alone! He came to comfort and rescue them because He loved them. The Lord of glory committed Himself to them in their hour of crisis — because they were totally committed to Him.

The truth is, our Lord does not commit Himself to every person's crisis. Scripture says when He was in Jerusalem at the Passover, ". . . many believed in his name, when they saw the miracles which he did. But Jesus did not commit himself unto them, because he knew all men, and...knew what was in man" *(John 2:23-25)*.

Jesus knows the deception in people's hearts. He knows many are willing to acknowledge Him as God — but are not willing to commit the keeping of their lives into His hands!

It is one thing to believe Jesus is God and Savior — but quite another to commit everything to Him. To commit means to "entrust or give charge." So, commitment to Christ is all about giving your life completely to Him — entrusting your whole being to His care. And, in turn, He commits Himself to those who are totally committed to Him.

We live in a society bogged down by one crisis after another. Do you know anyone who is *not* facing a crisis or hasn't just come out of one? Personally, I know many Christians who are facing deep troubles that threaten to overwhelm and ruin them.

What kind of crisis are you facing? Is it spiritual, financial, mental, physical? Is it in your marriage, your job, your business? I am talking about circumstances so serious, only a miracle can get you out — a situation that looks hopeless. When you are in such a crisis, you need Jesus to come into it and walk through it with you. Only the Son of the Living God can solve your problem — do the impossible — rescue you out of your furnace of affliction!

You may answer, "Yes, I need Jesus to walk with me through this. I need Him to come into my crisis as He did for the Hebrew men. But how can I do that? How can I get Him to commit to my crisis?"

You can do it in the same way Shadrach, Meshach and Abednego brought Christ into their crisis. These men made three notable commitments:

1. They Committed Themselves to a Pure, Undefiled Lifestyle in the Midst of a Wicked Society.

"But Daniel purposed in his heart that he would not defile himself with the portion of the king's meat, nor with the wine which he drank: therefore he requested of the prince of the eunuchs that he might not defile himself" *(Daniel 1:8)*.

The word defile here suggests "freeing through repudiation." Daniel was saying, in other words, "Any compromise of my standards will rob me of my freedom."

So Daniel committed to eat only beans and drink only water for ten days. There was no filet mignon from the king's table, no expensive wine. When he told the prince of eunuchs this, the prince answered, "You're going to cost me my life! You'll look sickly at the end of ten days. Your cheeks will be sunken — and the king will surely notice. Here, eat just a little meat. You need the protein. Drink the wine to build up your blood. Eat some of these sweets to give you energy."

As I studied this passage, I wondered: Why did Daniel go on this kind of fast? These Hebrew men weren't vegetarians. The answer probably is that, before going to the king's table, the wine, meat and delicacies were blessed by idolatrous priests. Therefore, the food was ceremonially unclean to the Jewish youths.

Yet I believe Daniel and these others had something more in mind —

that their commitment went way beyond ceremonial uncleanness. What I am about to tell you didn't come from any commentary. I believe the Holy Spirit revealed it to me. Why did these four Hebrew men refuse to eat the king's food?

First, these men had been taken captive along with thousands of their countrymen. The prophet Jeremiah had encouraged these Jewish captives to settle and build in Babylon for seventy years, until God would bring them back. But, in keeping with Israel's history of backsliding, the people likely were swept up with the covetousness rampant in that land. No doubt, Daniel and his friends saw how quickly and easily these early captives had compromised. The fast life of Babylon had ensnared them.

These four men must have been shocked beyond belief at what they saw when they first arrived in Babylon. There were brazen harlots on the streets, pagan shrines and altars on every corner, open drunkenness and debauchery everywhere, officials and leaders staggering down streets, dim-witted and stupefied from wine and alcohol. It was a society so loose, immoral and full of cursing, these four men's spiritual sensibilities were assailed.

Now, Daniel was a student of the prophets. He had Jeremiah's writings with him, and those prophecies ultimately led him to conclude that Israel would be in captivity for seventy years. He knew they were living in an important time in history! And, sometime during their introduction to Babylon, Daniel had made a commitment with "...the men that were with me..." *(Daniel 10:7)* — the three other Hebrews who stood with him both in body and in spirit. I imagine them having a conference, sharing their grief over Israel's compromise. Then Daniel stands up and says:

"You saw what I saw on these streets! Yet what seems so shocking to us now will soon be normal among our people, if we do not determine to live differently. It won't be long before our countrymen will look, talk and live like the Chaldeans. Everyone will be caught up in sensuality — our shepherds seeking ease and prosperity, our leaders settling for compromise. Our synagogues will be full of mixture, defilement, double standards. Everyone will hold to a form of faith, but will lose all power with God.

"We have to take a stand! God is going to need voices in this time of backsliding. We're going to have to lay our lives on the line — lest the light of Israel go out completely!"

So the four made a commitment. They told each other, "We dare not compromise. We dare not adopt these moral standards. We dare not soil our spirits with pagan music, alcohol, a devilish lifestyle. We dare not let the spirit of Babylon taint our faith. We will be separate. And we will be disciplined in our walk of faith."

These four Hebrew men remained free by repudiating the Babylonian lifestyle. It was not merely an issue of food — it was something that encompassed their entire way of living. It was about having a hidden life of separation! Yet these men did not go about preaching their lifestyle to others. They did not advertise their disciplined walk. It was strictly a matter between them and God.

I ask you: When God was ready to speak to that nation and its people, whom did He choose to be His mouthpiece? Who became the Lord's voice — His untainted testimony to a doomed empire? It was these four committed men!

As I look at our own doomed society, I see a nation disintegrating so fast it's appalling. And this includes the body of Christ! The church has been infiltrated by the Babylonian spirit — a message of mixture, with multitudes conforming to worldly standards. I cry out often in my secret closet, "Oh, God, where are Your voices in the land? Where are Your people who live separated lives — who'll stand up and speak a prophetic word? Where are Your unbending spokesmen?"

In this time when everything around us is crumbling, where are such voices? Where are the congregations, the believers who will step out and be a voice for God on their job, within their family, in their daily walk?

That is what the four Hebrew men asked themselves. And it is why they committed themselves to a pure lifestyle. Their bold decision — and their testimony of a holy walk — had to have made an incredible impact on little Ezra, Nehemiah and Zerubbabel. It may have been what inspired the 43,000 who later stood strong. Yes, these four men's holy lives raised up a godly remnant.

Beloved, you cannot be a voice for God unless you lead a separated, holy life. God cannot use you if your heart is soiled and tainted by this wicked age. It takes a decisive commitment! I ask you: When you're in a crisis, do you cry out, "Lord, where are You when I need You? Aren't You committed to my deliverance?"

But what if the Lord should say to you, "Where are you when I need a voice? I need voices in these sinful times, pure vessels through whom I can speak. You say you want Me to come to you in your crisis — yet you remain a part of the wicked, wordly system. Tell Me — are you committed to My purposes?"

2. They Committed to Become Seekers After God — Men Who Pray!

"And I set my face unto the Lord God, to seek by prayer and supplications...And I prayed unto the Lord my God, and made my confession...And whiles I was speaking, and praying, and confessing my sin and the sin of my people Israel..." *(Daniel 9:3-4, 20)*. Here is the proof — these were praying men!

You see, the first commitment they had made — to live a separated life — had to be backed up by a second commitment: to be seekers after God. It is impossible to live a holy life without spending much time on your knees, seeking God for the power and authority to lead such a life. Don't be mistaken — faithful praying will not keep you out of a crisis. On the contrary, it most likely will bring you to a fired-up furnace and a lion's den. But prayer will prepare you to face it all with trust — to become a living sacrifice for Jesus' sake.

Daniel's praying led him straight to the lion's den. And this test came years after that of the Hebrew men — when Daniel was in his eighties. This may frighten you, if you wonder how long it will be before you stop having crises. Perhaps you thought you'd learned all your "important" tests after a certain number of years in the Lord. Yet here God is allowing one of His greatest prayer warriors — a man of a quiet, tender spirit — to face the crisis of his life after decades of faithful intercession.

Beloved, the testing ends only when Jesus comes — or when you die in Christ. The time will never come when you no longer have to face a fiery furnace or a lion's den. That won't happen until you lay your head on His bosom! This is why prayer is so important. You can make a commitment to live an undefiled life — but that commitment is impossible to fulfill without also having a commitment to seek God. All the convicting sermons, all the powerful books on holiness, all the exhortations in the world can't keep you committed to a separated, holy life. Everything will fail — unless you have committed yourself to be a dedicated seeker after God.

A few weeks ago I went to the Father asking, "Lord, why do You require prayer for everything? Why is it You won't do anything except by prayer?"

The Lord answered, "David, it is impossible to love Me without seeking Me. How can a child of Mine say he loves Me when he neglects Me for days on end? Prayer is the barometer of devotion to Me. True love will draw My children to My presence!"

Of course, faith must be sparked by the Word of God; after all, faith comes by hearing. But once faith is sparked, prayer sets it aflame. It explodes our faith. Talk about a furnace turned up seven times hotter: Prayer turned up the faith of the four Hebrew men until it was hotter than the fiery flames.

When King Nebuchadnezzar called those men out of the furnace, he said: "...Blessed be (your) God...who hath sent his angel, and delivered his servants that trusted in him...and yielded their bodies, that they might not serve nor worship any god, except their own God" *(3:28)*. Again, the testimony came from pagan lips: These men had yielded their bodies to God!

Yet they had done this long before they faced the furnace. Prayer is the process of yielding up our bodies to the Lord — of becoming a living sacrifice. And these men sacrificed daily in this way. They remained in prayer for days, weeks, becoming intimate with the Lord. After a while, they understood that to die was gain. Death would only bring them closer to Him whom they so loved!

3. They Made a Commitment to Wholly Trust God — Live or Die!

"Nebuchadnezzar spake and said unto them...if ye worship not, ye shall be cast the same hour into the midst of a burning fiery furnace; and who is that God that shall deliver you out of my hands?" *(Daniel 3:14-15)*. These men were facing the worst possible crisis any human could face. If God didn't come and deliver them by a miracle, they were dead!

And that's exactly the kind of crisis I'm talking about with you. Perhaps you have a severe physical affliction. Maybe your marriage is in a crisis beyond your power to solve or heal it. You say, "I've prayed, I've fasted, I've done everything. If God doesn't come on the scene now, I won't make it!"

What will bring Christ into your crisis? He comes when you make the same commitment the three Hebrew men made: "(They)...said to the king, O Nebuchadnezzar, we are not careful to answer thee in this matter. If it be so, our God whom we serve is able to deliver us from the burning fiery furnace, and he will deliver us out of thine hand...But if not, be it known unto thee, O king, that we will not serve thy gods, nor worship the golden image which thou hast set up" *(verses 16-18)*.

In other words: "It looks hopeless. Without God performing a miracle for us, we are dead. Yet our God is able to deliver us from this fiery crisis!

But even if He doesn't, we still will not quit on Him. Live or die, we will trust Him!"

Beloved, this is the kind of faith that causes angels to rejoice and blesses the very heart of God. It is a faith that says, "Lord, I am convinced, fully persuaded, that You are able to deliver me. If You just speak a word, it will all be over. But, if not — I'm not going to run. I won't accuse You of abandoning me. I will remain faithful and true. Your ways are higher than mine, Lord — and my life is in Your hands. Though You slay me, yet will I trust You."

This is what brings Christ into our crisis — the full confidence that He is able to rescue and deliver us out of any crisis. It is a confidence that, no matter what comes, we are in His hands.

Please understand — God could have delivered these three men in any number of ways. He simply could have changed Nebuchadnezzar's mind. Or, He could have allowed them to escape. After all, Moses had escaped, as had Joseph and David. Yet these three Hebrew men had a special kind of faith that the Lord responds to very quickly: They had faith in the faithfulness of God! They were persuaded He would do what was best for them and for His own glory.

That is why you do not see them "claiming their rights" as believers. Nor did they spend their time trying to build up each other's faith by quoting promises. No, they went with quiet dignity toward the furnace, saying, "God is able! But if not..." Undoubtedly, this last phrase will make many people indignant. I can almost hear them saying: "Oh, no, pastor — that is negative! It leaves room for doubt. We should only say, 'God is able' — period!"

I believe with all my heart that the Lord is able. I believe He could speak a word and deliver anyone in a moment. Yet, consider this: If these Hebrew men had not been able to say, "But, if not..." — if they had not had such faith — what would they have done in their moment of crisis? Would they have begun protesting the closer they got to the fire? Would they have ended up crying, "God, You failed to keep Your Word. You let us down!"

No — they were prepared to die! They could say, "Lord, even if I have to suffer — if my body ignites and my burning flesh fills the air with stench — I will go out trusting You. I will believe You, even if I don't get the answer to my prayer!"

Most of us don't have a faith that would use the daring words these men used: "But, if not..." I ask you — what will you do if you don't get your answer? Will you accuse God of failing you, of not loving you? What a tragedy to go into your furnace crying, "God, where are You? You've failed me!"

The three Hebrew men went into the fire with their bodies already dead to the world. They were able to offer their bodies joyfully, as living sacrifices. And Jesus literally met them in their crisis! What an incredible reward — to have Christ walk with them through their most difficult time.

What do you think they said to Jesus when He showed up in the furnace? "Oh, thank You, Lord! Thank You for not letting us feel the pain. Thank You for giving us another chance — for a few more years!"

No! I believe they said, "Lord, take us with You! Don't leave us here. We have touched the ecstasy, the glory — and we don't want to go back. Walk us home to be with You." They would have preferred to be with Him. Jesus knows this kind of heart — and it is to such that He commits Himself.

Are you able to say, "Lord, walk me home"? Perhaps you've never learned to commit your body, your business, your marriage, your crisis into God's hands. Yes, we are always to pray in faith, believing that God will answer; yet we also are to trust Him completely with our situation, saying in our hearts, "But if not, Lord — I'm still going to trust You!"

Pray with me now: "Lord, You are able to deliver me from this fiery furnace. But if not — I will still believe! Even if I have to continue in this horrible trial — if I have to face more suffering, more testing — I commit everything to You. Just come and walk through it with Me!"

I promise you — Jesus Christ will come into your crisis. He will take you by your hand and lead you through the fire. I consider the coming of Christ into your crisis to be the greatest answer to prayer possible — because when He comes, His presence lifts you above all your pain, all your hurt, all your confusion. When Jesus appears at your side, He takes you by the hand and makes you stand strong!

3

Right Song — Wrong Side!

Learning to Sing in the Midst of Hard Times

The children of Israel were in a hopeless predicament! The Red Sea was before them; the mountains were to the left and right; and Pharaoh and his iron chariots were closing in from the rear. God's people seemed helplessly trapped — like sitting ducks, just waiting to be cut down. Yet believe it or not, God purposely had led them into this precarious spot!

It was panic time in the camp of Israel. Men shook with fear, and women and children wept as they huddled around grandparents and relatives. Suddenly, Moses was mobbed by irate family leaders who cried, "Surely this is the end! Weren't there enough graves in Egypt to bury us there? You had to drag us out here to die. We told you in Egypt to let us alone. It was better to be slaves there than to die in this miserable wilderness!"

I wonder if even Moses had a moment of trepidation about their circumstances. Yet when this man of God wept, the Lord seems to have chided him: "Wherefore criest thou unto me?..." *(Exodus 14:15).* No one in Israel could have known what a great deliverance God was about to bring to them! Suddenly the winds parted the sea, and the people walked through the parted waves on dry ground. When Pharaoh and his powerful army tried to follow, the waters began to rage again — closing in and drowning them all.

What a sight it must have been! The people of God looked back from the other side and saw their mighty enemy destroyed like tin soldiers. Then a song went up in the camp as, once again, they realized God had delivered them from impossible circumstances. Scripture records their reaction — and the song they sang:

"Israel saw that great work which the Lord did upon the Egyptians: and the people feared the Lord, and believed the Lord, and his servant Moses. Then sang Moses and the children of Israel this song unto the Lord, and spake, saying, I will sing unto the Lord, for he hath triumphed gloriously: the horse and his rider hath he thrown into the sea. The Lord is my strength and song, and he is become my salvation: he is my God, and I will prepare him an habitation; my father's God, and I will exalt him" *(14:31, 15:1-2)*.

You may know this glorious song of victory, taken directly from the Scriptures. Christians lift up their voices to sing it in many churches today. But, beloved, note the following words and emphasis in this passage of Scripture — because they are the heart of this message: "Israel saw that great work which the Lord did upon the Egyptians....THEN sang Moses and the children of Israel this song"...*(same verses, emphasis mine)*. They sang the right song — but they sang it on the wrong side! Israel's song was not sung in true faith, because they sang it only on the other side of the Red Sea — the side of victory and not of testing.

You see, there are two sides to all our trials and temptations: the testing side and the breakthrough side; the east side of darkness and hopelessness, and the west side of victory and deliverance. Any doubter can sing after the testing has passed and the victory has come. Rather, it's on the testing side that the Lord wants us to learn to sing His praises. He deserves our worship in the darkest moment, when there appears to be no way out, when it is absolutely hopeless — and He alone can deliver!

You can imagine the scene in Israel after their victory: Miriam dancing with all the maidens, tambourines shaking, everyone singing and shouting praises to God. Scripture says they exclaimed boldly: "The people shall hear, and be afraid...the dukes of Edom shall be amazed; the mighty men of Moab, trembling shall take hold upon them; all the inhabitants of Canaan shall melt away" *(15:14-15)*.

How secure and powerful they must have felt. But the victory was hollow — because Israel had already failed the test that day. Only Moses had a right to sing on the west side. Before the waters parted, the people had moaned and groaned and complained and cried.

The Great Need of This Hour Is for Christians to Learn to Sing The Song of Deliverance on the Testing Side of Their Trouble.

God's purposes in allowing us to stumble into hopeless crises is to test us — to build in us a foundation of trust in Him. How else will His people be able to trust Him for all the battles that lie ahead?

We've all heard a lot recently about ministers falling into sins such as adultery and financial scandal. But much worse in God's eyes is the growing number of ministers who walk away from the ministry because they've allowed doubt and fear to overcome them. We receive letters from all over the country, telling us whole congregations are falling into temptation and ruin because the pastor who once preached faith gave up and left. He couldn't sing the right song on the right side.

Beloved, every crisis you face right now is an opportunity to learn to trust God — to build a foundation for everything that comes at you for the rest of your life. This test was an opportunity for Israel to put a mirror to their heart and show them the doubt inside — so they might turn to God in faith. If only they had remembered the miracles they'd witnessed in Egypt, they would have been able to say, "Live or die, we are the Lord's!" They could have encouraged one another by lifting up a song of praise — the same song they eventually sang on the other side: "Great is our God, and greatly to be praised...." It could have spread throughout the camp and ignited their faith. And that would have established a foundation for an abiding faith in God. It would have begun a faith so fire-tested and unshakable that it would have seen them through the hardships of the wilderness and the battles of Canaan. It would have established them as the people of God on earth — a light unto the nations.

But Israel did not sing. They lost all confidence in the love of their heavenly Father — and they accused God of neglecting them!

A dear brother in the Lord recently unburdened his heart with me about a deep, dark trial he has endured for some time now. About a year ago he gave up a well-paying job because he saw that in the near future he would have to compromise to remain there. For months he has sent out numerous resumes, but nothing has opened up for him.

This has been a time of severe testing for him, and he has received all sorts of advice from well-meaning Christian friends. Some tell him there must be sin in his life — that that's why God hasn't opened a door. Others say, "If you just have enough faith ..." But this brother told me, "If God is trying to tell me something in all this, I'm just not getting the message. I don't see the purpose yet. It's okay for people to encourage someone like me who is hurting — but until you go through it yourself, you just can't know the pain. I love the Lord, but it looks so hopeless. This trial just keeps dragging on — and I keep hitting dead ends everywhere I turn!"

Then he said something that struck me deep within — and it became the spark for this message: "I want to come out of this trial with a testimony. I don't want God just to give me another job, deliver me from my troubles, and allow me to continue on without my having learned anything of Him. People all around are watching me — and I want them to see a testimony to God. I want to come through tested and tried. Otherwise, all I've learned about trusting the Lord is nothing but empty theory. Unless it works in hard times, it's useless!"

The Flesh Argues, "Who Can Sing When You're Hurting So Badly?"

Some would say, "But it's not natural to sing songs of deliverance in such pain. If we'd been in Israel's shoes, we'd have cried in fear, too. It's only human to worry when you think of your spouse and family — when you're unemployed, your children are in trouble and all kinds of problems are facing you."

Brothers and sisters, God doesn't see it that way. His perspective is vastly different from ours. Was He heartless to say as He did to Moses, "Why are you crying out to Me? Tell the people to move on!" Does this mean He doesn't care about our human passions and hurts?

No! Scripture says, "Thou hast seen how that the Lord thy God bear thee, as a man doth bear his son, in all the way that ye went...." *(Deuteronomy 1:31)*. He was a loving, caring Father. And He didn't take kindly to their endless insults and insinuations that He had forsaken them!

You may have teenagers in your family. As you see what's happening in our country, our cities, our schools, you may wonder if God is able to hold things together. But don't even begin to think our loving, heavenly Father doesn't hear your prayers and won't keep a wall of fire around your children! The Lord told Israel, "Moreover your little ones, which ye said should be a prey, and your children, which in that day had no knowledge between good and evil, they shall go in thither, and unto them will I give it, and they shall possess it" *(verse 39)*. God delivered the children — but not the adults who refused to trust Him!

There's nothing wrong with going to the Lord when you're hurting, and crying, "Help!" God understands when you're heartbroken and things look black. David said, "In my distress...I cried unto my God..." *(Psalm 18:6)*.

But the time comes when the Holy Spirit meets you in the prayer closet and says, as He did to Moses, "Why are you still crying? When will faith rise up in your heart?" You see, God knows you're not in danger. He knows the way He's going to deliver you. In fact, He has a million ways to do it. You just can't see them when your back is to the wall!

For the children of Israel, that wall was the Red Sea. If they'd have tried going into the mountains, the lions and beasts would have devoured them. They were stuck, trapped — right where God wanted them.

They received God's deliverance that day — and they sang afterward. But their song was shallow, without foundation. Here is the proof that it was shallow: Three days later they were back to their old ways of doubt and fear! All they had done in their hour of crisis was to suppress their fear. They had pushed it down inside and slapped on a coating of praise. They never dealt a death-blow to doubt. Yet that was the whole purpose behind the crisis!

The World Requires of Us a Song In the Midst of Hard Times.

Beloved, there is a song that can be sung — and it must be sung on the right side. You can be sure that if the world knows you're a Christian, they will demand it of you.

The Psalmist says, "They that carried us away required of us a song; and they that wasted us required of us mirth, saying, Sing us one of the songs of Zion. How shall we sing the Lord's song in a strange land?" *(Psalm 137:3-4)*. The people of God were in the hardest place of their lifetime. And as they were being carried away, their captors required of them a song. Yet there was no life in them anymore — nothing but depression, despair, hopelessness.

Multitudes of Christians are in the same position today. You may be trapped by your circumstances. The devil is chasing you down, coming at you ninety miles per hour with an old temptation. You're on the edge of giving up, thinking, "I can't make it. In spite of all my crying and praying, it looks like I'll be this way as long as I live. That old bondage is going to hound me forever!"

When Israel fell into the Babylonian bondage, their captors cried to them, "Sing for us — play for us! We've heard all about you and what your God did for you. Our spies told us everything. Now take out your tambourines and bring out your harps. Play us a song! Show us your joy in your God!"

I don't believe this demand was made only in mockery. I believe it was also a pitiful plea. The Babylonians' gods had left them empty and dry. They had no hope. But they had heard Israel singing to their God — a God who had seen them through impossible circumstances. They said, "These people have a God who can open a sea for them. His fire comes down from heaven. He stands against their enemies. There's got to be something to this God of theirs."

Like all the world, they wanted to see a people who endured the same problems they endured and faced the same battles they faced — yet who could sing and shout and hold their faith in the darkest of hours. The Babylonians demanded a song because there's something in every person's heart that cries out, "Where on the face of the earth is there something that can make you sing even when you've lost everything?" They needed a testimony. And it is important that the children of God, wherever they are at whatever time, sing the songs of Zion: "God, I believe You, no matter what is happening!"

The world is not going to respond to just another testimony, however. Church programs often leave people dead and dry. Even healings nowadays can have little impact because the world has seen so much of "miracle medicine" — heart transplants, limb transplants, eye transplants. No, the world is shouting to us, "You can show us a miracle! It isn't the Red Sea opening up that impresses us. It's not seeing the blind given sight or the lame healed. It's that you can look at the darkest hour of your life, a situation that's hopeless to all human reasoning — and yet you smile with joy, singing praises to God! That's the miracle we want to see!"

Your Doubts Must Be Dealt a Death-Blow on the Testing Side — Or You Will Become a Confirmed Murmurer!

If you don't deal with your doubts, you'll be given over to a spirit of murmuring and complaining. You'll live and die that way. Your doubts cannot simply be suppressed. They have to be pulled out by the roots!

Let's look at Israel just three days after their deliverance from Egypt. They had been singing, shaking their tambourines and testifying to the power and strength of a mighty God, boasting that He was leading and protecting them. Then they arrived at Marah, which means "waters of bitterness." This was to be another testing place for them.

God just keeps allowing crisis after crisis until we finally get the lesson. If we keep refusing to learn it, a time comes when He gives us over to our own bitterness and murmuring. "And they went three days in the wilderness, and found no water.... And the people murmured against Moses, saying, What shall we drink?" *(Exodus 15:22, 24)*.

On Sunday, they were having a great time — singing, dancing and praising. But now it's Wednesday — and they're already in trouble. It's another crisis, and they're falling apart!

How could a people lose their confidence so quickly? They never had any to begin with! They never had that foundation built under them. So again they failed the test. They had learned absolutely nothing from their previous crisis — and again they missed an opportunity to shine forth the greatness of their God.

From that day on Israel was beyond learning anything from God. They even began to take His goodness for granted. They had no food, so He sent them manna from heaven. He dropped quails out of the sky, piling them up outside of the camp three feet high. But not a word of thanksgiving was heard. Instead, the people turned to greed, hoarding all that God gave them. Israel became stiff-necked!

Oh, what a shame it is to go from crisis to crisis and learn nothing in the process. It carries with it a curse — that you will be given over to a spirit of murmuring!

Four Great Deliverances Later, They Were Given One Last Chance.

Israel had witnessed God's miracle at the Red Sea. They'd seen the healing waters at Marah. They had seen the water flow from the rock on Mount Horeb. And they'd seen manna and quails appear from heaven.

Now they were poised and ready to go into the Promised Land. God had given them one final opportunity to come to the ground of trust and faith in Him. They had sent twelve spies into Canaan — and ten had come back with an evil report: "Surely it floweth with milk and honey....(But) the cities are walled, and very great.... We be not able to go up against the people; for they are stronger than we.... The land eateth up the inhabitants...and all the people that we saw in it are men of a great stature. And there we saw the giants...and we were in our own sight as grasshoppers..." *(Numbers 13:27-28, 31-33)*.

The report caused utter chaos in the camp of Israel. Every pent-up emotion, every doubt and fear that had built up inside, came churning out in anger at God. When Joshua stood up and said, "God is with us! God is able!", they all wanted to stone him.

The people didn't know it at the time, but this testing was to prepare them for their first battle in Canaan, at Jericho. The spies told them, "The first thing you're going to find there is a walled city called Jericho. It's

impenetrable. There's simply no way in! We have no weapons, no battering rams. It's useless, hopeless. Why even try to go over there?"

That talk came right out of hell! And that is exactly what the devil
wants you to think about your problems: "There's no way out of this." Yet
you know God already has a plan. You just can't see it. All you can see is
that wall ahead of you. But God sees infinitely more than you do. It's an
easy thing for Him to go right through it. There are no complications
involved for Him, because He doesn't recognize the power of the enemy.
It's time to begin to trust Him!

For Israel, this was a final chance. It was a time to rise up and sing, to
show God their trust. It was time for someone to stand up and say, "We
thought we were dead at the Red Sea — and He delivered us! We thought
it was the end for us at the bitter waters of Marah — and He delivered us!
We thought we were dying of hunger in the wilderness — and He delivered us! We thought it was all over many times. But every time God brought
us out of danger. He has brought us safely thus far. Let us testify to the
world that our God is able!"

Yet no one did. Israel failed her final test. Where was the victory, the
song? There was none! Israel only wept! "And all the congregation lifted
up their voice, and cried; and the people wept that night. And all the children of Israel murmured against Moses and against Aaron: and the whole
congregation said unto them, Would God that we had died in the land of
Egypt! Or would God we had died in this wilderness! And wherefore hath
the Lord brought us unto this land, to fall by the sword, that our wives and
our children should be a prey? Were it not better for us to return to Egypt?
And they said to one another, Let us make a captain, and let us return into
Egypt.

"Then Moses and Aaron fell on their faces before all the assembly of
the congregation of the children of Israel.... And the Lord said unto Moses,
How long will this people provoke me? And how long will it be ere they
believe me, for all the signs which I have shewed among them?" *(14:1-5, 11)*.

Finally, God's patience ended. Listen to what He said to the confirmed
murmurers: "Tomorrow turn you, and get you into the wilderness by the
way of the Red Sea.... Your children shall wander in the wilderness forty
years...until your carcases be wasted in the wilderness" *(verses 14:25, 33)*.

The New Testament Gives Us the Same Message.

"Ask in faith, nothing wavering. For he that wavereth is like a wave of the sea driven with the wind and tossed. For let not that man think that he shall receive any thing of the Lord" *(James 1:6-7)*.

The world is full of Christians today who will not hold onto God's holy Word. They think it is an innocent thing to sit at the table in the house of God and murmur and complain, as if God doesn't hear. But God does hear our murmurings! They are accusations that He does not care — insinuations that He has let us down.

God has warned me not to give voice to nagging doubts and fears — not to my wife, not to friends, not to loved ones, not to colleagues. God says to take those doubts to the Cross and say, "Jesus, heal my unbelief! Take it out!"

Israel spent the next forty years in turmoil — backbiting, complaining, jealous, full of bitterness. What a miserable existence they led — still claiming to be the children of God, still claiming to be holy. But that was their testimony — not God's.

There is no job, no deliverance, for a man or woman who complains continually before God. You'll stay unemployed the rest of your life. Or if you do get a job, it'll be a yoke around your neck. This is a matter of life or death. You must come to a place where you learn to trust Him. If you learn it now, the next time a crisis comes you'll sing and shout with praises to your Deliverer. Oh, the victory will be there — but more importantly, you'll have dealt a death-blow to all doubt, fear and unbelief.

Where do you start? You begin by looking straight into the mirror of God's Word! Consider your words and actions over the last thirty days: Have you been murmuring, complaining? You may answer, "Yes — but I haven't been murmuring at God." Oh yes, you have! No matter where or to whom you complain, it's all directed at God!

Every place I turn in the Bible, I see: "Trust Me, and I will see you through. Just commit your ways to Me." What does that require? Simply this: Stand still and see the salvation of the Lord. You ask, "But what if nothing happens?" That response reveals doubt and fear!

Dear saint, turn to God today and say, "Lord, I've done everything I know to do in my situation. I know there's nothing I can do to fix the problem anyway. I'm going to trust You — and wait for Your victory." Let God make you a testimony to the world — a witness of His faithfulness. Love Him with all your heart right now. Give Him all your problems, all your faith and trust — and He will give you the right song on the right side!

The Queen in Gold

4

The Bride of Christ

The 45th Psalm provides us with a beautiful picture of Christ and His bride. A great marriage is about to take place, and the writer is "boiling over" with ecstasy and excitement: "My heart is inditing [boiling over] a good matter..." *(Psalm 45:1)*. The psalmist can hardly contain himself. He is trying to describe something he sees in his mind's eye — an incredible ceremony, with a grand and glorious Bridegroom, and a beautiful bride dressed in gold.

Several years ago, the entire world was mesmerized by the royal wedding in England. Millions around the globe were glued to TV sets as Princess Diana and Prince Charles were married. It was one of the most glamorous and celebrated weddings in modern history. TV networks had "color commentators" who described every detail of the proceedings. News clips showed the princely, regal life of Charles — his polo matches, his duties as prince, and his inheritance as the next king of England — his throne, his riches, his palace. The commentators also described in exquisite detail everything about Princess Di. And the picture was incredible: her hairstyle, royal gown, retinue, shoes, ornaments, ring, flowers, royal carriage. Even during the wedding ceremony, as the couple stood together at the altar, a commentator whispered details into a microphone: "Isn't she beautiful? Look at her shoes, her flowers...."

It was romantic, breathtaking — a prince and a princess united in holy marriage "until death do us part." People all over the globe wept at the sight. But today we have lived to see this marriage disintegrate into one of the most sordid, ugly breakups on the face of the earth.

The marriage described in Psalm 45, on the other hand, is a union far more glorious and grand. It, too, is full of romance, beauty, majesty — but it is a marriage that will never end. It is meant for eternal glory!

This Wedding Is All About King Jesus Taking a Bride!

At this very moment, you and I are seated in heavenly places with King Jesus. Yet, much greater than that, we are engaged to Him. And soon a grand and glorious marriage will take place — a majestic royal wedding beyond anything this world has ever seen. The commentator for this marriage is the Holy Spirit, who unfolds to us a glorious scene:

● King Jesus is standing before His throne — His royal scepter in His hand, His garments full of the wonderful aroma of myrrh and aloes. He has come from the ivory palace of His Father, where He has been anointed with the oil of gladness.

● He is dressed in His full military regalia. His glittering sword is strapped upon His thigh. He has conquered all His enemies, and His kingdom is secure. He reigns in peace and power, Victor over all. And, Scripture says, He is "...fairer than the children of men: grace is poured into thy lips..." *(Psalm 45:2)*.

● Every battle this King has fought — every enemy He has laid low, every act of grace and mercy He has provided — has been for His bride. It all has been meant for this moment. And now He is ecstatic, beaming with joy, full of excitement — because He anticipates being joined to His beautiful bride. He gazes down the long corridor of the palace, waiting for her to approach with all her retinue!

The psalmist tells us that the Bridegroom could have chosen a bride from many honorable daughters in the kingdom. "Kings' daughters were among thy honourable women..." *(verse 45:9)*. But He chose only one: "...upon thy right hand did stand the queen in gold of Ophir" *(same verse)*.

Now, Ophir gold was the purest, most refined gold made in those days. And this bride is adorned in it. What a sight she is, as she is "... brought unto the king..." *(verse 14)*. She absolutely glows, because her heart is pure. Her golden gown glistens with incredible needlework. This isn't some broadcloth picked out of endless yards; it has been intricately interwoven with threads of the purest gold. And its gold ornaments shine forth spectacularly.

The queen in gold marches toward the King with great fanfare. And what a glorious sound — tambourines, trumpets, stringed instruments. Behind her, as far as the eye can see, is her retinue — an army of virgins, all dressed in white, singing, dancing, praising with great joy. The bride is leading the whole procession — and they're coming to meet the King of Kings and Lord of Lords.

Finally, the queen takes her place at the King's right hand. And everyone is rejoicing — because this is the royal wedding of eternity. "...The virgins her companions that follow her shall be brought unto thee. With gladness and rejoicing shall they be brought: they shall enter into the king's palace" *(verses 14-15)*.

Talk about a Holy-Ghost revival meeting! Can you imagine the scene? This wedding is the purpose, the highlight, of all Creation. There stands King Jesus, His heart full of joy. And here comes His bride — the redeemed of mankind — dressed in pure gold, the righteousness of Christ.

Yet, I want to stop here for a moment. So far, this looks like another romantic, royal wedding. My question is: Just who is this bride in gold? Some commentators say this psalm merely describes an historical marriage between King Joram of Judah and Athaliah. Scholarship shows that there was a great, royal wedding at the time. But to say this psalm is about that wedding is mere conjecture. I agree with most spiritually-minded scholars that this psalm is messianic. And I believe its message is very clear: It's about Jesus and His bride. The Bridegroom is our King and Lord, Jesus Christ. And the bride is His church — believers who have prepared themselves for His coming — who yearn for Him with great expectancy, and whose hearts are without spot or wrinkle.

"And I John saw the holy city, new Jerusalem, coming down from God out of heaven, prepared as a bride adorned for her husband....And there came unto me one of the seven angels which had the seven vials full of the seven last plagues, and talked with me, saying, Come hither, I will shew thee the bride, the Lamb's wife.

"And he carried me away in the spirit to a great and high mountain, and shewed me that great city, the holy Jerusalem, descending out of heaven from God, having the glory of God: and her light was like unto a stone most precious, even like a jasper stone, clear as crystal" *(Revelation 21:2, 9-11)*.

This picture in Revelation 21 is a beautiful picture of the last-day church of Jesus Christ. The great, holy city descending out of heaven is His spotless bride — the overcoming church seated with Him right now in heavenly places. This church is built upon the foundation of gospel truths of the twelve apostles. It is surrounded by walls and gates that keep out everything impure and uninvited.

Scripture also speaks of a pure, crystal water, which represents a clear conscience. And that is another component of this last-day church: It is transparent, pure, walking in the light — with no other temple but Christ!

As the Queen Stands Before Her Bridegroom, the Wedding About to Begin, the Voice of a Third Party Is Heard.

The queen in gold is honored, favored, greatly adorned. Now she stands at her Beloved's right hand, the marriage about to be performed. But before the ceremony begins, a voice whispers an admonition to her: "Hearken, O daughter, and consider..." *(Psalm 45:10).*

I believe this voice is the Holy Ghost, warning all who are called by His name. He is speaking a word to overcomers — to those most in love with Jesus — saying, "Harken, consider, listen!" This voice comes to the bride in the final moments just before the marriage is to be consummated.

You must understand — the queen has already been chosen. Her heart has already been won to her Bridegroom. She has left her home, family and country and has committed herself to Him. She is full of joy because she passionately loves the King.

Now, let me ask you: Do you think of yourself as chosen by the Lord? Are you the blood-covered, redeemed apple of His eye? Do you love Him with all your heart? Have you forsaken all the world, all your past, for Him? Can you say, "He is mine, and I am committed to Him. Lord, I love You with all my heart!"

My point is this: If you want to be in the bride of Christ, you must be concerned with more than simply escaping a godless hell. Rather, you must desire not to be absent on that great wedding day! You must shudder at the very thought of not being His bride — of not being in His embrace, not spending eternity with Him. The Holy Ghost's message to the bride was: "...forget also thine own people, and thy father's house" *(verse 10).* The still, small voice was whispering, "It's not enough just to leave your past behind. You must also forget it all. Put out of your mind all past loves and distractions!"

Jesus said, "...whosoever he be of you that forsaketh not all that he hath, he cannot be my disciple" *(Luke 14:33).* The messenger here is saying to the bride, "Are you counting the cost as you prepare to be united to Him? Or are you going to give Him mere lip service after the wedding? Have you started a commitment you're willing to finish? Or does your mind wander back to things of your past — old friends, old habits, old loves? If you commit to this marriage, you must not only leave your past behind — you must forget it completely!"

Are the Holy Spirit's words a call for us to physically leave family, job, career? No — never! His warning isn't an excuse to escape the obligations of marriage or family. In fact, the Bible is full of commands and warnings about providing for our household. We are to cling to our mate, care for our relatives and raise our children in the fear of God.

This isn't just a physical call. When Jesus speaks of some people "not forsaking all," He is speaking of those who turn from Him and cling to idols. An idol is anything that becomes the sole focus of our devotion — anything that possesses our time, attention, money, love, interest.

"And they forsook the Lord God of their fathers...and followed other gods..." *(Judges 2:12)*.

I Want to Speak Particularly to Husbands and Wives.

I'll address husbands first. Many men can rightly say they are good providers. They work long and hard, don't waste their money, dress their children adequately and spend quality time with their family. But how much time do they devote to Jesus? Do they have what I call a "leaving-and-forgetting time" — a time when they mentally leave and forget everything, setting aside quality time for Jesus alone?

A man can do this on the job, while driving to work, anytime. It's a time to set aside all thoughts of work, family, children and say, "This is Your time, Jesus. I'm Yours alone right now. No one is more important to me."

Please don't misunderstand me: The problem isn't business or family or career. Rather, it is "loitering" — idle, aimless, lounging around and wasting time. Multitudes of God's people spend their time endlessly loitering — idly spending time with friends or lolling in front of a TV. We loiter away so many precious hours — while we neglect our Lord and Savior!

Now I want to speak to wives: You have given your husband and children the best years of your life. You are hard-working and faithful. You take good care of your family. Yet, I ask you: How much "leaving-and-forgetting time" do you give to Jesus? How many hours a week do you shut out the world and draw close to Him?

Grandfathers, grandmothers, singles, everyone — one day you're going to stand before the judgment seat to account for your time. And God keeps accurate books. He knows exactly how many hours you've spent on "good" things — your children, your spouse, your interests. But He is going to place that on His scales — and then measure it against the few hours you gave Him. Do you think those scales will even move?

How jealous the Lord must be over all our other loves — all the things that eat up our time and attention. The old adage is true: It's not the "bad" that is the enemy of the Christian, but the "good": It's family, career, job, children. These things in themselves don't stand between us and the Lord. Rather, it's our loitering! We could easily take hold of our time for Jesus' sake — but we don't. And now the Lord stands before us, asking: "...lovest thou me more than these?..." *(John 21:15)*.

Whatever You Love Most Will Get Most of Your Time and Attention.

God is a jealous lover: "...for the Lord, whose name is Jealous, is a jealous God" *(Exodus 34:14)*. It is possible for us to provoke Him to jealousy: "Do we provoke the Lord to jealousy?..." *(1 Corinthians 10:22)*. Paul is asking: "You have testified that you love Him. You've even taken His name. Yet, has someone or something else stolen your heart?"

As a faithful shepherd, I am called by the Spirit of God to warn you: When the day of judgment comes, you may not be in the bride of Christ. And when you stand before the Bridegroom, He won't say, "Here is My beloved, who spent so much time with Me. You couldn't wait to wake up to meet Me, and You didn't go to bed without talking to Me. You have been waiting for Me expectantly — and now we are one. Nothing will part us!"

Instead, Jesus will turn His face away from you. He will say, "You loved Me with words — but your heart was far from Me. You went to church and called that 'quality time' with Me. But there was no intimacy, no private time. You were seldom with Me, seldom in My presence. I don't know you. Depart from Me!" "Can a maid forget her ornaments, or a bride her attire? Yet my people have forgotten me days without number" *(Jeremiah 2:32)*. "How shall we escape, if we neglect so great salvation...?" *(Hebrews 2:3)*.

You can say you love Jesus; you can go to church every time the doors are open. But do you seek Him when your time is your own? How many books do you devour — how many magazines and newspapers, how much TV and radio — and yet you never give a thought to spending time with Christ? Time is running out! Soon you'll stand before Jesus. And how will you escape His judgment then, when you have been given every opportunity to know Him now?

Think of whole nations begging for Bibles — old Russian mothers who cry for even a New Testament. Think of the thousands of Eastern European pastors and believers who now sit devouring the Word, weeping at its glorious truth. Then think of your own Bible (if you even know where it is) — and how you neglect it!

Preachers search their Bibles for sermons. Sunday-school teachers study it for lessons. But why do we not turn to it for recreational reading, to be refreshed by our Lord? Why don't we open it to learn of Him, to love Him? The Bible is Jesus — God's own Word! It is the full revelation of His heart. Everything about Him is unmasked there. And I would think that if you truly love Him — if you expect to spend eternity as His bride — then you'd want to learn everything about Him that you can.

Right now many Christians are being branded in their very souls. Perhaps you are one. Will you go to the judgment with these words marking you: "Christ Neglecter"? Have you rejected Him, making no time for prayer or His Word? If so, how will you escape?

Many Have Had Their Hearts Won to the Lord — But Have Never Been Satisfied by Him.

It's not enough for Jesus to win your heart. He also has to be the satisfaction of your heart. Yet, there are many believers who have never been satisfied with Jesus. They're always up or down according to their circumstances. That is not a suitable bride for this Bridegroom. A certain beauty must adorn His bride in order to attract Him: "So shall the king greatly desire thy beauty..." *(Psalm 45:11)*. But what is this beauty?

You probably have sung of the beauty of holiness: "...worship the Lord in the beauty of holiness" *(29:2)*. This beauty is beheld in God's eyes; it is what Jesus sees in us that attracts Him. It is what is beautiful about us in His eyes!

And the Holy Ghost is saying to the bride in gold, "If you will lay aside everything, forget all others and adorn yourself for Him alone — then He will desire your beauty!" This means no job, no person, no relationship can come between you.

I heard a godly wife say, "The more godly my husband becomes, the more attractive he is to me." That is what a godly marriage is all about. Likewise, the more you give yourself in entire devotion to the Lord, the more attractive and beautiful you become to Him.

"So shall the king greatly desire thy beauty..." *(45:11)*. What an incredible thought: Jesus will not be able to stay away from you! In fact, the Hebrew meaning of beauty here includes the word lust (with righteous connotations). It signifies a strong yearning and desire. In other words, Jesus will draw close to you — overflowing with desire for you!

I have performed many weddings in my lifetime. And there was never a groom who didn't smile with delight at his bride, thinking, "She's all mine!" That is the beauty I'm talking about. Our Bridegroom rejoices, saying of His bride, "I'm the apple of her eye. She'd rather spend time with Me than with anyone else. And that makes her beautiful to Me."

I want to be beautiful in Jesus' eyes. I want to worship Him in the beauty of holiness. He is not merely "first" in my life; He is everything. And the Bible says He is drawn to me because of that.

The bride in gold has an inner beauty that makes her outwardly beautiful. She is "...all glorious within..." *(verse 13)* because she is devoted to her Bridegroom. He knows beyond any shadow of a doubt, "She is all Mine — devoted only to Me. She worships Me and is submissive to Me. I am the only One in her life, the sole focus of her attention. She makes time for Me, is overjoyed in My presence, and desires to be with Me continually. What beautiful devotion!"

A Final Important
Question for You:

If Jesus were to come tonight, would you be in the great marriage procession, approaching the throne? Or would you find yourself standing before a jealous, jilted Lover? Our Lord yearns after us, wanting our time and attention — and yet He sees us spending all our time on other people, other things. And that makes Him burn with jealousy! The day is coming when His jealousy will "smoke" against those who turn to vain idols *(Deuteronomy 29:20)*. It will burst into flames of judgment.

When that day comes, will Jesus take your hand with delight and whisper, "At last — we're together! You have desired Me so. You have given Me the best of your life, your time, your attention. Come, now — let us be one!" Or, will He say to you: "I'm sorry — I don't know you. You said you loved Me, but your actions never matched your words. You had time for a lot of things — family, children, grandchildren, loved ones, career. But you neglected Me. We were never intimate; I never had your heart. And now it's too late."

How will you stand before Him on that day? Everything of this world is going to burn. But what about your intimacy with Him? Will you be able to stand before Him, because you shut out the world and cried, "Jesus, I want to know You!" The Holy Spirit is whispering to you right now: "Harken — listen! Forget everything else, and start anew today. If you have missed Him altogether, confess it to your heavenly Father. Repent — and devote yourself wholly to your Bridegroom."

Pray with me right now: "O blessed Lamb of God, I want to be beautiful in Your sight! Forgive me for neglecting Your Word, for rejecting Your revealed heart. Forgive me for spending so much time on everything else but You. And give me a new heart to know You. I want to grow in intimacy with You."

Give the Lord all your devotion — your time, your attention, your thoughts, your finances — and He will take care of all such things. You won't have to seek after them as the heathen do; instead, He will add them to your life liberally. The Lord has promised to take care of you. And if you turn to Him with your whole heart, He will walk in covenant with you and your family. So give Him your wholehearted attention. Act as His bride — and you will become beautiful in His sight!

5

Getting Back Your Fight

Paying the Cost of Prevailing Prayer

Paul said: **"Fight the good fight of faith, lay hold on eternal life"** *(1 Timothy 6:12)*. Near the end of his ministry, the apostle could boast, "I have fought a good fight, I have finished my course, I have kept the faith..." *(2 Timothy 4:7)*.

Paul never lost his fight — he was filled with it to his dying day. And many of our other spiritual fathers died fighting as well. The writer to the Hebrews said of the elders of the church, "[They] waxed valiant in fight, turned to flight the armies of the aliens" *(Hebrews 11:34)*. Men like Joshua and Caleb were mighty warriors to the very end.

What kind of fight have you been putting up in the past year? Have you been so overwhelmed at times you've lost your fight? Have you become a weak, passive soldier of the Cross — discouraged, wounded, perplexed? I pray this message from the Holy Spirit will put the fight back in you — that once more you'll be fearless against the devil's weapons. It's time for you to get back up and fight the good fight!

Jacob is our example of how to get back our fight — and how to prevail with God. When the prophet Hosea wanted to warn Israel about their cowardly spiritual condition, he reminded them of their father Jacob. The crux of the message is, "You've become weak, passive. And now the enemy is overwhelming you. You claim to be Jacob's seed — but I want to show you how far you've strayed from his example. I want to show you how Jacob prevailed — how he had power with God!"

Hosea told the Isrealites this about Jacob: "He took his brother by the heel in the womb, and by his strength he had power with God: yea, he had power of the angel, and prevailed: he wept, and made supplication unto him: he found him in Bethel, and there he spake with us" *(Hosea 12:3-4)*.

In this very brief passage about Jacob, Hosea sums up three secrets to getting back our fight — and how to overcome and prevail with God. Let me list them for you:

1. "He Took His Brother by the Heel in the Womb" *(Hosea 12:3)*.

Esau came forth from his mother's womb first — a baby covered with man's hair! (His name means "hairy man.") But his twin, Jacob, had grabbed his heel while still in the womb. What a shock the midwife must have had as she delivered Esau. As he came forth, a tiny hand had a grip on his heel!

The Israelites listening to Hosea who recounted this story must have looked at each other in bewilderment. "What does this have to do with us?" they probably asked. "What does it have to do with fighting the enemy?"

Hosea's message to them was very simple: "Here was a man greedy for God — hungry for everything God had for him!" Jacob came out of the womb in a fighting mood, greedy for the blessings of God. There was something of a godly instinct in this child. It was as if he were saying, "Brother, if you don't want the fullness of God, I do. Get out of my way! I won't be left behind in God's blessings."

The birthright and blessing Jacob desired throughout his life represent all the blessings that are in Christ Jesus. Yet it wasn't the double portion of his father's wealth that Jacob was after; it wasn't the promise of the land. He proved that wasn't so by laboring under Laban for fourteen years by the sweat of his brow. No, Jacob wanted something more. He wanted the blessing of God so he could be in the lineage of the Messiah. And he wanted the priestly blessing. This meant not only being priest of the clan — but also being able to bless others!

We see this priestly ministry throughout Genesis 27, and as Isaac laid hands on Jacob and blessed him: "...that my soul may bless thee..." *(verses 4, 19, 27)*. It meant the high honor of having God's hand on him — and being given the power to bless others.

This is what is being required of believers in these last days. God is wanting to raise up a people who aren't concerned only about making their own living, owning a house or driving a nice car. He is seeking those who are greedy for the blessing of God — not to consume it on themselves, but to be used of Him to help others.

Jacob's brother Esau represents everything that God hates in humankind. He lived only for himself — for immediate pleasure and self-satisfaction. He never considered God's eternal purposes. And God said of him: "...yet I loved Jacob, and I hated Esau..." *(Malachi 1:2-3)*.

But Jacob lived for God's purposes. And his hand on Esau's heel was a powerful statement. It said: "I will not be held by sin's grip — I am more than a conqueror! I will lay hold of all that is of Satan and resist, fight and be victorious. I want God's hand on me — I want His blessing at any cost. I was born to be a channel of His blessing."

Hosea used this to chide Israel: "You claim to be children of Jacob, but you know nothing of his consuming hunger for the things of God. You're carnal, lazy — you're careless about seeking His fullness. Your hands reach out for selfish things. You are nothing like your father, Jacob!"

Jacob spent years fighting to get and keep the blessing of God. And that same desire ought to put a fight in all of God's people. If you don't hunger for Jesus — if you only want to make it to heaven and not be bothered by the needs of others — then you have nothing to fight for. You are a powder-puff Christian, an easy mark for the devil.

This is why so many followers of Jesus are in bondage to lusts and habits of all kinds. They have no fight. They refuse to grab the heel of their sin and cast it down through the power of God. Instead they claim, "I can't help my sin." But that is not so. There is great victory for all who will fight their besetting sin!

A young man who was flirting with homosexuality recently told me, "I really don't fight it. In fact, I kind of like it." He can never be delivered until he sees it as evil — as sin — and until he stands up and fights. You've got to get a grip on the heel of your sin! You've got to grab hold of it and say, "God, I want Your blessing. I want victory over everything in my life that is unlike You!"

2. "And by His Strength He Had Power With God" *(Hosea 12:3)*.

Jacob had labored under Laban for fourteen years. During that time, Laban changed his wages ten times. But Jacob was very prosperous because God's hand was on him. Now Laban's sons wanted to kill him because, they said, "He's stealing us blind!"

Jacob became concerned for his family's safety. And Scripture says God came to Jacob in the middle of the night: "And the Lord said unto Jacob, Return unto the land of thy fathers, and to thy kindred; and I will be with thee" *(Genesis 31:3)*. Jacob immediately obeyed. He gathered his family and flocks and set out on a journey home.

Please understand this: Jacob went in God's time, in God's way, with God's calling and mandate — and with His promise ringing in his ears: "I will go with you." God made him go!

Yet in spite of all this — in spite of being in God's perfect will, having a clear word from Him and obeying Him completely — Jacob suddenly entered into some of the hardest times a man of God ever experienced. He was hungry for God — worshiping the Lord, spending time at the altar, walking in complete obedience. But suddenly everything began spinning out of control.

First, he received word Esau was coming — racing toward him with 400 rough riders, appearing set for revenge. "Then Jacob was greatly afraid and distressed…" *(32:7)*. So Jacob divided his entourage into groups and droves of cattle. He sent the first group forth to meet Esau, instructing them, "Tell Esau all these camels and donkeys and sheep are his — a gift from his brother, Jacob." Jacob then told the other groups to flee if the first group met with the sword. Finally, he sent his two wives, two women servants and eleven sons over the brook Jabbok — and he was left all alone.

We need only to look into our own hearts to know what must have gone through Jacob's mind in that lonely hour. I see him pacing back and forth, his arms flailing in frustration. He was weeping, crying, wailing before God: "O God — it must have been the enemy who gave me the word to do this! How could You put Your obedient servant through such a trial? First, You gave me a clear word telling me to go. And I obeyed You — I did exactly what You told me. But now I've ended up facing an army of powerful enemies! My whole family is in the crisis of their lives. And I'm about to lose everything. My very life is on the line! What kind of guidance is this, God? You called me out here — and now You've abandoned me!"

Beloved, this was not the worst part. At the very depth of his despair and deepest confusion, when Jacob needed the comforting Word of God — the Lord came toward him as if an enemy, to fight him! "And Jacob was left alone; and there wrestled a man with him until the breaking of the day" *(verse 24)*. Try to imagine the scene. Jacob sees the form of a man coming at him, with fists raised and a challenge: "Come on, Jacob — fight!"

If ever a man seemed to have a reason to give up, it was Jacob. He was as low and confused at this point as he could ever get. And instead of getting an encouraging word from God, he was called out to fight. Jacob could have said, "That's it — no more! I can't take it. I've tried, I've obeyed, but everything is spinning out of control. All my circumstances tell me I'm not in God's will. I'm at my wits' end. God, You told me You

48

would go with me. But instead You've come at me only to pin me to the ground. I'm about to die, and You say, 'Fight!' No man can take this. You can do what You want. You won't get any fight out of me!"

Beloved — I have been there! I remember once standing by a window overlooking this city. On one side a death angel whispered, "Your daughter is next." And on the other side Satan whispered, "I'll wreck your home and cause you to reproach God's name." Everything seemed to be unraveling. My own body was heavy with pain, fear, trembling — and accusing demons on all sides!

I know what it's like to scream at God, "What's going on? I'm not living in sin. I've obeyed You! I came to New York in faithfulness to You. I haven't done anything to deserve any of this. But it looks like You've allowed the devil to get to me. Is this what happens when I obey You, God? If I've done wrong, show me. But don't let this go on any longer!"

To make matters worse, the Lord didn't come to me with outstretched arms of comfort. I heard no soft whisper of reassurance. Instead, He came at me with fists clenched, commanding me, "Stand up, David — fight!"

It's Not Esau That Is Coming at Jacob; It Is Life, the Future!

Jacob wasn't in any trouble with Esau. If he were, God would have delivered him. God had already promised Jacob at Bethel He would go with him to the very end. He'd even shown him a vision of a host of angels all around him. No, Jacob was in no danger from Esau. He was in danger from his own weakness to face the rest of his life!

So God came as Jacob's fight trainer — as a sparring partner to make him into a strong warrior who could prevail over any enemy. Think of it this way:

Suppose a boxing trainer took his fighter to an isolated training camp. Then he spent the whole training season psyching up his man for the big fight. He tells him: "I'll be with you at ringside. I'll never leave you nor forsake you. Here is a list of great boxers of the past. Study their every move. You don't have to suffer through hard workouts. I told you you're a winner — and my word is all you need. And when you step into the ring with Monster Man, I'll give you some diagrams on how to defeat him."

What kind of a trainer is this? Utterly foolish? Absolutely! I ask you — what would a good trainer do? He would find the best boxer he could, put him in the ring with his man and let them have it out.

Yet, how many Christians who call themselves warriors have never been tested or trained? We hear so much about the many prayer warriors in this nation. But the sad truth is, the vast majority of them have never been in battle. They've not been trained — and they're not ready to fight!

Recently, I asked the Lord why so many true believers are going through such heavy, hard times. "Why such deep suffering?" I wondered. "Why are so many being tested to their limits?" It is because the majority of Christians have quit the battle! They refuse to fight the devil or do battle against his kingdom. And when God does find a believer with a hunger and a desire for His blessing, He puts him into the ring.

You see, God knows Satan is going to be loosed on the earth for his last hour of warfare. And the Lord is going to need well-trained warriors who will prevail over all the powers of hell. Right now He is doing a quick work in His remnant. It's called crisis training!

These suffering, deeply tested saints are becoming the captains of His last-day army. God is putting Holy-Ghost fight in them — and He's bringing forth warriors who are tested and tried, because they've wrestled with God. The more they suffer, and the more intense their trial, the greater the work He has for them to do!

This kind of training calls for physical discipline as well as spiritual. Jacob threw his whole body into the battle, all his human ability. A fighting spirit had risen up in him — and, Scripture says, "by his strength he had power with God" *(Hosea 12:3)*. This verse has great meaning for all who want to prevail in prayer. It says Jacob prevailed and won the battle "by his strength." Likewise, if you're going to prevail in these last days, you're going to have to put all your body and physical strength into it.

Many Christians expect God somehow to save their family, reconcile relationships, do miracles — all at no cost to them. They just want to rest — to sit in their rocking chair and "believe God for it all." But this matter of prevailing in prayer — "breaking through" to God, getting answers and seeing results — is going to cost your flesh something. Consider what it cost Jesus: "Who in the days of his flesh, when he had offered up prayers and supplications with strong crying and tears..." *(Hebrews 5:7)*. Even though Jesus knew He was God in the flesh, He wept and cried out before the Father.

Jacob also "...wept, and made supplication unto him..." *(Hosea 12:4)*. And when Jacob did this, he was ninety-seven years old. He wasn't "just getting by," drifting along in some passive apathy. No! God's Spirit came upon him, and he dug in to lay hold of what God promised. He fought, wept and begged before God!

Jacob Realized His Battle Was Not With Esau
— But With the Lord!

This is one of the greatest lessons we can ever learn. Our battle is never with people — not our coworkers, not our neighbors, not our unsaved loved ones — but with God! If you settle things with God, everything else has to fall in line. When you're right before God — sprinkled with Christ's blood, having no sin in your life, prevailing in prayer — all the demons in hell can't make a dent in what God wants to do. He wants you to have that kind of strength — holy strength — and that means putting your flesh into it.

Hosea said, "The Lord hath also a controversy with Judah [His people] ..." *(Hosea 12:2)*. What is this controversy God has with His church? It is spiritual laziness! We want miracles, blessings, deliverances — but all at no cost, no effort. Hosea said to Israel, "All you want is prosperity and security. You're not willing to take a stand. You don't want to live for Jehovah's pleasure, but for your own!"

Who among God's people today prays all night — wrestling, fighting, weeping, crying out to God? Who disciplines their flesh to seek God, bringing their body under subjection to spend hours in prayer until breaking through? Who wants holiness, purity and Christlikeness so much they're willing to shut themselves in with God until they prevail? Who is so consumed with pleasing God that they're desperate to be delivered from all habits, all lusts — and they cry out, fight and wrestle with God until He breaks all chains?

Jacob prevailed "by his strength" — and so must you and I! We have His strength, but we just don't use it. "Strengthened with all might, according to his glorious power, unto all patience and long-suffering with joyfulness" *(Colossians 1:11)*. "That he would grant you, according to the riches of his glory, to be strengthened with might by his Spirit in the inner man" *(Ephesians 3:16)*.

The church of Jesus Christ is never going to see what God has for His body — until He sees us seeking Him in earnest, "The effectual fervent prayer of a righteous man availeth much" *(James 5:16)*. God wants you to lay hold of Him — because He loves you! He is saying, "Here it is. If you want it, come and get it." He wants to make a soldier out of you — to make you strong for His army!

3. "He Found Him in Bethel, and There He
Spake With Us" *(Hosea 12:4)*.

This verse does not say God spoke to Jacob at Bethel. It says, rather, "He spake with us." Hosea was talking about Israel — and about us, His church, today. He is saying God wants to speak to us at Bethel!

God met Jacob at Bethel on two occasions:

• The first time, Jacob was running from Esau, having stolen the birthright. He stopped at one point and piled up stones for a pillow. And as he slept, he dreamed of a ladder reaching into heaven, with angels ascending and descending. That was the first time God said to him: "And behold, I am with thee, and will keep thee in all places whither thou goest..." *(Genesis 28:15)*. In other words: "I'm with you from this day on — wherever you go!"

Jacob awoke and said: "Surely the Lord is in this place.... How dreadful is this place! This is none other but the house of God, and this is the gate of heaven.... And he called the name of that place Bethel..." *(verses 16-19)*. Bethel means "house of God" — a place to meet God!

• The second time God met Jacob at Bethel was after two of his sons committed a heinous act. Simeon and Levi were angry that Shechem the Hivite had raped their sister Dinah. So they took revenge and slew the entire town.

Jacob said to them, "... Ye have troubled me to make me stink among the inhabitants of the land... they shall gather themselves together against me, and slay me; and I shall be destroyed, I and my house" *(34:30)*.

Jacob was in a terrible crisis once again — and he didn't know what to do. Then, the Bible says: "... God said unto Jacob, Arise, go up to Bethel, and dwell there..." *(35:1)*. "Then Jacob said... let us arise, and go up to Bethel; and I will make there an altar unto God, who answered me in the day of my distress, and was with me in the way which I went" *(verses 2-3)*.

That's what Bethel is — a place to go in our time of distress! And the lesson for Israel and for us today is this: Whenever Jacob was in trouble or danger — when things looked foreboding and hopeless — he knew where to go and what to do. God was saying to Jacob, "You know where I'll speak to you, where you'll hear My voice. Go back to Bethel! Go to the altar where I met you. Get down on your face before Me. And cleanse your house of all idolatry."

Jacob called his sons to bring forth all their idols, and he buried them under an oak tree. Then he led his family to Bethel, where he erected an altar before God. Again God told Jacob, "I am with you." Then, Scripture

52

says, "…the terror of God was upon the cities that were round about them, and they did not pursue after the sons of Jacob" *(verse 5)*. The surrounding cities were afraid of Jacob — this little Jewish clan — because God put a dread in them!

Beloved, the Lord is still God of Bethel! And He is saying to us, "Go to Bethel — because that's where I'm going to meet you. Every time you're in trouble or distress, run to the altar. Cry out — get alone with Me!" He is waiting for us to meet Him in the secret closet of prayer.

But few Christians run to Bethel when they're in trouble or overwhelmed. Prayer isn't the first thing they do; it's the last! Instead, they try to "ride it out." They run to friends and counselors — and they drag about in despair. Some even go across the country to hear so-called prophets give them a "personal word."

But Jacob knew where to go to get a clear word from God Himself. He went to Bethel — to the altar. He shut himself in with God in a secret place!

Of course I believe God talks to us. I believe He gives us words. But it happens on our knees! That's where God says He will meet us.

A Final Word for Some Readers Today:

I believe God gave me this word to you for this very day: God is calling you today to get your eyes off all circumstances. Don't judge anything by your present condition. Don't try to figure it all out. Don't let fear cast you down. God will meet you in prayer! He will soon bring forth His word to you. He will not keep you in the dark. He knows you're being obedient to Him.

Just accept that you're being trained. Throw off your passive, defeated countenance. Cast aside all feelings of defeat — and stand up and fight! He has given you the strength. You just haven't used it! You're not going to hear God's voice until you're shut in with Him alone at your Bethel — down on your face before Him, weeping, crying out, "Lord, I'm not letting go until I hear Your voice!"

Right now God is saying, "Come on, fight!" — because He loves you. He wants you to claim all His blessings. So, rise up in faith and lay hold of His promise. Stand up and fight. You have His strength — use it!

A Place Called Wit's End

6

Trusting God in Hopeless Situations

They that go down to the sea in ships, that do business in great waters; these see the works of the Lord, and his wonders in the deep. For he commandeth, and raiseth the stormy wind, which lifteth up the waves thereof. "They mount up to the heaven, they go down again to the depths: their soul is melted because of trouble. They reel to and fro, and stagger like a drunken man, and are at their wit's end" *(Psalm 107:23-27)*.

In this psalm, the place called "wit's end" is on a ship's deck in a storm-tossed sea. Giant waves carry the ship up to the heavens, then drop it down to the depths. Powerful winds toss it back and forth so that none of the sailors can find their "sea legs." They stagger across the deck like drunken men.

The ship's sails are tattered and ripped, and wave after powerful wave crashes onto the deck. The sailors have to struggle just to hold on. It looks like it's all over for them — and they're in total despair. They are helpless — vulnerable to the power of the elements, unable to stop the storm, powerless to save themselves.

These sailors have come to a place called "wit's end." It is a condition that afflicts all Christians at one time or another. This phrase means simply, "having lost or exhausted any possibility of perceiving or thinking of a way out." In short, it is the end of all human ability and resources. There is no escape — no help, no deliverance, other than in God Himself.

Perhaps You Have Already Arrived at "Wit's End"!

Like the sailors aboard the ship, you have simply been going about your business, moving on in your walk with Jesus. Then one day, out of nowhere, a storm hit — and waves of trouble came crashing down on you from all sides!

Life's troubles seldom come one at a time. They're like the waves in a storm — coming one after another, fast and furious, mounting higher and higher. It's as if the sun has gone down, the air has turned cold and icy, and the winds of trouble have begun beating down. Like the sailors in Psalm 107, your "...soul is melted because of trouble..." *(verse 26)*. (The Hebrew word for melted here means "fainting with fear.")

I must note: God Himself has initiated this storm. "...For he commandeth, and raiseth the stormy wind..." *(verse 25)*. He's the One who brought the sailors to this place. He's the One raising the wind, stirring up the waves, tossing the ship. It is all His doing!

Yet this can be a great encouragement to our faith whenever troubles hit us from all sides. We have the knowledge that all troubles and storms in life have been ordained by God, for those who walk in righteousness. They aren't caused by the devil or some particular sin. Rather, the Lord has brought us to wit's end — and He has a purpose in it all.

"Beloved, think it not strange concerning the fiery trial which is to try you, as though some strange thing happened unto you: but rejoice, inasmuch as ye are partakers of Christ's sufferings; that, when his glory shall be revealed, ye may be glad also with exceeding joy" *(1 Peter 4:12-13)*. God is not surprised by your ordeal. In fact, it is happening because He wants to produce something in your heart — to reveal His glory in you.

Yet you may feel it is absolutely the worst storm in your life! Your trial may be a financial struggle, business troubles, slander, family problems or a personal tragedy. You go to bed at night with a restlessness inside and a cloud hanging over you. When you awaken, the dull ache is still with you. And it keeps hanging on until one day you wake up, crying, "God, how much more do I have to endure? How long will You allow me to go through this? When will it all end?"

When did the storm stop for the sailors in Psalm 107? When did God bring them into their desired safe haven? According to the psalmist, two things happened:

● First, the sailors came to their wit's end, giving up on all human hope or help. They said, "There's no way we can save ourselves. Nobody on earth can get us out of this!"

● Second, they cried to the Lord in the midst of their trouble — turning to Him alone for help.

"Then they cry unto the Lord in their trouble, and he bringeth them out of their distresses. He maketh the storm a calm, so that the waves thereof are still. Then are they glad because they be quiet; so he bringeth them unto their desired haven" *(Psalm 107:28-30).*

If you are a true child of God — if you're set on allowing Him to mold you into the image of His Son — then your battle won't stop until you give up trying to figure it all out and throw yourself completely into God's care. Until He has accomplished His eternal purposes in you, your troubles will only continue to rage!

Right now, you could be keeping your storm raging, your troubles piling up. You could be missing the calm that God wants to bring to you. How does this happen? It happens when you keep questioning the Lord in the midst of your crisis; when you keep murmuring and complaining; when you phone a friend whom you think has the answer for you; when you turn to counselors, psychologists, lawyers, experts; when you go to a Christian bookstore and buy stacks of self-help books and tapes; when you keep looking for that one secret, that one plan, to deliver you from your trouble.

Beloved, you're only prolonging your trial! It sounds simple, but from the very beginning God has been wanting our childlike trust and confidence. And you're only keeping the storm raging and the waves piling up when you refuse to cry out, "Lord, I'm in a mess — and the only way out is You!"

God Keeps Bringing Us to Wit's End Until We Learn to Trust Him Completely — No Matter How Hopeless Things Appear!

We see this happen time after time with the children of Israel in the wilderness. Again and again God brought them to wit's end — to test them, to see if they would trust Him. But each time they refused!

First the Lord brought them to a place called Pihahiroth, between Migdol and the sea. He had shut them in — the sea in front, the mountains on both sides, and Pharaoh behind. God had actually led them to a place of human hopelessness — to wit's end!

Had the Israelites simply believed one promise God had made to them, they could have been free from all worry and fear. God had told them: "...the Lord thy God bare [carried] thee...the Lord your God...went in the way before you, to search you out a place to pitch your tents in...to shew you by what way ye should go..." *(Deuteronomy 1:31-33).*

God was saying, in other words, "I will go with you! I will carry you as a man carries his son. I will walk before you and find places for you to pitch your tents. Wherever the cloud I have provided for you stops, that's where you are to stop."

It happened that the cloud stopped between Migdol and the sea — a place of total befuddlement, of wit's end. There was no way Israel could figure their way through the Red Sea. And now Pharaoh's army was fast approaching.

Are you in a hard place right now, with a storm brewing? I ask you: How did you get there? Do you think the devil put you there? My answer to you is this: "The steps of a good man are ordered by the Lord..." *(Psalm 37:23)*. No matter what storm you're going through, no matter how black things seem, God has put you in that place — at wit's end!

Please understand: God is never caught by surprise. He doesn't have to ad lib His divine direction whenever troubles befall us. He doesn't flip some cosmic coin to determine His actions on our behalf. No — long before Israel left Egypt and arrived at Migdol, God's plan for them was already set. He had already commanded the winds to blow at a certain hour, to wall up the Red Sea. He had known all along exactly what He was going to do.

Likewise today, God has a plan to bring you out of your storm. In fact, He devised that plan long before your trouble even started. Yet He will hold it back to the very last moment, waiting for you to trust Him. He wants to see if you'll put your life into His hands and say, "Live or die, I will trust the Lord!"

Israel failed this test. They became fearful, fainting at wit's end. Yet God still did for them what He had planned all along. He delivered Israel with a mighty miracle. But the result was, the people sang their song of faith on the wrong side of the Red Sea. Had they simply believed God's promise — "I will go before you and carry you as a man carries his son" — they would have passed the test!

If you panic at wit's end as Israel did — fainting, accusing God of not caring — He nevertheless will move in at the last moment and deliver you. But, afterward, He will take you into another wit's-end experience — because you did not come through the last one trusting in Him!

Indeed, just three days after their Red Sea deliverance, Israel was back in the middle of another big crisis. The people were hot, exhausted, overcome by thirst. Their scouts now came back crying, "There is water ahead at Marah, but we can't drink it. It's too bitter!"

Scripture makes it very clear: It wasn't the devil who had led Israel to this testing place. It was the cloud that had led them here. Once more, the people were at wit's end. And what a wailing went up from the camp — what awful accusations against Moses and God: "You've brought us here to die!"

Did God know these waters at Marah were bitter? Of course He did! But He had a plan. There was a certain living tree near that bitter pond — and He would use it to purify the waters for Israel.

I wonder — how many years before had God planted that tree in that spot? And how many times had the hot sun beaten on that tree to wither it? How many worms had tried to kill it? How many passersby had tried to cut it down? I tell you, nobody could have touched it — because God had a plan for it! He said, "One day My children are going to come here, and these waters will need to be purified. I have a plan to deliver them — and it's going to involve this tree!"

Of course, this tree in the desert represents the Cross. And, beloved, God has already planted a tree of deliverance for you. He knows exactly what to do about your problem, and the exact hour He will do it. All He wants from you is a quiet trust. He wants you to say, "My God is with me. He knows the way out of my trouble!"

Wit's End Is a Place of Suffering, Pain and Insecurity.

We see this illustrated in Israel's experience at Rephidim:

"And all the congregation of the children of Israel journeyed from the wilderness of Sin...according to the commandment of the Lord, and pitched in Rephidim: and there was no water for the people to drink.... And...the people murmured against Moses, and said, Wherefore is this that thou hast brought us up out of Egypt, to kill us and our children and our cattle with thirst? And Moses cried unto the Lord, saying, What shall I do unto this people? They be almost ready to stone me" *(Exodus 17:1-4).*

God had led Israel to the driest place in the whole wilderness. It was a testing place — with no stream, no well, not even a trickle of water. Most baffling of all, Israel was led there "...according to the commandment of the Lord..." *(verse 1).*

God Himself had allowed His people to grow thirsty: "And the people thirsted there for water..." *(verse 3).* Babies were crying, children wailing, grandparents suffering parched throats. Parents looked at their families and thought, "In a few days we'll all be dead." So they turned in anger to

Moses, crying, "Give us water to drink!" They were still depending on man — on the flesh!

I want to stop here to point out something. First, God took Israel to Migdol by the sea, to test them — and they failed to trust Him there. Next, He took them to Marah, where He had another plan of deliverance — and they failed the test again. Now He brought them to Rephidim for more testing. Do you see the pattern? If you don't learn to trust the Lord in simple, childlike faith when you're being tested, He will bring you back to yet another testing ground. You'll go from one test to another!

Israel was in just such a place once again. They were hot, thirsty, angry. But God already had a plan. He wasn't going to let them die. He had chosen beforehand to have them walk up Mount Horeb to a reservoir of water that He had prepared long before. And that source would last not just a day, a week or a month — but thirty-eight years!

Yet God was waiting for a response of faith from Israel. He was saying, "I have taken you through all of these things, but you've refused to learn. Will you trust Me now? How many more problems do I have to allow in your life before you'll trust Me?"

Many Christians are being tested and tried right now through unemployment. They have sent out resumes in every direction, but weeks roll by and nothing turns up. They've used up all their savings, and now they're surrounded by creditors. Their situation looks totally hopeless. There is pain and suffering involved; it is never easy.

Others have jobs but are underemployed. They don't earn enough to make ends meet. Many working young people have had to move back in with their parents. And thousands of single mothers are scraping by on a tiny income.

Numerous business owners are barely surviving. Many have trouble sleeping at night because the business world is so crazy, with skyrocketing taxes, increasing regulations, shaky profits. The competition is growing, and they have exhausted all their ideas and alternatives. Now they lie awake worrying about what to do.

These suffering, anxiety-ridden people come to church and raise their hands in praises to the Lord. They put on big smiles and hug each other. Yet they are going through awful pain and insecurity. They are troubled — completely at wit's end.

I ask you: As God's children, do we have no option but fear — sleepless nights, restless days, endless times of questioning God and living in utter turmoil? Consider Israel: Was their fretting and grumbling the only response possible? Was it simply human for them to react as they did, out of concern for their families?

Let me answer these questions by raising another one: Hasn't God always known what He was going to do in each of these cases? Hasn't He always had a plan? Think about it: Didn't God already plan to have the winds open the Red Sea? Didn't He already preserve a tree at Marah that would heal the waters? Didn't He already choose a rock on Mount Horeb, out of which He would supply Israel's water for decades?

Our loving, heavenly Father would never lead His children into a dry desert only to let them die of thirst — especially when He has a reservoir stored in a nearby rock! God has always had a plan for His people. And He has a plan for you right now, to deliver you from your present trouble. There is no problem you have that He can't unravel.

Let me show you why God had to bring Israel to the brink of disaster before He miraculously met their need:

God Brought Israel to Wit's End to Try to Induce Faith Through the Miraculous — and It Didn't Work!

I want to talk to you about the limitations of the miraculous. Many Christians travel thousands of miles each year to witness supernatural works — miracles, manifestations, signs, wonders. Yet, ironically, these sign-seeking addicts never develop a lasting faith — because miracles rarely produce that. Instead, they always need a bigger, more spectacular miracle.

Nobody had ever seen as many supernatural works as Israel. God provided miracle after miracle for them — and yet each work left the people as faithless and unbelieving as the first. You'd think that the ten plagues on Egypt would have produced faith in the Israelites. When Egypt was afflicted with flies, there were none to be found in Israel's camp. When Egypt fell under total darkness, there was no darkness in Israel. Yet none of their deliverances from these miraculous plagues produced faith of any kind.

Even after God opened the Red Sea, Israel's faith lasted only three days. Scripture says: "...they remembered not the multitude of thy mercies; but provoked him at the sea, even at the Red Sea" *(Psalm 106:7)*. The psalmist is saying here: "They even doubted God at the Red Sea —

the place where He performed His greatest miracle!"

The elders who watched Moses strike the rock at Marah saw water come flowing out. Indeed, all of Israel drank to the full — and yet that miracle didn't produce any faith. Then God sent hordes of quail to Israel. Hundreds of thousands of birds fell from the sky into the midst of their camp, and the people cooked them for meat. Still they had no faith. The next morning, when Israel came out of their tents, the ground was covered with manna, miraculously sent from heaven. Yet even this didn't produce faith.

On the contrary, after all these glorious miracles, God's children wrung their hands in despair, crying, "...Is the Lord among us, or not?" *(Exodus 17:7)*. In other words: "Is God even with us? How could He be leading us when we have so much trouble?"

Israel had received forty years of miracle food, miracle water, a miracle cloud by day, miracle fire by night, miracle protection, miracle clothes that never wore out. Moses told them: "...These forty years the Lord thy God hath been with thee; thou hast lacked nothing" *(Deuteronomy 2:7)*. And yet still they doubted Him. In fact, all but two of those who had witnessed these miracles died in the wilderness — in total unbelief!

We are so like Israel. We want God to speak a word, grant us a miraculous deliverance, quickly meet our needs, remove all our pain and suffering. In fact, you may be saying right now, "If God would just get me out of this mess — if He'd give me this one miracle — I'd never doubt Him again!" Yet, what about all the miracles He has performed for you already? They haven't produced in you any faith to help you in your present trouble.

Recently, two precious men of God from the Zulu tribe in Africa visited Times Square Church. An incredible revival is taking place among the 8 million Zulus today, and God is doing miraculous things among them. For example, more than ten cases have been documented of the dead being raised. Yet that is not what these men wanted to talk about. Rather, what has impressed them most about the revival are the "over-comer Zulus" — those who take a stand for Christ, burning witchcraft books and witnessing boldly even though they're being tested and tried severely. These people were once evil, with murderous spirits — and now they're being transformed into the image of Jesus.

I believe the greatest sign or wonder to the world in these last days isn't a person who's been raised from the dead. No, what truly makes an impact on the mind and spirit of the ungodly is the Christian who endures all trials, storms, pain and suffering with a confident faith. Such a believer emerges from his troubles stronger in character, stronger in faith, stronger in Christ.

I recently read of a foggy little town of 4,000 people in Hungary with an alarming suicide rate. The newspaper headline read: "Suicide Stalks Isolated Village." Residents there have committed suicide in every conceivable manner. One man tossed himself into an abandoned well. Another hanged himself. Some people have overdosed. Others cut their wrists, swallowed pesticides, jumped in front of trains. Entire families have taken their lives, from teenagers to grandparents.

The town is Asotthalom, one hundred miles south of Budapest, and it is a desolate, lonely place. A doctor named Ulloh runs a psychiatric clinic there, and he told a reporter, "Some people call the road here the 'narrow road to the cursed place.' …It is ingrained in the people that God doesn't very much like us."

Beloved, that is the destructive power of unbelief! There is no worse despair than to believe God has it in for you. This was Israel's problem, and too often it is ours as well. We have an unspoken sense that all our suffering and troubles are the result of God's displeasure with us.

When You Are at Wit's End, One of Two Things Will Happen to You:

Every Christian emerges from wit's end either trusting in man, or trusting fully in God — that is, either cursed or blessed. Which way will you respond in your time of trouble?

Jeremiah writes: "Thus saith the Lord; Cursed be the man that trusteth in man, and maketh flesh his arm, and whose heart departeth from the Lord. For he shall be like the heath in the desert, and shall not see when good cometh; but shall inhabit the parched places in the wilderness, in a salt land and not inhabited. Blessed is the man that trusteth in the Lord, and whose hope the Lord is. For he shall be as a tree planted by the waters, and that spreadeth out her roots by the river, and shall not see when heat cometh, but her leaf shall be green; and shall not be careful in the year of drought, neither shall cease from yielding fruit" *(Jeremiah 17:5-8)*.

The first person Jeremiah talks about here doesn't wait for God to move. He takes matters into his own hands — making his own plans, turning to people he thinks have clout, taking shortcuts. He is always scheming, planning, manipulating. His philosophy is, "It's not what you know that counts, it's who you know." And he's forever looking for that special "who" to solve his problems.

Scripture says a spiritual dryness sets into this person's life: "...He shall be like the heath [shrub] in the desert..." *(verse 6)*. He looks barely alive — with no fruit, no wellspring of life. He's always on the brink of dying! "...he...shall not see when good cometh..." *(same verse)*. He never partakes in the joy of being delivered by God's hand. And everything he thinks looks good turns into misery. He is isolated, existing only in "...parched places..." *(same verse)*. He keeps withering away — sweating it out, always frantic.

But consider the one who trusts God in the hard places, at wit's end: "Blessed is the man that trusteth in the Lord, and whose hope the Lord is" *(verse 7)*. This Christian is "planted." He has roots, stability, a reservoir of Living Water. He is always "spreading out," fruitful and green with fresh life. Scripture says "...he...shall not be careful [fearful] in the year of drought..." *(verse 8)*. When things get hot and bothersome, he won't be afraid! This person says, "Jesus, I give up looking to any person to bring me out of my trial. I turn to You alone. You're my only keeper, my only hope. I look to You to bring me out of this!"

The Lord desires this kind of faith from us in everyday matters. You may object, "But, Brother Dave, I'm still unemployed, still having trouble." Yet I have to believe God's Word: "Trust Me, and you'll be blessed!"

You may answer, "But I don't know what I'm going to do. The storm is still raging. It looks so hopeless. I don't see any sign of help or deliverance." To all these things God still says, "Trust Me, My child — and you will be blessed!"

It doesn't matter whether your trial is with your family, with your business, or with putting food on the table. If you put your total trust in His Word and His faithfulness, God has promised to bless you — and He cannot lie! When the heat comes, you won't even be bothered. When the wind comes, you'll stand strong — because you will have learned to trust Him in spite of all unnerving circumstances. You'll be a green tree bearing the abundant fruit of confidence — and everyone around you will be given hope and encouragement as they behold your quiet trust.

God, help us all to surrender our wills, our personal agendas, when we come to this place called wit's end. May it become a place of renewed faith and trust in our loving Father.

The Solomon Church

7

How to Tell a Holy-Ghost Church From a Laodicean Church

I **believe Solomon represents the spirit and nature of the modern, last-day Laodicean church.** And this church — here in America and throughout the world — is headed for the same ruin Solomon faced!

Scripture tells us: "And Solomon the son of David was strengthened in his kingdom, and the Lord his God was with him, and magnified him exceedingly" *(2 Chronicles 1:1)*.

The church of Jesus Christ today has been strengthened and blessed mightily by God. Provision has been made for endeavors of all kinds. Consider the big, beautiful edifices being built in the land. One large Pentecostal church was built recently at a cost of $28 million. There are other church complexes worth $40-50 million.

Consider also the church's great financial blessings. Millions are spent on televangelism, books, records and tapes, missions, institutions, colleges and parachurch ministries of all kinds. Think of all the huge conventions, the well-attended seminars, the religious pomp and ceremony attending megachurch services and programs.

When all these works began, each one had something of God's anointing. Indeed, most started out with the same blessings that God poured out upon Solomon. Think about it: Solomon was well-organized. He was much more educated than his father, David. And he did everything bigger and better than any previous generation ever could have conceived. Solomon's organizational skills were so great — his pomp and ceremony so gorgeous and breathtaking — that when the Queen of Sheba watched him merely ascend into the temple, she nearly fainted at the sight.

Yet the driving force behind Solomon was wisdom and knowledge. This was his heart-cry to God: "Give me now wisdom and knowledge, that I may go out and come in before this people: for who can judge this thy people, that is so great?" *(verse 10)*.

Isn't this a wonderful prayer? It sounds so good, and God was pleased he did not ask for selfish gain. Yet there's a problem: It's totally man-centered! This very talented, self-confident king was saying, in essence, "Just give me the tools, God, and I'll get the job done. Give me the wisdom and knowledge, and I'll set everything in order among this people. I'll accomplish it all!"

Solomon's prayer was not the prayer of his father, David, a man who was after God's own heart. No, Solomon's prayer was that of a new generation — an educated people with new ideas and skills. And his cry was, "I need wisdom and knowledge!"

We Have Become the Church of the Floppy Disk!

The driving force behind the modern-day, Laodicean church is wisdom and knowledge. What great rivers of information flow through this last-day church: computers with countless megabytes, computerized Bibles, computerized commentaries, software programs on philosophy, counseling, fund-raising, child care. All you have to do is insert a little disk in your computer, press a button, and the answers pop up right in front of you.

I am not against computers or software programs. Our own ministry would not function as well without them. But I am amused by all the young ministers who spend much of their time punching keyboards and utilizing fax machines to spit out reams of information, ideas, networking and strategies. They preach a computerized gospel — yet so few people are ever saved or delivered through them!

There is an insatiable thirst today for information, wisdom and knowledge like never before. Never have there been so many seminars and massive teaching conventions. Huge screens are needed just to show who the teacher is on the distant stage. And afterward people flock to sale tables to buy hundreds of dollars' worth of tapes.

The emphasis is on more tools, more information, more wisdom. The thinking is, "If we just have enough knowledge on these subjects — enough books, enough seminars, enough teaching — we'll get the job done. Just give us the tools, God, and we'll evangelize the world!"

Recently, I heard the leader of a youth organization say, "If I had $100 million, I could win the world." He was traveling across the country trying to raise that amount. He was saying, "If we just have enough money, knowledge, networking and strategy, we can evangelize the entire world for God."

Beloved, we will never accomplish anything for God by wisdom alone, no matter how important and necessary it is. His Word says: "For after that in the wisdom of God the world by wisdom knew not God, it pleased God by the foolishness of preaching to save them that believe" *(1 Corinthians 1:21)*. All the true treasures of wisdom and knowledge are hidden in Jesus Christ. "In whom are hid all the treasures of wisdom and knowledge" *(Colossians 2:3)*.

Yet Solomon's gospel was different. It was said of Solomon: "And he spake three thousand proverbs: and his songs were a thousand and five. And he spake of trees, from the cedar tree that is in Lebanon even unto the hyssop that springeth out of the wall: he spake also of beasts, and of fowl, and of creeping things, and of fishes" *(1 Kings 4:32-33)*.

This was Solomon's gospel — 3,000 short sermonettes of practical knowledge and wisdom! He created new songs, wonderful stories, great applications of truth on human nature and behavior. You can read many of his words of wisdom throughout the book of Proverbs. He offered practical instruction on marriage and child-rearing. He gave clear directions on how to cope, how to behave, how to be blessed. And everyone loved his preaching. It was so concise, so to the point.

But, beloved, unless the Spirit of God anoints the preaching or teaching, it remains dead. It becomes dead-letter unless the Spirit ignites it! In the end, Solomon delivered an absolutely powerless message — because he had no power to practice what he preached. He gave himself to strange women. He raised wicked children, including a devil who succeeded him to the throne. Indeed, Solomon ended up a decrepit, anguished idolater, living out his days in a sensuous cesspool of immorality. And his entire generation became harlot-chasing reprobates — in spite of all his wisdom, teaching and 3,000 proverbs!

Now, don't think for a minute that today's, "sinner-friendly," Laodicean church does not have good, insightful, thoughtful preaching. The sermons of this last-day church are concise, homiletically correct, centered on how to cope with the problems of life. They are mostly fifteen-minute messages, illustrated with clear points and packed with lots of truth. Yet so many of them are not producing life! Divorce is still rampant, even among the shepherds. Fornication and infidelity are commonplace. Teenagers smoke, drink and sleep around. People's lives are not being changed. Why? It is because knowledge in itself is unable to save or change anybody — including those who preach it!

A church's services may be well-organized, with excellent, new, contemporary music. The choir may sing a thousand new songs. The pastor may condemn sin and point out the right way clearly. But without the Holy Ghost, it all becomes a letter that kills!

Solomon had a head full of wisdom and a mouth full of songs. He could preach and teach with incredible skill. He had a well-organized operation, with talented leaders. Everything about his church appeared to be decent and in order. But everything Solomon did ended up in Ecclesiastes, in the phrase, "All is vanity and despair!"

The Solomon church has all the answers. It looks great on the outside. But it is absolutely lifeless! And it ends up in vanity, idolatry, sensuality, emptiness and despair.

Compare the Church of Solomon With David's Church of Zion.

The driving force behind David's church was total dependence on the Holy Spirit. Here is what distinguished David: "Then Samuel took the horn of oil, and anointed him in the midst of his brethren: and the Spirit of the Lord came upon David from that day forward..." *(1 Samuel 16:13)*.

When David was on his deathbed, he said to his son Solomon, in so many words: "I want to tell you why God has blessed me. I want you to know the secret of my ministry — why the kingdom is at peace and why God has been with me everywhere I've gone." Listen to David's last words to his son: "The Spirit of the Lord spake by me, and his word was in my tongue" *(2 Samuel 23:2)*.

David was saying, "I didn't trust in my knowledge and wisdom. I didn't trust in any part of my flesh. I was a weak man — but I depended on the Holy Ghost! Every word I spoke was under His unction and anointing. His words filled my mouth!"

Thirty-five years ago, when we opened the ministry doors at 416 Clinton Avenue to drug addicts and alcoholics here in New York City, our motto was, "The Holy Ghost is in charge here." You see, it wasn't "how to cope" preaching that saved gang members like Nicky Cruz and Israel. They didn't fall on their knees because we preached concise, pithy sermons. They weren't convicted by pointed illustrations and nature stories. No — these former drug addicts testified to their friends, "I once was on the street, like you. But look at me now. The Spirit of God changed me!"

It was the power and demonstration of the Holy Ghost that brought Nicky and Israel to their knees before God. The Spirit came down — and those hardened criminals fell on their faces and cried out to God for mercy!

Solomon spoke of trees, hyssop, beasts, creeping things, fish. But David spoke of intimacy with the Lord, of brokenness and contriteness. He spoke of "the Rock" which is Christ. And David was convicted and changed by his own preaching. He so valued the presence of the Holy Spirit in his life, he asked the Lord never to take His Spirit from him. David knew he was nothing without the Holy Ghost.

In Solomon's church, however, a preacher merely gathers truthful, biblical information and creates a sermon out of it. Then he throws it out to the congregation and tells himself, "It's the Word — it has to have impact. It has to cause growth and change in my hearers, because it's God's powerful Word." Not so! You can throw out as much Word as you please — sermon upon sermon, teaching upon teaching, wisdom and knowledge in abundance. But if it isn't anointed by the Holy Ghost, it is a dead word! If a preacher doesn't spend time on his face before God, he won't have the fire of God in his soul. And there will be no unction of the Holy Ghost in his words, no matter how wise and knowledgeable they sound. They simply won't produce life.

Paul said, "And my speech and my preaching was not with enticing words of man's wisdom, but in demonstration of the Spirit and of power: that your faith should not stand in the wisdom of men, but in the power of God" *(1 Corinthians 2:4-5)*. "...we speak, not in the words which man's wisdom teacheth, but which the Holy Ghost teacheth....But the natural man receiveth not the things of the Spirit of God: for they are foolishness unto him: neither can he know them, because they are spiritually discerned" *(verses 13-14)*.

You should never go to church without praying, "God, give me Holy-Ghost ears to hear. Help me to hear, understand and apply Your Word to my life!" You must have Holy Ghost-hearing ears as much as a pastor has to have a Holy Ghost-speaking tongue!

How to Tell a Holy-Ghost David Church From a Laodicean Solomon Church.

In a Holy-Ghost church you will always hear a gut-wrenching cry of repentance. In fact, you cannot be a Holy-Ghost person until you "cry out from your guts" yourself. And that is something Solomon never did!

We never read of Solomon crying out his guts before God. Instead, at the dedication of the temple, he stood with kingly robes on his back and prayed a gracious, majestic, high-sounding prayer. It was all sincere, precise and orderly. But it wasn't a gut-cry — and it didn't penetrate his own heart!

In his prayer, Solomon admonished the congregation: "Let your heart therefore be perfect with the Lord our God, to walk in his statutes, and to keep his commandments, as at this day" *(1 Kings 8:61)*. Solomon knew the statutes of which he spoke. Among them were these warnings in Deuteronomy to every king of Israel:

● "But he shall not multiply horses to himself, nor cause the people to return to Egypt, to the end that he should multiply horses..."

● "Neither shall he multiply wives to himself, that his heart turn not away."

● "Neither shall he greatly multiply to himself silver and gold" *(Deuteronomy 17:16-17)*.

These were very clear, direct statutes. Yet no sooner had Solomon become king than he violated all three!

● "And Solomon had horses brought out of Egypt..." *(1 Kings 10:28)*.

● "But king Solomon loved many strange women, together with the daughter of Pharaoh, women of the Moabites, Ammonites, Edomites, Zidonians, and Hittites. ... Solomon clave unto these in love" *(11:1-2)*.

● "And the king made silver to be in Jerusalem as stones..." *(10:27)*. "And king Solomon passed all the kings of the earth in riches and wisdom" *(2 Chronicles 9:22)*.

Solomon's prayer to walk perfectly before God had no effect on his own life — because he had no conviction of sin in his heart: "And Solomon did evil in the sight of the Lord, and went not fully after the Lord, as did David his father" *(1 Kings 11:6)*. Where there is no Holy Ghost-anointed preaching, there is no conviction for sin — no fully going after the Lord!

Solomon sinned without remorse even while he preached against sin. He could read in the Scriptures that he was not to go down to Egypt to buy horses — and then immediately he would begin negotiating to buy a thousand new horses and chariots. He could hear a prophet preach that the king was not to multiply wives to himself — and yet immediately he would go out to inspect a harem for prospective wives. Solomon showed no evidence of sorrow, no sign of repentance. He could openly indulge in all this gross sin and immorality, and yet go back to his chamber and write another proverb.

Yet compare Solomon's indifference toward sin to David's total sorrow and brokenness for having sinned against God. David's church was not perfect; in fact, it was a Corinthian church. David committed adultery. He killed an innocent man. He walked for a season in horrible deception. Yet after David sinned, he uttered this rending cry from his innermost being: "Wash me throughly from mine iniquity, and cleanse me from my sin. For I acknowledge my transgressions: and my sin is ever before me. Against thee, thee only, have I sinned, and done this evil in thy sight.... Cast me not away from thy presence; and take not thy holy spirit from me" *(Psalm 51:2-4, 11)*.

David later sinned again by numbering the people of Israel, which he had been commanded not to do. He had just defeated all the giants and the remnant of Gath. He had driven out the Assyrians, and the entire land was at peace. In that moment, David enjoyed great blessing and victory. And yet he was deceived by the devil! David was so blinded by his sin, no amount of reasoning could change him. Joab, who had seen David's deception, warned him, "Why do you insist on going through with this sin?" But David persisted, saying, "I want to know how many fighting men I have!"

Beloved, this is a sobering thought — that a righteous, God-fearing servant could be deceived by sin! David lived under the deception for almost ten months. Yet, this time, no prophet had to come to him to expose his sin. It was the Holy Ghost who convicted him. Soon after the count had begun, David lost heart; he didn't even finish counting. He was now gray-haired and old, and he had become sensitive to the voice of the Spirit. The Bible tells us: "And David's heart smote him..." *(2 Samuel 24:10)*. The Hebrew here suggests: "Oh God, I am wounded in my heart for what I've done against You!"

That is the mark of the Holy-Ghost David church: a heartrending cry! Of course, there are many Christians who fail and who live in deception. But, like David, they have become so sensitive to the work and moving of the Holy Spirit. They don't always need a prophet to tell them they've sinned. They repent even before a prophet comes to them, because they feel wounded by their sin.

In Solomon's church, deception is never dealt with. Eventually, it leads to blindness and ruin. But in David's church, there is a cry of godly sorrow, a cry for deliverance — a wounded, grieving heart for having sinned against God!

David said of his sin: "The sorrows of hell compassed me about; the snares of death prevented me; in my distress I called upon the Lord, and cried to my God: and he did hear my voice out of his temple, and my cry did enter his ears . . . . He sent from above, he took me; he drew me out of many waters; he delivered me from my strong enemy, and from them that hated me: for they were too strong for me" *(22:6-7, 17-18)*.

Here Is the Tragic End of the Gospel According to Solomon!

After all that Solomon wrote and sang about, he concluded his life with these tragic words:

"All his days are sorrows, and his travail grief; yea, his heart taketh not rest in the night. . . . There is nothing better for a man, than that he should eat and drink, and that he should make his soul enjoy good in his labour. . . ." *(Ecclesiastes 2:23-24)*.

Solomon was saying philosophically, "You're going to have sleepless nights. And you won't be able to do anything about the despair. You won't be able to change your feeling that everything is vanity. So the best thing you can do is to grab all the gusto you can and squeeze everything you can out of life. Just enjoy yourself!"

That is how Solomon died. And that is the gospel of this present-day, Solomon age! Everything ends in Ecclesiastes, in emptiness and despair. Many people end up wondering, "What is life all about? Where am I headed? Who am I?"

Yet David's gospel says, "I cried unto the Lord with my voice, and he heard me out of his holy hill. I laid me down and slept. . ." *(Psalm 3:4-5)*. If you've got the Holy Ghost, you will know God's voice and He will know yours. And you'll be able to sleep soundly.

Now consider this prophecy from the New Testament: "After this I will return, and will build again the tabernacle of David, which is fallen down; and I will build again the ruins thereof, and I will set it up" *(Acts 15:16)*.

God is going to bring the Solomon church to ruin — and He is going to resurrect David's church from out of those ruins! This remnant church will have a godly sorrow for sin. It will cry out in anguish and repentance. And it will be wholly dependent upon the Holy Spirit!

Two years before the PTL ministry fell, the Spirit of God came upon me and instructed me to write a long letter to Jim Bakker. I wrote, "In two years, by March 15, PTL will be dead." I described a vision of emptiness — of weeds growing tall and bats nesting in the buildings.

Jim read the letter and called me, asking, "What must I do?" I told him first to get rid of all the homosexuals in his ministry. Yet, not long after that conversation, Jim appeared on television mocking every word I said. Two years later, to the very day, the Lord's word about PTL happened — just as He had told me.

To hear the Solomon gospel that's preached on much of Christian TV today, you'd think Jesus is going to return to the earth in Beverly Hills driving a Rolls Royce. This image of Christianity is the most abominable thing I've ever seen or heard. And God says He has to bring it to ruin — because He's going to build His David house upon those ruins!

Right now I sense in my spirit that in less than five years, there will be no more so-called gospel television networks. They will all fall into bankruptcy and absolute ruin. The only thing left will be some local television programs with true men of God preaching the gospel. And all the phony smiles, the ungodly fund-raising circuses, the pop theology, the preaching of prosperity are going to come down.

Most of the so-called spiritual revivals today are mere cardboard structures. They're all going to burn in the chaotic days ahead. What Christian will be laughing when our cities are in flames? Who will be giddy and foolish when the economy collapses?

The Bible says of the Jews in the last days: "And...in that day...I will pour upon the house of David...the spirit of grace and of supplications: and they shall look upon me whom they have pierced, and they shall mourn for him, as one mourneth for his only son, and shall be in bitterness for him, as one that is in bitterness for his firstborn" *(Zechariah 12:9-10)*.

Right now there are Jews mourning and weeping for their Messiah at the Wailing Wall in Jerusalem. And not long ago some 10,000 Lubavitcher Jews held a march in Brooklyn, crying, "This is the year of our Messiah!" Their hands were upraised, tears rolled down their faces, and they wept and cried out for their Messiah.

When I think of the 25 million babies aborted in this country and all the lost people who are going to hell, I don't understand why multitudes of Christians are laughing. Why are millions of Jews weeping and millions of hellbound sinners crying themselves to sleep, while charismatics are laughing? When the revival comes, the joy will be because of repentance and because of the ingathering of the last harvest of lost souls!

"I...will build again the tabernacle of David..." *(Acts 15:16)*. God is going to build His church in the last days on the ruins. That means He must ruin the evil taking place in His church and bring down all abominations. And on those ruins He will raise up a holy, repentant church that utters gut-wrenching cries of repentance!

I thank God for the David church He is building right now out of heaps of ruin. Indeed, many who read this message have come from ruined backgrounds. Dear saint, if that describes you, then rest assured — God is using you to build His David church!

If you've got an overwhelming sin problem, don't go to some book or tape that's supposedly full of wisdom and knowledge. Instead, get on your face and have it out with God. Be a Holy-Ghost David Christian and cry out to the Lord with all your heart. He is building His church on your very cries!

God Over-Answers Prayer

8

Our Lord Delights in Answering Us

One of the most often-heard phrases in the church is, **"God answers prayer!"** Yet that is only half the truth. The whole truth is, "God *over*-answers prayer!"

I want to act now as a lawyer before you. I'm going to build a case that will prove to you that in every generation — all through the Bible and continuing to the present day — God always over-answers the prayers of His children. He continually gives much more than we ask for — and often things we wouldn't think to request!

I'll go straight to the biblical record to make my case. It is built on precedent after precedent in history — all proving that God over-answers prayer!

1. God Over-Answered Israel in Hosea 14.

Here is a very clear picture of how God not only answered prayer — but over-answered! Hosea prophesied to Israel, "You're backslidden — but you're still God's people. Now return to the Lord and pray." "Take with you words, and…say unto him, Take away all iniquity, and receive us graciously…" *(Hosea 14:2)*.

Their prayer was simple. All Israel asked God to do was to take away their sin and receive them graciously. "Lord, have mercy. Cleanse us — receive us back into Your grace."

Yet God not only forgave their iniquities — He not only cleansed them and received them back graciously — He also added blessings beyond imagination! "I will heal their backsliding, I will love them freely…I will be as the dew unto Israel: he shall grow as the lily, and cast forth his roots as Lebanon. His branches shall spread, and his beauty shall be as the olive tree, and his smell as Lebanon. They that dwell under his shadow shall return; they shall revive as the corn, and grow as the vine: the scent thereof shall be as the wine of Lebanon" *(verses 4-7)*.

Now, the "dew of heaven" is the presence of the Lord. Up to this point there had been drought; everything was dying because God's favor had been taken away. But now, because of true repentance and a heartfelt prayer, God said He would cause life to spring up on all sides. Israel not only would be forgiven, but revived as well. They would grow, become well-rooted, spread out, thrive. All they asked for was mercy, forgiveness and acceptance. But instead, God opened the windows of heaven and poured on them blessings they dared not even hope for. God largely over-answered their prayer!

Beloved, God has done the same for you. When you repented, all you asked God for was a clean heart, forgiveness and peace. Yet look at how He has over-answered you:

• He gave you a hungering heart — a thirst for more and more of Jesus! He gave you eyes to see and ears to hear. He gave you a love for His body.

• He has put in you a hatred for sin. He has protected you from a raging, mad devil. He has flooded your soul with hope, joy and gladness.

• Jesus has become your morning dew! He waters your soul daily with His Word. And you are growing. You're not dead or dying, but very much alive in Him!

You asked only to be saved and cleansed. But God has poured out blessing upon blessing to you. He has over-answered you!

2. God Over-Answered Solomon's Prayer.

"Give therefore thy servant an understanding heart to judge thy people, that I may discern between good and bad: for who is able to judge this thy so great a people?" *(1 Kings 3:9).*

Solomon prayed, "Lord, all I want is wisdom to know how to handle Your people. I only want to be a just king and lord over them." It was a simple, direct request. But God answered Solomon's prayer in an incredible way: "And God said unto him, Because thou hast asked this thing... behold, I have done according to thy words: lo, I have given thee a wise and understanding heart; so that there was none like thee before thee, neither after thee shall any arise like unto thee" *(verses 11-12).*

Here we see how anxious God is to over-answer unselfish prayers. Solomon asked only for an understanding heart of discernment. But God not only gave him the heart he asked for — He also promised to make him wiser than anyone else in the history of humankind!

Yet God didn't stop there. He told Solomon: "And I have also given thee that which thou hast not asked, both riches, and honour: so that there shall not be any among the kings like unto thee all thy days...then I will lengthen thy days" *(verses 13-14)*.

What an incredible response! God added to Solomon's wisdom blessings, honor and riches such as no other man had ever received. And on top of that, He gave him a prolonged life: "I will lengthen thy days!" It was another prayer greatly over-answered!

3. God Over-Answered Israel Regarding the Ammonites.

"Moreover the children of Ammon passed over Jordan to fight...so that Israel was sore distressed" *(Judges 10:9)*.

Ammon had been used by God to correct Israel's sins. And now their army was marching toward Israel. God's people were perplexed and downcast — and they began to confess their sins: "And the children of Israel said unto the Lord, We have sinned: do thou unto us whatsoever seemeth good unto thee; deliver us only, we pray thee, this day" *(verse 15)*.

They were so haunted by their sin, they couldn't conceive of asking God for anything more than just to spare them. Theirs was the simplest of prayers: "Lord, deliver us — just this one time! Don't let us be defeated or overrun by our enemy." They prayed for a single victory. But God had something more in mind, and He over-answered their prayer mightily. Not only did Israel get protection — but they got the upper hand. They totally subdued the Ammonites! "So Jephthah passed over unto the children of Ammon to fight against them; and the Lord delivered them into his hands. And he smote them from Aroer, even till thou come to Minnith, even twenty cities....Thus the children of Ammon were subdued before the children of Israel" *(11:32-33)*.

Not only did God deliver Israel — but He also gave them the courage and the direction to defeat the Ammonites. They subdued them from that time on — and they were never troubled by them again. They had total victory!

That is just how God wants to over-answer His people today. Most Christians pray, "Lord, just give me victory in this one battle." But the Lord responds, "I'll give you that — yet I have much more in store for you as well. I want to subdue your enemy so you won't have to get just one victory at a time. I want you to have a total victory!"

Beloved, He wants to give you power not just to overcome — but to subdue every enemy! He wants you not just to conquer sin — but to be more than a conqueror! He wants you not just to have life — but life more abundantly! He wants you not just to have joy — but joy unspeakable and full of glory! He wants you to be free of fear not just for a day, a week or a month — but for all the days of your life!

4. God Over-Answered David's Prayer for Life.

"He asked life of thee..." *(Psalm 21:4)*. David's request was simple : He asked God to save him from dying. And God answered his prayer: "...and thou gavest it him, even length of days for ever and ever" *(verse 4)*.

But God went much further in over-answering David's prayer. He not only gave him life — but He also put a crown on his head, making him king of Israel. And He poured out on him honor and majesty: "...thou settest a crown of pure gold on his head....honour and majesty hast thou laid upon him" *(verses 3, 5)*. David exclaimed, "Lord, You've really laid it on me!" Yet to top it all off, God added "exceeding gladness": "For thou hast made him most blessed for ever: thou hast made him exceeding glad with thy countenance" *(verse 6)*.

It is no wonder David wrote, "...with him is plenteous redemption" *(Psalm 130:7)*. He said, "Lord, You not only saved me — but You poured out Your redemption on me!"

The Old Testament patriarchs and prophets knew all about this most generous inclination of God. They knew He delights in being plenteous, abundant, overflowing with blessings to us. Isaiah said: "Let the wicked forsake his way, and the unrighteous man his thoughts: and let him return unto the Lord, and he will have mercy upon him; and to our God, for he will abundantly pardon" *(Isaiah 55:7)*. God not only forgives sin — but He over-answers our cry for forgiveness with abundant mercy and pardon!

We Should Not Be Surprised By God's Delight in Over-Answering and Over-Giving—Because Men and Women Often Do It as Well!

People have over-answered in their giving. How much more will our God do so?

• A godly husband and wife in Shunem prepared a prophet's chamber in their home for Elisha to use. Elisha was so grateful he sent his servant

Gehazi to ask, "You have cared for us. Now what can we do for you?" But the wife answered, "Nothing."

The servant came back and told Elisha she didn't want anything. But something in the prophet's heart wasn't satisfied. He said, "She's done so much for me!"

Suddenly, the servant remembered: She was childless and desired a child. That was it! So Elisha called her: "...And when he had called her, she stood in the door. And he said, About this season, according to the time of life, thou shalt embrace a son..." *(2 Kings 4:15-16)*.

Elisha got hold of God, the Lord heard his prayer — and the woman birthed a son! Although she never asked for anything, she got the desire of her heart!

● Perhaps you remember Naaman, who was healed of leprosy. Elisha told him, "I don't want anything from you. This is a free gift from God." But later Gehazi, in covetousness, stopped Naaman and said, "My master has had a change of heart. He would like to have a talent of silver, and two changes of garments" *(see 2 Kings 5:22)*.

Now, a talent was a lot of money at that time. It probably could have bought a whole farm. Yet Naaman immediately answered, "...take two talents..." *(verse 23)*. The Lord had so touched Naaman — he was so happy and blessed — that he desired to over-answer the request. Something in his heart wished to bless Elisha!

I ask you — how is it we can credit men like Elisha and Naaman with over-giving and yet believe God is any less kind and loving toward us? We often act as if He's stingy! We think we have to pull things out of Him, to agonize before we can get what we desire. No — our Father loves to give to us! He loves to over-answer our cry! "If ye then, being evil, know how to give good gifts unto your children, how much more shall your Father which is in heaven give good things to them that ask him?" *(Matthew 7:11)*.

Let Us Consider an Even More Glorious Vision of God's Over-Answering Nature!

Consider these examples:

1. What about the man, sick with palsy, who was brought to Jesus on a bed?

"And, behold, they brought to him a man sick of the palsy, lying on a bed..." *(Matthew 9:2)*. This paralyzed man sought Jesus for healing — but Jesus over-answered his prayer! "Son, be of good cheer; thy sins be forgiven thee....Then saith he to the sick of palsy. Arise, take up thy bed, and go unto thine house" *(verses 2, 6).*

The sick man asked for healing — but Jesus gave him much more. He added the greatest gift He could possibly give! The man got his healing — but even better, he received forgiveness, eternal life, and good cheer to replace his years of sadness.

Jesus had known all along what He was going to do; He knew this man would walk again. But He said, "First, I want to bless you — I want to over-answer you. Yes, I'll heal your body — but I'll also heal your soul and your mind. Now, take up your bed and go home!"

2. What about the thief on the cross?

The thief who hung next to Christ asked only one thing of Him: "...Remember me when thou comest into thy kingdom" *(Luke 23:42).* His request was simple: "Think about me."

Jesus truly over-answered this man's request: "And Jesus said unto him, Verily I say unto thee, To day shalt thou be with me in paradise" *(verse 43).* He said, "I'll remember you — because you're coming with Me!"

Talk about an over-answered prayer! This evil thief could not even conceive of being saved. But he was told he would be waking up in a few hours in paradise — beside Jesus!

3. What about the crippled beggar who asked alms of Peter and John as they entered the temple?

"A certain lame man...seeing Peter and John about to go into the temple asked an alms" *(Acts 3:2-3).* Again, it was a simple request — just a little money. Yet what a glorious answer this beggar got!

Scripture says, "Peter fasten(ed) his eyes upon him..." *(verse 4).* The beggar probably thought, "I'm going to get a quarter — maybe a dollar. This may be my lucky day." Instead, he got something all the money in the world couldn't buy — a new body!

"Then Peter said, Silver and gold have I none; but such as I have give I thee: In the name of Jesus Christ of Nazareth rise up and walk...and immediately his feet and ankle bones received strength. And he leaping up stood, and walked, and entered with them into the temple, walking, and leaping, and praising God" *(verses 6-8).*

This beggar not only was healed — but he also received an outpouring of the Holy Ghost! The spirit of praise came upon him, and he danced and worshiped. That surely is an over-answered prayer!

4. Cornelius prayed diligently for a revelation of God's Word — and God marvelously over-answered his prayer!

The Lord had spoken to Cornelius about Peter in a vision. So the centurion sent three servants to Joppa to fetch Peter, "...to hear words of thee" *(10:22)*. This was Cornelius' only request — to hear the gospel: "We want to hear the word of the Lord." Yet look at how God over-answered his request: "While Peter yet spake these words, the Holy Ghost fell on all them which heard the word. And...on the Gentiles also was poured out the gift of the Holy Ghost. For they heard them speak with tongues, and magnify God..." *(verses 44-46)*.

It was as if God was so excited He couldn't wait for Peter to stop preaching — and He moved in to over-answer! The people standing nearby not only got the Word — they also got the Holy Ghost. And they got not only the Holy Ghost but also the gift of tongues. And they got not only tongues but water baptism. "And (Peter) commanded them to be baptized in the name of the Lord..." *(verse 48)*.

Cornelius only wanted the gospel — but God poured out heaven on him!

The New Testament Is Filled With Promises Proving That God Loves to Over-Answer the Prayers of His People!

The most familiar promise of all is Ephesians 3:20. We all know it well — yet few of us live as if we believe it: "Now unto him that is able to do exceeding abundantly above all that we ask or think, according to the power that worketh in us...."

God isn't just able to answer our prayers. He wants to do for us exceeding abundantly above all we can even imagine. He wants to answer us not according to our puny requests, but according to His riches and might. He wants to give till it runs out!

The Bible tells us elsewhere He is inclined to answer us with abundantly more:

• "Give, and it shall be given unto you; good measure, pressed down, and shaken together, and running over..." *(Luke 6:38)*.

• "But as it is written, Eye hath not seen, nor ear heard, neither have entered into the heart of man, the things which God hath prepared for them that love him. But God hath revealed them unto us by his Spirit..." *(1 Corinthians 2:9-10)*.

• "Whereby are given unto us exceeding great and precious promises: that by these ye might be partakers of the divine nature, having escaped the corruption that is in the world through lust" *(2 Peter 1:4)*.

• "...the living God, who giveth us richly all things to enjoy..." *(1 Timothy 6:17)*.

God is virtually begging us to ask for great things!

We like to call the Lord "our King." But do we pray large requests worthy of our King's greatness? A king is obligated to care for his subjects. And his people honor him by asking largely, believing he has all they need and will provide it abundantly. Dear saint, you can't call God "King" and then accuse Him of letting one of His subjects continue in need!

A well-known philosopher approached Alexander the Great to make a request because he'd done a good deed for him. He asked the king for a gift of one hundred talents — a fortune in silver — for his daughters.

Everyone present was aghast. But Alexander had a big smile on his face. He said, "Give it to him! It is a request worthy of King Alexander. It is worthy of my wealth and my ability to give."

I ask you — have you embarrassed God by your puny requests? "...prove me now herewith, saith the Lord of hosts, if I will not open you the windows of heaven, and pour you out a blessing, that there shall not be room enough to receive it" *(Malachi 3:10)*.

We Can Grieve God — Even Anger Him — By Not Asking!

We think it is spiritual to say, "I just worship the Lord. I don't ask Him for anything. Whatever He wants for me is good enough." That may sound holy — but it is not, according to the Word of God!

Again and again Jesus implores us, "Ask! Ask in My name! Ask, and you shall receive. Ask anything — whatsoever you ask. Ask what you will. You have not because you ask not. God gives good things to those who ask. He knows what you need even before you ask. Ask the Father in My name, and He will give it to you." But we don't have the faith to ask!

"And it shall come to pass, that before they call, I will answer; and while they are yet speaking, I will hear" *(Isaiah 65:24)*. God says, "You don't have the faith or courage to ask for what I really want to give you. So I'm going to beat you to the punch! I'm going to answer you before you even ask, because your thinking is too small. I know your request won't come near to what I want to do!"

"Moreover the Lord spake again unto Ahaz, saying, Ask thee a sign of the Lord thy God; ask it either in the depth, or in the height above. But

Ahaz said, I will not ask, neither will I tempt the Lord" *(Isaiah 7:10-12)*.

Ahaz's response may have sounded holy — "I won't tempt God." But it angered the Lord. It was hypocritical — because God knew Ahaz had lost his faith long before then! Ahaz didn't want to have his faith tested because he didn't have any. And many Christians today don't ask God for anything because it will test a faith they don't have!

Ahaz represents the backslidden church — Christians who have lost their faith in God, who don't believe in His great resources. They say, "Don't ask God for healing. You're tempting God." That sounds good — but it is hypocritical!

You see, at this point Israel needed deliverance. So God invited Ahaz to ask for confirmation of His faithfulness by any sign the king could think of, from heaven to hell. But Ahaz already had planned to call on King Tigath-Pilneser and Samaria for help. God said, "No! I'm going to fight your battle. I want you to trust in Me!" "Hear ye now, O house of David; Is it a small thing for you to weary men, but will ye weary my God also?" *(verse 13)*.

The Hebrew word for "weary" means "disgust." God was saying, "How long are you going to keep disgusting Me because you're afraid to stand on My Word? When will you ever learn that I have everything you need — that I will take care of you because I'm King and Lord?"

Isaiah told Israel, "You didn't ask for a sign — but God is going to give you one anyway." "Therefore the Lord himself shall give you a sign; Behold, a virgin shall conceive, and bear a son, and shall call his name Immanuel" *(verse 14)*.

Beloved, this was the greatest over-answer of any prayer in history! The people had cried, "Send us a deliverer," hoping for some man. But God answered, "I'll give you a man. And yes, He will be a deliverer — for all humankind!" God over-answered by promising Immanuel!

In Jesus Christ — Immanuel — we have God's most glorious over-answer of all. He is the fullness of God. In Him all riches and blessings abound. He is our great resource. And in Him is exceeding abundantly more than we could ask or think!

"And Samuel Grew, and the Lord Was With Him, and Did Let None of His Words Fall to the Ground"
(1 Samuel 3:19).

This verse means Samuel's prayers as well as his prophecies. None of them fell useless to the ground. Not one prayer went unanswered. Every word of God's promises that Samuel repeated in prayer was a seed that brought forth fruit exceeding abundantly!

Dear saint, when you go to your secret closet, remember: "...he that cometh to God must believe that he is, and that he is a rewarder of them that diligently seek him" *(Hebrews 11:6)*. Always quote that verse — work it into your system, praying: "I come to You, Jesus, because I know You are God Almighty. You have all the resources I'll ever need. You are beyond my comprehension in greatness — but I believe You reward those who diligently seek You!"

Bring all your requests to God. Pray, believing He delights to over-answer you in His own way and time. Start asking today for the healing of those whom you thought were hopelessly beyond help. Trust Him for your hopeless financial situation, your unsaved loved ones. He is going to give to you — to over-answer your prayer — exceeding abundantly above all you could ask or think!

The Salvation of Your Face

9

You Need a Holy Ghost Face-Lift!

David boldly declared, "…God…is the health of my countenance…" *(Psalm 42:11)*. And he repeats the same statement in another psalm: "…God…is the health of my countenance…" *(43:5)*. In the original Hebrew, the proper rendering of both these verses is, "God is the salvation of my face!"

I believe David is saying something very important here. You see, your face is a billboard that advertises what's going on in your heart. All the joy or turmoil that's inside you is reflected in your countenance. When I speak of countenance, I'm talking about facial expression, body language, tone of voice. For example, when my mind is loaded down with the cares of our church — sermon messages, finances, relationships — I have a tendency to slouch. I look preoccupied. My brow is furrowed. Some people even tell me I look sad.

Not long ago I was walking along 52nd Street near Hannah House, totally absorbed with church business and probably slouched over. I came upon a crack house where a woman sat on the stoop, smiling from ear to ear. I could see she was high on crack. She watched me approaching — and as I got nearer she spoke up, "Mister, it can't be that bad."

I was flabbergasted! I thought, "Here is this woman, high on crack — and here I am, a man of God. She's smiling and looking good — and I'm slouched over, as if all hope is gone." What a rebuke it was to me!

Now, I thank God for His great salvation — for redeeming our soul, our spirit, even our body. But many of us need to get our faces saved! We need a Holy Ghost face-lift — because our faces are giving the wrong message to the world!

You've probably heard that an aspirin a day is good for the heart. It helps stop blood clotting, which can cause heart attacks. But now research has led to "aspirin face-lifts." Dr. Nageena Malik, a research scientist in Oxford, England, conducted a study recently that produced some amazing results. Her research shows that aspirin helps to prevent wrinkles by keeping the skin flexible, preventing collagen stiffening, and blocking some of sugar's bad effects on the body.

So, now science says you can actually look younger by taking aspirin. Or, if you want a more radical change in your appearance and can afford it, you can pay a plastic surgeon to alter your facial features.

But, beloved, it doesn't matter what kind of face-lift you get — medicinal, surgical or any other kind. Your countenance will still reflect what is going on inside your heart! You cannot hide your inner emotions. Your face is the index of your soul!

Nothing Hardens a Face as Much as Sin and Worry!

"A wicked man hardeneth his face..." *(Proverbs 21:29).* If you live in New York City, all you have to do is look around you on the streets, and you'll see faces aged and hardened by sin. Visitors from the Midwest can't understand it. The people here look twenty to thirty years older than their actual age. Sin ages people fast!

I recall about ten years ago, a young film actress — a rising star in her twenties — had just recovered from a long addiction to crack. The newspapers reported that she was trying to get back into movies — but her face had aged about thirty years. I saw a photo of her, and indeed, her face was etched with sin and hardness. Eventually she had to accept older roles, because her skin had become hardened and wrinkled.

On the other hand, I see miraculous changes in the faces of the men and women we take in at our Timothy and Hannah Houses. They enter our programs with a fallen countenance — and within days, as Jesus heals their inner man, they begin to shine. They look as if they've had face-lifts — literal, Holy Ghost surgery!

One young woman came into Hannah House a year or so ago with lines of sin etched deeply in her face. Her countenance was extremely hard. Yet, two weeks after she was saved, no one could believe the change. I didn't even recognize her!

Why such a change of countenance? "...a man's wisdom maketh his face to shine, and the boldness of his face shall be changed" *(Ecclesiastes 8:1).* I take "wisdom" in this verse to mean Jesus Christ. Indeed, the very presence of Christ in your heart has a direct impact on your face! It affects your walk, your talk, the very tone of your voice.

Worry can also harden a person's face, just as much as gross sin can. We all know that as Christians we aren't to worry. Our Lord is fully aware of all our needs and problems. Yet, you may say, "Come on, Brother Dave. You worry, don't you?" Of course I do — but I'm not supposed to. (And I wonder how many wrinkles on my face are the result of worry!)

I believe ours is "a religion of the face." When we allow Jesus to be Lord of all — when we cast all our cares upon Him, trusting fully in His Word and resting in His love — our appearance should undergo a deep change. A quiet calm should begin to radiate from our countenance.

Scripture gives us many examples of this:

• When Hannah laid her burden down, "...her countenance was no more sad" *(1 Samuel 1:18)*. Her face was no longer etched with sorrow or sadness. Joy radiated from her!

• When Stephen stood before hostile, angry men in the Sanhedrin, "...his face [shone] as it had been the face of an angel" *(Acts 6:15)*. Stephen stood among unbelievers with the shine of Jesus Christ — and the difference was clear to all!

• The men in that synagogue council were so angry at Stephen, "...they gnashed on him with their teeth" *(Acts 7:54)*. Have you ever had angry people grit their teeth at you? If so, you probably remember exactly what their faces reflected!

There Are Many Sad, Downcast, Despondent, Wrinkled Countenances in the House of God!

I'm convinced we have a duty to let our countenance speak of God's faithfulness in our lives. But the problem is, our facial features and body language often say just the opposite. Many believers' faces say, "My God has failed me! He doesn't care for me anymore. I have to carry all my burdens and problems alone. I grieve and weep — I have to decide my own fate, plan my own deliverance — because God doesn't come through for me!"

You may not consciously say such things to yourself — but they show on your face! Perhaps at this very moment you have a troubled look. It may be because of family problems — your marriage, children, finances. Every day, you wake up and these problems hit you in the face. They hang over you like a dark cloud.

I want to show you from God's Word that what you are going through is not new. Someone else has been exactly where you are:

"...my sore ran in the night, and ceased not: my soul refused to be comforted....I complained, and my spirit was overwhelmed....Thou holdest mine eyes waking: I am so troubled that I cannot speak. I have considered the days of old, the years of ancient times. I call to remembrance my song in the night... Will the Lord cast off forever? And will he be favourable no more? Is his mercy clean gone for ever? Doth his promise fail for evermore? Hath God forgotten to be gracious? Hath he in anger shut up his tender mercies?...And I said, This is my infirmity..." *(Psalm 77:2-10)*.

When the psalmist says, "This is my infirmity," he means, literally, "This is what I have to endure." I ask you: Could your condition possibly be worse than this man's? In his own words, he is beyond all comfort. His spirit is overwhelmed. He can't sleep. He is so troubled he can't speak. He has to jog his memory to think of better times. He feels cast off and alone, forgotten by God, haunted by memories of better days. Yet the psalmist eventually comes out of his trouble with his happy countenance restored. Why? It is because, he says, "I cried unto God with my voice...in the day of my trouble..." *(verses 1-2)*.

There are many Christians who believe in Jesus and take Him at His Word — and yet they continue suffering day after day, year after year, because they won't take their problems to Him. How many homes are miserable because one spouse is wrapped up in his own problems or his children's, and he forgets the needs of his spouse? For example — a wife may carry her children's problems for so long that they actually become etched on her face. Year after year, her husband hears only complaints from her — he never sees joy in her face — because she is bound by her children's burdens. The husband tries to hold on in love, but her obsession gradually wears him down. Living with her becomes like living in a morgue.

This wife is slowly ruining her marriage — embittering her patient husband — because she is enslaved by her problems. She has no peace, no calm, no smile, no normal days or nights. She is consumed with sorrow, and she can't lay it down. Day after day, it's the same old story: She sleeps with it, eats with it, talks about it — and she stays forever depressed.

Even her friends are eventually turned off by her. They try to offer her strength through prayer. But their counseling and encouragement to turn it all over to Jesus goes unheeded. It's as if this woman never hears a word. And, little by little, her friends drop away. Eventually, all that's left in this woman's life is her own little world — all wrapped up in somebody else's problems!

Many such people come to their wits' end and end up divorced or having a nervous breakdown. Their faces are etched with the lines of sadness. And their worry has devastating effects on their children and even their grandchildren. If this describes you, I beg you: Today, this very day, get alone somewhere with the Lord and cry out to Him! Tell Him all your problems — everything about you. Tell Him you're at the end of your rope, that you can't take it anymore, that you're ready to lay it all on His shoulders. Have it out with God!

It amazes me that so many people who say they're in love with Jesus come to a hard place and yet won't turn to Him. Why won't we shut ourselves into His presence and pour out our hearts to Him? You may answer, "I'm just not in the habit of doing that. I'm not much of a praying person. Instead of going to God, I carry the whole load myself."

Indeed, when a sin problem or crisis hits, many Christians have a tendency — like Adam and Eve — to run and hide. But, beloved, the best time to learn to run to Jesus is at such a time — when you're in great need! David said that was his secret of deliverance in time of trouble: "Deliver me, O Lord, from mine enemies: I flee unto thee to hide me" *(Psalm 143:9)*.

You can start doing that today. And as you do, you'll see a miracle take place: Your load will be lifted. Your heart will change. You will experience a whole new realm of victory — and you'll get a face-lift in the process!

Now, let me get to the heart of my message:

I Want to Talk About the "No-Name Infirmity."

There is an unexplainable spiritual depression that comes upon the holiest of God's servants at one time or another. The psalmist says: "Why art thou cast down, O my soul? And why art thou disquieted in me?... O my God, my soul is cast down within me..." *(Psalm 42:5-6)*.

Scholars aren't certain who the writer of this psalm is. But we do know for sure that something is bothering him. His soul is deeply disturbed — but he can't explain why. This psalmist is on fire for God. He pants after the Lord the way a deer pants for water *(verse 1)* — thirsting after Him, yearning for intimacy. He asks, "...when shall I come and appear before God?" *(verse 2)*.

We never do learn what the psalmist's infirmity is. No doubt, he tried to figure it out himself, crying out to God, "Why, Lord? Why this unexplainable spiritual depression in me? I love You more than I ever have. My heart pants after You. But for some reason I'm going through this depression. I feel so down — but I don't know what's bothering me. I can't explain it!" "My tears have been my meat day and night..." *(verse 3).*

Have you ever experienced this kind of unexplainable melancholy — an unexpected, unnamed spiritual blues? You're doing fine one day, with no known sin in your life. But one day you wake up with a disturbance deep in your soul. Some kind of depression has come over you — and you can't put your finger on it!

There is a dear Jewish brother named Joel who attends our church. He's a poet, and I know he has a sensitive spirit. I saw him one day as he was entering the subway, and I greeted him with, "How's it going?" Joel answered with a half-smile. Then, with a quizzical look, he said, "Okay, I guess. I'm feeling something I can't explain."

I knew just what he meant — because I personally have just come out of such an experience. I can say with the psalmist that I hunger and thirst for God, that my soul pants for intimacy with Him. I have no family or personal problems that might cause a disturbance in my soul. In fact, I have never felt closer to the Lord.

But out of nowhere came an unnamed infirmity! I felt a sense of worthlessness — a boredom and monotony. I felt also that perhaps I wasn't accomplishing much. My mind was in the doldrums, and I couldn't figure it out. I didn't feel like praying at all.

Beloved, this affected my face! My countenance was sad, and the feeling hung on for days. Finally, I prayed, "Lord, what's going on? Why do I feel this way? I know You love me — but I feel like a total failure!" All day long I felt my eyes welling up — and a few times I let the tears flow freely. I ended up saying with the psalmist, "Why are you cast down, O my soul? Why are you disturbed? Why the inner mourning?"

A woman minister once told me, "Occasionally I wake up with an empty feeling. Now, I realize I am very secure in the Lord, and I have a wonderful intimacy with Him. I believe my spirit is strong. But I experience these depressing feelings when I wake in the morning, and I just can't explain it. I feel my life is on hold — as if I'm operating on three wheels instead of four."

This affliction is widespread among men and women in ministry. One pastor's wife told me, "My husband has a good church and is well-respected. God has opened many doors for us, and our needs are well-supplied. My husband has everything he has ever wanted —- all he has ever prayed for. But at times, something comes over him, and it concerns me.

He gets restless and tells me he doesn't feel like he's accomplishing much. He can't explain what comes over him — and it makes me feel really insecure."

I believe this no-name infirmity is behind many "two-year teachers" and "four-year preachers." These are ministers who remain in a church for a certain period, then become restless and leave. Or, sometimes they stay but feel compelled to "make something happen" in the congregation. A strange restlessness overtakes them.

It is often during such times that a pastor decides to launch his church into a huge building project. One prayer group in a certain city has written to our ministry, requesting prayer for their pastor. They write: "Something is going on in our pastor that we can't explain. He wants to build a gymnasium — and our congregation is mostly over sixty years of age! Everybody is wondering what in the world we would do with a gymnasium. No one wants it. Our pastor can't explain why he wants a gym, and his wife doesn't know what's behind it, either. Please pray that he'll get over this soon — before he builds it!"

There are many others in ministry who are just like this man. But now let's talk about you. Do you feel that your life is on hold? Are you cast down, troubled at heart, with all kinds of sad, confusing thoughts in your soul — all unexplainable? Do your prayers go unanswered? Do your dreams not come to fruition? And do you feel it is affecting your countenance, your face?

I've got good news for you: This is an infirmity of the righteous! It strikes only those who hunger after Jesus. We are not to be afraid of such an infirmity — because the Holy Spirit has a part in it!

I am now in my sixties, and I have experienced enough of life to know that a time comes when this happens to every Christian. But we mustn't try to figure it out — because we can't! The psalmist never did get his "why" answers. And there isn't a book, counselor or psychologist on earth who can tell you why an unnamed infirmity has come upon you.

I believe this strange infirmity is "the sighing of the Holy Spirit" within us. He is letting us know what it feels like to be without God — to be on our own, without comfort, hope or guidance. He allows us to experience just a taste of such an awful, horrible condition. You see, our bodies are His temple — and He has been sent to prepare us as a chaste bride to Christ. He knows what it takes to keep us unspotted for the Bridegroom. And He knows how important it is for us to cry out to God for daily strength and for power over every besetting sin. We simply cannot stand in these times unless we are intimate with the Lord — trusting in Him fully and constantly fleeing into His presence.

The Holy Spirit also knows the mind of God and the way out of every problem. He has the power to deliver us out of any burden or difficulty. And from His holy sanctuary in our heart, He breathes His influence on all our emotions — wooing, pleading, encouraging, comforting, convicting, guiding, teaching, reproving, manifesting the reality of Christ.

Yet we neglect this wonderful gift inside us. We ignore God's Spirit completely. We go about our daily affairs as if He doesn't abide in us. And the evidence is in our faces — our heavy, drooping countenances!

It's Sad to Say — But Many Christians Neglect Seeking God!

Many of us read the Bible with boredom. We open God's Word only because we know we should, and its message doesn't register with us. It brings no quickening life. We also pray less and less. We no longer look forward to shutting ourselves in to talk to our Lord.

Beloved, the gift of the Holy Spirit within us provides us with all the power, resources, hope, grace and peace we will ever need. And yet we subject Him to the awful abuse of neglect! It is absolute abuse against the Spirit for us to carry unnecessary burdens — to walk before a wicked world fretting and looking downcast, as if God were dead.

That is why the Holy Spirit sighs and groans in our spirit, with unutterable groanings. He sighs within us as He withdraws for a season. No, He doesn't totally abandon us — but at times He does remove Himself for a season to test our faith. Why does He sigh? It is because, rather than running to Him, we stay up all night talking to friends, reading how-to books, trying to find some answers. And all the while we neglect His presence! He sits in the very sanctuary of our heart, offering us everything we need. But we insist on crying our needs to others and walking around with a heavy countenance.

When the Holy Ghost sighed in my life, I used to examine myself, asking, "Lord, what did I do wrong? Is there some hidden sin in me?" I have dug and dug for answers — reading books, doing word studies. I've tried desperately to discover why I was going through an unnamed infirmity.

Sometimes this overwhelming spirit still comes over me. But now I know what it's all about — and I'm not afraid of it anymore. I know it has nothing to do with being in sin. Rather, it is the Holy Spirit at work in me. He is sighing so that I'll run back into Jesus' arms!

That is exactly the effect the Spirit's sighing had on the psalmist. It gave him a renewed hunger for God:

• "And I said, This is my infirmity: but I will remember the years of the right hand of the most High. I will remember the works of the Lord: surely I will remember thy wonders of old. I will meditate also of all thy work, and talk of thy doings. Thy way, O God, is in the sanctuary: who is so great a God as our God? Thou art the God that doest wonders: thou hast declared thy strength among the people" *(Psalm 77:10-14)*.

• "...bring me unto thy holy hill, and to thy tabernacles. Then will I go unto the altar of God, unto God my exceeding joy..." *(43:3-4)*.

The Spirit allows this no-name infirmity to plague our lives until we say, "I can't figure this thing out! I know I can't fight the devil in my own power, and I can't overcome any temptation without the Holy Ghost. I'm tired of going to others to try to get an answer. Oh Lord — I'm calling out to You now. I can't do anything without You. Holy Spirit, take over!"

Simply put, what we experience in this infirmity is a loneliness for Jesus. It really isn't a depression. No — it's a yearning to enjoy our Savior's presence! That's what the sighing and groaning are all about. You see, when we don't have His presence, it shows on our face. And the psalmist wrote, "...they continually say unto me, Where is thy God?" *(Psalm 42:3)*. Evidently he was so downcast, it was reflected in his face and body language. Seeing him in such sorrow and hopelessness, others said to him, "You're supposed to be a person of faith. So, where is your God?"

Beloved, if you don't run to the Lord and your face reflects that — then the world has every right to ask you the same question: "Look at you! You look awful — so sad, so hopeless. Where is your God? Where is the Christ you preach so much about?"

Does your face say to a lost, confused generation, "My soul is at rest, my mind at peace — because I have dwelling in me the very Spirit of God Himself. He is guiding me, comforting my troubled soul. And I need fear no evil — because I sleep and wake in the saving power of the Holy Ghost, who lives in me!"

How God Brought Me
Out of My Infirmity

I was going through just such a time of heavy sighing and groaning recently when God sent me a special word from heaven. As I was walking through the hills in Pennsylvania, the Lord dropped this word into my heart — and I repeated it again and again until my unnamed infirmity was lifted and gone. The word was a simple verse: "Casting all your care upon him; for he careth for you" *(1 Peter 5:7)*.

It is one thing to quote this verse — and another to believe it! As I walked through the woods, I was reminded that the Lord cares all about me and what I'm going through. He is touched by my infirmites. And I cried, "Oh Lord, You do care for me. You do love me. You watch over me continuously!"

Suddenly the Holy Spirit whispered to my soul: "That's the secret! It is why the Father has sent Me — to help convince you of this Word. You've got to believe that no matter what you're going through, no matter what your burden is, He cares! God is not mad at you. He is not hiding from you. On the contrary, His heart is moved toward you. He cares about everything affecting you. Will you believe it, David? Will you cast all your cares on Him — all your sins, failures, troubles and needs?"

Dear saint, if you truly believe God loves you, and you lay all your cares on Him, you can walk in glorious freedom. Your face will be lifted, as mine has been. Now, as I walk the cold, uncaring streets of New York City, I lay all my cares on the Lord. And I am reminded, "My heavenly Father watches over me. He loves me — and He cares!"

The next time I see that crack-addicted woman on 52nd Street, I can say, "You're right — it really isn't that bad at all. It's good because of my God!"

Taking Up the Towel

10

Offering the Comfort of the Holy Ghost

In a famous passage in John 13, Jesus took a towel and a basin and washed the feet of His disciples. He told them: "If I then, your Lord and Master, have washed your feet; ye also ought to wash one another's feet" *(John 13:14)*.

Some devout Christians take this verse literally. They have made it their custom to have "foot washing" services. This is commendable — yet, if it remains only a ritual, the true meaning of foot washing has been lost.

After Jesus washed the disciples' feet, He put His garment back on, sat down and asked them, "Do you know what I've just done to you?" In other words: "Do you understand the spiritual significance of foot washing?"

I believe the Lord's question is for us today as well. Indeed, something very powerful and profound was taking place; Christ was teaching His church one of its most important lessons. Yet, do we understand the depths of what Jesus did in washing the disciples' feet?

Jesus was not instituting an ordinance to be carried on throughout the church ages, such as communion or water baptism. If that were so, He would have instituted it at the beginning of the disciples' training. And He would have submitted to a foot washing Himself, as He had done with water baptism. I pored over my Bible commentaries to see what the church fathers have said about this scene. Almost without exception, they wrote that its significance is in Jesus' example of humility. He took the lowly place to show us how to be humble.

Yet I believe this interpretation misses the meaning of the passage entirely. After all, Jesus had already set an example of humility by taking on human form — by laying aside His glory and coming to earth as a servant.

No — this passage says so much more than that. I believe Jesus was giving us an example of the kind of physical manifestation He desires most — that of "taking up the towel"!

Today, when we speak of manifestations, we think of people in church meetings falling to the ground. To many, that kind of manifestation seems strange. Yet, as you study the Word of God, you learn that Jesus talked a lot about unusual physical manifestations. No, He didn't talk about falling to the ground. But He did speak of falling into the ground and dying — to bear fruit! He spoke of the manifestation of taking up a cross — of cutting off an offending hand, plucking out an offensive eye, going an extra mile.

Yet one of the most unusual of all the manifestations Christ talked about is His call to take up the towel. Throughout my years in ministry, many people have asked, "Why don't we wash each other's feet in church, as Jesus told us to? He said, 'If I do it, you should do it, too.'" I usually answered, "What Jesus is talking about is primarily a spiritual thing, and not just physical." Yet even as I said this, I had no concept of the spiritual meaning of foot washing.

We gloss over certain truths in the Bible because we don't understand their meaning — and for years we miss the power of these passages. For example, Scripture tells us: "...by love serve one another" *(Galatians 5:13)*. And: "(Submit) yourselves one to another in the fear of God" *(Ephesians 5:21)*.

How many of us really know what it means to serve one another in love? And how are we supposed to submit to one another in the fear of God? It's easy enough to understand how a wife is to submit to the spiritual authority of a godly husband. And the same is true for children submitting to godly parents. But in what practical ways do we serve and submit to one another in the house of God?

I believe that if we understand what Jesus did in washing His disciples' feet, we will understand these concepts of service and submission. You see, serving one another in love and submitting to one another in godly fear mean much more than taking orders from or being accountable to a higher authority. Rather, these glorious truths are unlocked only in the context of "taking up the towel."

While I was in prayer recently, the Holy Spirit gave me three words to open my understanding about this matter of taking up the towel. The three words are dirt, comfort and unity. Hopefully, as we examine these words, the Holy Ghost will reveal to us His truth.

1. Let Us Begin With the Matter of Dirt Clinging to a Christian Brother or Sister.

The disciples were twelve men beloved of God — precious in His eyes, full of love for His Son, pure-hearted, in full communion with Jesus. Yet they had dirt on their feet! Jesus, in essence, was saying to these men, "Your hearts and hands are clean, but your feet are not. They've gotten dirty in your daily walk with Me. You don't need your whole body to be washed — only your feet."

The dirt Jesus mentions here has nothing to do with natural dirt. It's all about sin — our faults and failures, our giving in to temptations. And no matter how dusty and dirty the roads were in ancient Jerusalem, no age was ever as filthy as ours.

I wonder how many people reading this message right now have some dirt clinging to them. Perhaps this past week you fell into a temptation or failed God in some way. It's not that you've turned your back on the Lord. On the contrary — you love the Savior more passionately than ever. But you fell, and now you're grieving — because your feet are dirty!

Scripture tells us: "Brethren, if a man be overtaken in a fault, ye which are spiritual, restore such an one in the spirit of meekness; considering thyself, lest thou also be tempted" *(Galatians 6:1)*. The Greek word for *fault* here means "a fall, a sin, a transgression." We are to restore every Christian who falls into sin, if there is a repentant heart. And foot washing, in its deepest spiritual meaning, has to do with our attitude about the dirt we see on our brother or sister. So, I ask you: What do you do when you're face to face with someone who has fallen into a sin or transgression? What you do about the dirt on your brother or sister has everything to do with the ministry Jesus describes as "taking up the towel." It has everything to do with how you serve others in love and submit to others in the fear of God.

Let me say very clearly: Christians can be very cruel! In fact, believers often are more vicious and destructive than the wicked in the streets. And Jesus knew that. He knew how we react to the sight of dirt on someone else — how we put on a holier-than-thou attitude, judging, gossiping and slandering. Indeed, carnal Christians delight in seeing dirt on others. But their spreading of the dirt is the dirtiest sin of all!

In recent weeks, I've been trying to encourage a young pastor who resigned from his church after confessing a moral transgression. This dear man loves the Lord. He has a heart for people and for God's Word. But his feet got dirty! Yet he is totally repentant.

As soon as I heard about his fall and resignation, the Holy Spirit instructed me to get in touch with him immediately. I knew this young pastor was still a good man. He hadn't suddenly become wicked. His heart wasn't hardened over his sin. Yet his best friends forsook him. Those who claimed to love him most now ignored him, as if he had an infectious disease. To top it off, his denominational leaders demanded he make a video of his confession — giving every vivid detail of his transgression.

I called this dear brother — and I took a towel with me. I left a message on his answering machine, saying: "Brother, I want you to know I love you. God isn't finished with you. If you have a repentant heart, the Lord will restore you. And I'm going to stand with you!"

A friend of this pastor later called me. He said, "David, you will never know what your phone call meant to my friend — how blessed, encouraged and comforted he was. No one else has reached out to him. Your words gave him new hope."

Taking up a towel is an attitude, a commitment. It means doing all within our power to cleanse the dirt off our brother's feet. It says, "I'm committed to helping you clean off the dirt — to restore your reputation, your family — to do everything to keep you alive in Christ!" Scripture clearly states that whenever a brother or sister has been overtaken in a sin, we must restore that person — serving him in love, submitting to him in the fear of God. Yet, you may ask, how are we to do this?

We are to take up the towel of God's mercy and go to that hurting one. In the special love of Jesus, we are to submit all of our human inclinations to ignore him, judge him, expose him, lecture him and find fault with him — and, instead, we are to commit to being his friend. We are to help wash away his sins by sharing the correcting, healing, washing, comforting Word of God. This is not overlooking or winking at sin. It is not calling evil good. We're talking about fallen saints who have repentant hearts yet are without hope. They know they have grieved the Lord — and they live with fear, guilt, rejection.

It's a different matter entirely with those who have been warned two or three times yet persist in their sin. The Bible says we are to sharply rebuke such believers in public so that others may fear God. Often they must be disfellowshiped for a season, until they demonstrate godly sorrow. But those who acknowledge their sin — who confess it and forsake it — are in need of someone to bring the towel of mercy, to bring them cleansing and healing.

A few years ago, an associate pastor of a very large church called me in tears. He told me, "Brother David, I can't keep my head up, I'm so broken." He described to me the pain he experienced when his teenage daughter became pregnant outside of marriage. The senior pastor of the church demanded that this associate go before the congregation and tell them what his daughter had done. This dear man did just that — and it devastated his daughter. It broke the family's heart. But the congregation wallowed in all the details of the poor teenage girl's sin.

Then, a year later, the senior pastor's teenage daughter became pregnant. But this time, the senior pastor did everything in his power to cover it up.

God, have mercy on us — because we destroy people who get dirt on their feet! When will we ever learn to take up the towel of mercy — to commit ourselves to cleansing and restoring, rather than throwing dirt into the wind and destroying precious souls?

2. Those Who Take Up the Towel Are the True Comforters Whom the Holy Ghost Uses.

Do you know what it's like to be barefoot and have to walk through mud? The dirt that cakes on your feet can be truly miserable. You feel much better when your feet are washed and clean. When Jesus washed the dirt from His disciples' feet, they were comforted. But, spiritually speaking, Jesus was teaching the comfort of transgressions removed!

In 1 Corinthians 5, we read of a man in the church who fell into the terrible sin of incest. Evidently the man was unrepentant, and Paul directed the church to turn him over to Satan for the destruction of his flesh (that is, to the saving of his spirit). Paul was not saying the man was lost and going to hell. No — he only wanted him isolated from fellowship and given over to Satan's devices, so he would come to his wit's end and be driven to repentance.

Later, in 2 Corinthians 2, Paul found out the same man had become repentant and that the church had forgiven him. Satan had brought him to despair, and the lust in his flesh had been destroyed. The man had come back repentant. And now Paul wrote to the Corinthians: "...ye ought rather to forgive him, lest perhaps such a one should be swallowed up with overmuch sorrow. Wherefore I beseech you that ye would confirm your love toward him" *(2 Corinthians 2:7-8)*.

Paul knew this man was absolutely overwhelmed with grief and sorrow. Those in the church had seen his brokenness and humility, and they were overcome with a spirit of mercy. They encouraged him, were tender-hearted toward him and washed his feet. Now he was clean — and he was being restored to the body of Jesus Christ. What a wonderful picture!

There are many Christians today who are in the same condition as this man, after being overtaken by a sin. They say to themselves, "I have reproached my Savior. I've brought shame to His name!" Yet what they experience is nothing like what 2 Corinthians describes.

I want to show you a passage from a book I received not long ago. It was written by the daughter of a pastor who was overtaken by a sin several years ago. And for all those years, the family endured a nightmarish hell. She wrote:

"...(The press) followed us to our homes. We got phone calls from famous gossip tabloids offering large sums of money for a story. We'd finally succeed in getting Dad out of the house and into a restaurant, only to find ourselves the subject of people's conversations. It was horrible.

"But Reverend —— was never ashamed to identify with us. Dad would literally sit by the phone awaiting this man's call. He was overcome with guilt and shame....Dad had sunken into deep depression....People to whom he gave so much of himself were the ones who turned against him so harshly.

"New rumors were spread daily. Ministers wrote to one another, spreading those rumors....Only a select few proved true by showing Christian love and restoration, by calling us and remembering us in their prayers."

I know the man this daughter is describing. He is a dedicated man of God, a good father and a caring pastor. His heart is still passionately in love with Jesus. In fact, he has been restored and is pastoring a growing church. Yet, can you imagine how he has felt all these years? Everyone he'd ministered to for years turned against him — including those he'd won to Christ! He was devastated, overwhelmed with sorrow. At one point his daughter suggested to her husband that they take the gun out of the man's house, fearing that in his depression he might be overcome by thoughts of suicide.

This lonely, despairing man waited by the phone for a call from his faithful pastor friend. The loving, compassionate minister was the only one willing to bring a towel to his friend — a little comfort, a word of encouragement, a brief moment of laughter. Can you blame the fallen, dejected pastor for wanting just a little relief from the long years of pain inflicted by God's people and other ministers?

The World Outside the Church Has Become Demonized With the Spirit of Hate — Character Assassination, Slander, Destruction of Reputations and Families.

No sooner does a politician announce he's running for office than the press turns into a pack of vultures, digging into his past life just to find some dirt. And when they find it, they plaster it across the headlines, for all of America to wallow in. America has gone crazy with slander! TV is rife with talk shows featuring gossip, exposure, mockery. The wicked get their thrills from destroying people, families, good reputations. And the more lurid the dirt, the more the people love it.

But this kind of thing has no place in God's house. The church ought to be different. It ought to be a house of cleansing! The Gentiles in Ephesus honored God's people by calling them "Christians," meaning, "kind-hearted." They had seen how kindhearted these believers were toward others. "And be ye kind one to another, tenderhearted, forgiving one another, even as God for Christ's sake hath forgiven you" *(Ephesians 4:32)*.

If you want to be kindhearted — to take up the towel to restore a brother or sister — you don't need to know the details of how that person got dirty. Jesus did not ask His disciples, "How did you get such dirty feet?" He wanted only to get the dirt off of them. His love for them was unconditional. Likewise, those who walk in the fullness of Jesus Christ must also have this attitude of love toward those with dirty feet. We aren't to ask for details. Instead, we're to say, "Let's do something about the dirt!"

But too often, this isn't the case. Many Christians want to delve into all the gory details. They come to a believer who has dirty feet, saying, "I want to wash your feet. But, tell me — what happened? How'd you get so dirty?"

Then, at some point in the story of failure, the curious comforter realizes, "Oh, my — this is worse than I thought. I can't get involved in this. I can't handle it." And after two minutes of details, he comes to the end of his puny human mercy. He judges the person as too evil, beyond help — and chooses to ignore him. He drops his towel and goes his way.

Beloved, you can't wash feet in a judge's robes! You have to take off your self-righteous garments — your holier-than-thou attitude — before you can do any cleansing. Like Jesus, you must lay aside your outer garment and gird yourself with love. Off with all self-righteousness — all pride, all thoughts that you could never stoop so low! You must have an attitude that says, "I don't care what you did. If you're repentant and want to hear God's Word, I'll be kind and tenderhearted to you!"

Yet, you ask, what if the dirty person before you is a Judas — someone who has betrayed you? My answer to you is, Judas was in that room with the other disciples, and Jesus washed his feet too. Christ stooped to cleanse Judas' dirt, even though Satan had already put betrayal in his heart.

Indeed, modern-day Judases can be saved because of the Cross. Often we think of certain sinners, such as homosexuals or lesbians, as being hopelessly hooked. We think they can never be delivered. Yet Paul says of them: "Know ye not that the unrighteous shall not inherit the kingdom of God? Be not deceived: neither fornicators, nor idolaters, nor adulterers, nor effeminate, nor abusers of themselves with mankind [homosexuals], nor thieves, nor covetous, nor drunkards, nor revilers, nor extortioners, shall inherit the kingdom of God. And such were some of you: but ye are washed, but ye are sanctified, but ye are justified in the name of the Lord Jesus, and by the Spirit of our God" *(1 Corinthians 6:9-11)*.

Such were some of us — but we had our feet washed by Jesus! I ask you — if Jesus is willing to justify all sinners, why aren't we willing to wash those sinners' feet? Paul says we are to be gentle and patient with all people: "And the servant of the Lord must not strive; but be gentle unto all men, apt to teach, patient, in meekness instructing those that oppose themselves; if God peradventure will give them repentance to the acknowledging of the truth; and that they may recover themselves out of the snare of the devil, who are taken captive by him at his will" *(2 Timothy 2:24-26)*. Paul is saying, "You've got to be tenderhearted with everyone, to be willing to wash their feet. God may have mercy on them yet — and deliver them from their sin!"

Our church has spent almost thirty weeks now praying for revival in New York City. Yet, it doesn't matter how much a church prays; God will not plant new believers there if they're going to have to struggle amid a bunch of judging, self-centered Christians. You see, every new believer is going to get his feet dirty before he becomes established in the faith. And he needs people who are willing to go to him quickly to wash his feet and restore him. True revival reflects this spirit of kindness — a spirit that's willing to take up the towel to cleanse and restore dirty believers!

3. Finally, We Come to the Word "Unity."

I believe when Jesus washed the disciples' feet, He was teaching a profound lesson on how to obtain unity of fellowship in the body of Christ. As Jesus approached Peter to wash his feet, the disciple drew back. "...Peter saith unto him, Lord, dost thou wash my feet?" *(John 13:6)*. Peter asked in astonishment, "Lord, You aren't going to wash my feet, are You? Never, never!" Jesus answered, "...If I wash thee not, thou hast no part with me" *(verse 8)*. Jesus was saying, in essence, "Peter, if I wash your feet, we have precious grounds for fellowship, a basis for true unity." Likewise, no pastor can bring unity into a church simply by implementing programs or even by his fiery preaching. No — unity comes from taking up a towel!

After Jesus washed His disciples' feet, He asked them, "Do you understand what I have done to you?" If they had understood the spiritual significance of what He had just done — taking away the stain and guilt of their sin — it would have produced in them gratitude.

I ask you: What did Jesus do to you when He cleansed you? He wiped away all your fault and guilt — He cleansed the last remnants of sin — and you were made clean, whole. He put gratitude, thankfulness, joy in your soul. He filled you with such love for Him that you would follow Him anywhere and do anything for Him. All you wanted was communion with Him, because of what He did for you.

Beloved, that is the secret of unity! When you take up the towel of mercy for a hurting, fallen brother, you encourage him by embracing him in his hurt — by submitting in godly fear, washing away his feelings of worthlessness, anguish and despair, and by loving and caring for him. Yet what have you done to that person by washing his feet? You have constructed a firm foundation for true unity and glorious fellowship. You are one by your common experience — that is, by being washed by the water of the Word!

Talk about gratitude — that Christian will be your friend for life! He will defend you, love you, do anything for you. He'll say to you, "You stood with me in my hard times. And now I'll never let anyone do anything to you!"

Can you imagine a church filled with such caring people — who refuse to hear a single word about another's dirt; who hurt when another hurts;

who rally around every despairing, fault-ridden brother or sister with a word of love and hope? That is why we moved our ministry to New York City — to raise up a holy, godly remnant who would make up a strong, unified base of comforters — people who carry a towel in their hands!

You may ask, "But how do I find people whose feet need washing?" My answer to you is, "The same way you found them when you gossiped about them!" Now, whenever you hear anything negative about someone, merely ask, "Who are you talking about? Name only, please!" Then go to that hurting person quickly with your mercy towel — and start washing his feet. Tell the fallen one, "I care about you. And I want to pray for you — but I don't need to know any details. I just want you to know I still love you — and I'm going to stand with you."

This message is for me as much as for anyone else. I have just recently come into this convicting knowledge of what foot washing is truly about. And, by God's grace, I'll take up the towel of mercy along with others and seek out those hurting ones whose feet need cleansing from dirt.

Jesus said, "If I then, as your Lord and Master, have washed your feet; ye also ought to wash one another's feet....If ye know these things, happy are ye if ye do them" *(verses 14, 17)*.

Now that we "know these things," as Jesus said, we can do them. I ask you: Are you willing to do them? Are you ready to take up your towel in love?

The Joseph Company

11

Is Your Greatest Trial God's Word to You?

I know of one Bible scholar who has discovered more than a hundred ways in which Joseph was a type of Jesus Christ. Yet, as much as I believe Joseph was a type of Christ, I also believe He was a type of last-day remnant — a people whom God is raising up right now to show His church how to break out of its spiritual famine.

Let me show you the Joseph Company — a small body of last-day believers wholly given to the Lord. They commune with God daily. They are led by the Spirit in every detail of their lives. And at this moment they are coming out of great trials and testings to enter a place of revelation, wisdom and fruitfulness. God is working in them, giving them His truth and knowledge. And the time is coming soon when He is going to call upon them as He did Joseph!

Right now, the church of Jesus Christ is growing increasingly worldly, sensual, wicked and cold. Our ministry receives literally thousands of letters from pastors and laypeople who are burdened by the condition of their church. People complain that they don't hear convicting, life-changing sermons. Pastors complain that few want to hear the truth.

Yes, there are some powerful "lamp-stick" churches in America — full of light and glory and the holiness of God. The pastors are on fire, preaching righteousness, and God is moving mightily among the people. But for the most part, the church today is experiencing widespread spiritual famine: shallow sermons, dead hearers, "lively" worship that is not backed up by righteous living. A Laodicean blindness has fallen like a cloud over the eyes of multitudes who once were on fire for God.

Many true ministers of God are becoming disheartened. One pastor wrote recently: "A great number of godly pastors are being fired or forced out by their churches. I resigned from my church last December 31. A colleague just ten miles away also left his church under a cloud. A third pastor sixty miles away submitted his resignation under duress. A fourth was fired by his church in October.

"In my region, churches are not growing by making new converts, but from Christians moving around, shopping with a consumer mentality. It's a revolving door.... Please find out for yourself how many men of God are heartbroken, defeated, discouraged — yet also saying, 'Even so, come, Lord Jesus'!"

What Is God's Solution to Such Backsliding and Famine?

God has always been at work far in advance of every spiritual famine in His church. In every generation He has moved ahead to prepare a way out for His people!

The seventy-five members of Jacob's clan would have died in the great worldwide famine (and the promise of Israel would have been destroyed) had not God been working ahead of it all. In fact, some twenty years before the famine hit, God was already setting in motion a plan to save His people from destruction: He sent Joseph ahead to Egypt! For twenty years God worked on this man — isolating him, trying him, preparing him for a place of authority — because Joseph was to become the life-saver of God's chosen. He kept Joseph from the limelight — to be discipled for a coming day of chaos and death.

Beloved, just as surely as God isolated Joseph, He has a Joseph Company today that is hidden from all eyes. These are in the furnace of affliction, prisons of testing, battlegrounds of trials and temptation. They are dying to this world, wanting nothing of its fame, honor, money or pleasure. And they are growing hungry to become more intimate with Christ — to know His heart and His voice.

You may not understand all the mysterious testings, trials and troubles in your life. But if your heart is fully set on following Christ, you can rest assured God has purpose in it all: He is wanting to bring you into His Joseph Company!

There are three things that went into the making of Joseph as a tried and tested servant. And you too will experience these things if you are a part of this last-day company:

1. Joseph Responded to the Spirit's Call to a Holy, Separated Life.

God's Spirit has always been calling mankind to Himself — to holiness, purity of heart and a separated life. Tragically, few ever respond — but in every generation God has a small remnant who do answer His call. They separate themselves, purify their lives and give themselves wholly to Him.

Joseph responded to God's call at a very early age. And he had ten older brothers who received the same call to surrender, walk righteously and separate themselves. But they chose to remain in the world — and their walk with God was half-hearted.

There were at least two occasions when all of Jacob's sons received the Spirit's call very clearly. The first was at Shalem, in Shechem, where Jacob built an altar to THE GOD OF ISRAEL. Jacob called his sons to the altar to become worshipers with him — to kneel before the Lord and follow Him wholeheartedly. But Joseph's brothers instead turned to revenge and bloodshed. When a Shechemite defiled their sister Dinah, they rushed into the city, burning it down and killing every man, woman and child *(see Genesis 34)*. These ten brothers hadn't given themselves wholly to trust and serve God. No — their violence made Jacob a stench among the Canaanites!

Yet, God called out to them clearly once more, this time at Bethel. Jacob knew his sons were bound with idolatry and were rejecting God's call to purity and righteousness. So he warned them: "...Put away the strange gods that are among you, and be clean, and change your garments: and let us arise, and go up to Bethel; and I will make there an altar unto God..." *(Genesis 35:2-3)*.

Beloved, this is one of the clearest calls in all of God's Word! The phrase "change your garments" in Hebrew means a moral and spiritual purification of the mind and heart. Outwardly, Jacob's sons surrendered: "And they gave unto Jacob all the strange gods which were in their hand, and all their earrings..." *(verse 4)*. But their repentance was only on the surface; they never had a true heart-change. They went right back to their rebellion, becoming full of hate, envy and strife!

There was something different about Joseph: his repentance had been from the heart. He had responded to the Spirit's call — and from the age of seventeen, he was wholly set on following the Lord. In the midst of a wicked, evil environment, Joseph maintained clean hands and a pure heart.

Now, Jacob had other sons who were born to Bilhah and Zilpah, his maid and concubine. These sons cared for the family flocks, and Joseph was sent out to the fields to work among them. But he was soon grieved, because his brothers spoke and lived like heathen. His pure heart was crushed by the wickedness in his own family. "…and Joseph brought unto his father their evil report" *(37:2)*. Joseph revealed his heart to his father: "You wouldn't believe the way they live, Father. They speak against your God and mine. They're grieving Him!"

Beloved, this is a mark of the Joseph Company: they have a grief for sin! They have forsaken all idols and are in love with Jesus. Their hearts are aflame with His holiness. They see the sin in the land, but they are grieved most of all by the sin in the church. They cry out from their souls, "Oh, Father — look at what is happening among Your children!"

If you are a part of this last-day company, you can't overlook sin. Rather, something has to rise up in you that says, "Oh God, I can't stand what they're doing to Your name!" You begin to pray — not against people, but against the inroads of demonic powers into the church of Jesus Christ.

Joseph's Father Favored Him, Clothing Him With a Special Garment That Made Him Stand Out Among His Brethren.

Does our heavenly Father favor certain of His children? Or doesn't the Bible say God is no respecter of persons? When it comes to eternal salvation and His wonderful covenant promises, God treats all alike. But God also responds to all who respond wholeheartedly to His calling. He puts His special favor on those who yield their lives entirely to Him.

Job said: "Thou hast granted me life and favour…" *(Job 10:12)*. And David said: "For thou, Lord, wilt bless the righteous; with favour wilt thou compass him as with a shield" *(Psalm 5:12)*. "Lord, by thy favour thou hast made my mountain to stand strong…" *(30:7)*. Scripture also tells us: "And the child Samuel grew on, and was in favour both with the Lord, and also with men" *(1 Samuel 2:26)*.

The fact is, our heavenly Father puts a special garment on those who seek after Him and give Him their heart completely: "I will greatly rejoice in the Lord, my soul shall be joyful in my God; for he hath clothed me with garments of salvation, he hath covered me with the robe of righteous-ness…" *(Isaiah 61:10)*.

Joseph responded to the Spirit's call, surrendering all — and he received favor from his father. He was given a robe that set him apart. But that favor of his father was costly! It cost Joseph every relationship. It brought him rejection, misunderstanding, mockery: "All his brethren… hated him" *(Genesis 37:4)*.

Why did Joseph's brothers turn on him? The key is in verse 11: "His brethren envied him." When they saw the robe Joseph wore, they knew it spoke of favor, righteousness. And they hated it — because it reminded them of the Spirit's call they had rejected. Joseph was a reproach to their half-hearted life-style!

You see, Joseph's brothers sat around trading in petty gossip and self-centered talk. Their hearts were occupied with land, possessions, their future. But Joseph's mind was elswhere. He spoke of the things of God, of supernatural dealings. God had given him dreams, which in that day was synonymous with hearing the voice of God. Joseph was of a different cloth — and that difference made him hated and envied among his brothers. And, beloved, the same thing will happen to you if you have sold out to Jesus!

Lukewarm believers around you will want to talk about their cars, houses and jobs — but you'd rather talk about eternal things, about what God is saying to you. Soon you'll become a reproach to their half-heartedness. They'll envy you — because you represent the call of the Holy Ghost they turned down.

Indeed, those of the Joseph Company remnant know all about rejection. They know the pain of being tagged a fanatic, a spiritual kook, an "imbalanced" believer. Even preachers mock them, calling their separation and devotion to Jesus "spiritual pride." They tell their congregation, "This one is too far out. God does not expect such fanaticism!"

2. Joseph's Greatest Trial Was the Word of God He So Loved and Trusted.

"He sent a man before them, even Joseph, who was sold for a servant: whose feet they hurt with fetters: he was laid in iron: until the time that his word came: the word of the Lord tried him" *(Psalm 105:17-19)*. Joseph was tested and tried in many ways — but his greatest trial was the word he had received!

Consider everything Joseph endured: At only seventeen, he was stripped down and cast into a pit to starve to death. His cold-hearted brothers laughed at his pleas for mercy. He was sold to Ishmaelite traders, taken by caravan to an Egyptian slave market and then sold as a common slave. Yet Joseph's greatest trial wasn't his rejection by his brothers. It wasn't the human indignity of being made into a slave or being cast into prison. No — Joseph was confused and tried in spirit by the clear word he had heard from God!

God had revealed to Joseph through dreams that he would be given great authority, and that he would use it for God's glory. His brothers would bow before him; even the sun, moon and stars would bow! He would be a great deliverer of many people.

I believe none of this was an ego trip for Joseph. His heart was so set on God that this word instead gave him a humble sense of destiny: "Lord, You have put Your hand on me to have a part in Your great, eternal plan. Oh God — why choose me?" Joseph was blessed just by knowing he would play an important role in bringing God's will to pass.

But all the circumstances in Joseph's life were just the opposite of what God had put in his heart. He was the servant — and he had to bow! How could he hold to such a word from God, that he would one day deliver multitudes, when he was a slave himself? He must have thought, "This doesn't make sense. How could God be 'ordering my steps' into prison — into oblivion? He said I was going to be blessed. He didn't tell me this was going to happen!"

For ten years, Joseph served in Potiphar's house faithfully — but in the end he was misjudged and lied about. His victory over temptation with Potiphar's wife only landed him in jail. During such times he must have pondered the awful questions: "Did I hear correctly? Or did my pride invent these dreams? Could my brothers have been right — that I'm too given over to this word? Maybe all these things are happening to me as discipline for some kind of selfish desire...."

Beloved, there have been times when God has shown me things He has wanted for me — ministry, service, usefulness — yet my every circumstance was the very opposite of that word. At such times I thought, "Oh God, this can't be You speaking — it has to be my flesh." I was being tried by God's word to me! Consider, too, the following:

• I know a dear pastor who is being tried by God's Word. He believes what the Bible says about healing — yet, for the past five years he has watched his wife deteriorate with a rare disease. He prays for the sick at his church — and then he comes home to feed, dress and bathe his wife. He believes God for her healing, yet she grows worse every day. I see revealed in this man the grace and patience of Christ. He is one of the most loving, caring men of God I have ever met. And the tenderness he shows his wife now comes out in his ministry to his congregation.

• A dear sister wrote recently that over a year ago she finally determined to go all the way with Jesus. God began to reveal Christ in her — yet soon afterward, she discovered her husband was seeing prostitutes. He was staying out every night in bars and brothels. This woman was forced to leave her home and get a job to support her three children. The more devoted she became to Christ, the more her husband turned away from God. She couldn't understand why, when she set her heart on Christ, such an awful tragedy would happen. But I sensed in her letter a power, a heavenly strength. She, too, is being tried by the Word. God has given her His promises — yet her circumstances are the exact opposite!

Even in the Midst of Every Trial and Hard Place, God Prospers His Joseph Company!

Even while Joseph was a servant in Potiphar's house, he was blessed by God. And soon after he landed in prison, he prospered there as well. How did God prosper him? It wasn't with money or possessions; it wasn't with position. No — all along, God was prospering Joseph's spirit — speaking to his heart, giving him dreams and interpretations.

This is what kept Joseph going on with God. He had faith that, in spite of all his hardships and situations beyond his control, God was with him. Joseph was never for a moment without the manifest presence of the Lord — and that constant, abiding presence produced a peace within him.

I believe God must have longed to show Joseph the end of the story — to whisper to him, "Don't worry, Joseph. This is how it's going to end..." But He dared not — because Joseph was still in school!

You see, Joseph didn't know that one day he was going to "teach (Pharaoh's) senators wisdom" *(Psalm 105:22)*. Yet how could he teach God's wisdom to Egypt's leaders unless he first had learned it himself? God's children learn such lessons only by faith. We get God's wisdom through trials, tribulations, hardships and testings. We don't pray it down — we live it out!

If you are in God's last-day Joseph Company, then you are learning to lean on Him in your trials. You're learning to trust and not complain — to rest in Him completely. You may not comprehend all the mysterious ways God has led you. In fact, everything around you may seem the very opposite of the word God has given you. But you're learning that in all things, Christ is your resource. And God is keeping you in school for the day when He will call upon you!

3. The Day Came When It All Made Sense to Joseph! God Brought Everything Together — And Every Word and Promise Was Fulfilled to the Letter.

I believe it happened during Joseph's darkest hour — when he was lonely, downcast, about to give up his dreams, questioning his place in God. Suddenly, the call came from one of the king's guards: "Joseph! Get cleaned up. Pharaoh is calling for you!"

In that moment, the Spirit of God must have come upon Joseph mightily. I believe his heart leapt — an excitement grew within him: He was about to understand what it was all about! As Joseph shaved and trimmed his hair, he probably thought, "This is the beginning of what God promised me. Now I know I heard from Him! The devil was not in control — my life hasn't been wasted. God has been directing everything the entire time!"

In a matter of minutes, Joseph was standing before Pharaoh, listening to his dream. He gave the interpretation of the coming famine and told Pharaoh he had to gather and store the nation's grain: "Someone must be in charge of the storehouses. You have to find a man who's full of wisdom to oversee it all!" *(see Genesis 41)*. Pharaoh looked around — and then he turned to Joseph: "You, Joseph! I appoint you second ruler. Only I will have more power in the kingdom than you. You will oversee it all!"

How quickly things had changed! Within an hour, Joseph had gone from being a forsaken, unknown prisoner to the second most powerful man in Egypt. As he rode a royal chariot through the streets, the people were bowing before him — and suddenly he realized, his dream was being lived out.

I can just see Joseph riding along in deep but joyful contemplation. He must have relived every hard time of the past twenty years. He thought of all the trials and tests — of his brothers' rejection, and of being sold by them into slavery.

But now a joy came into his heart — because everything was coming together! He said, "Now I can see it. A famine is coming — and God is wanting to save my father and my brothers. He sent me ahead of them. This was His plan all along!"

The day came when Joseph stood before his brothers and was able to say: "But as for you, ye thought evil against me; but God meant it unto good, to bring to pass, as it is this day, to save much people alive" *(Genesis 50:20)*. "God sent me before you to preserve you a posterity in the earth, and to save your lives by a great deliverance. So now it was not you that sent me hither, but God: and he hath made me a father to Pharaoh, and lord of all his house, and a ruler throughout all the land of Egypt" *(45:7-8)*. Joseph was saying, "God was behind this, every step of the way! Every hardship the devil brought upon me — even the harm you meant to do to me — God turned to good and made a part of His eternal plan!"

Dear saint, if you are a part of this Joseph Company, very soon you're going to understand your present fiery trials. God is going to bring you into the promise He gave you — and suddenly it's all going to make sense. You'll see that He has never forsaken you. He had to take you this way — for He has been training you, preparing you, teaching you to trust Him for everything. He has planned a time for you to be used — and that time is just ahead!

The Last-Day Evangelists Will Not Be Primarily in Pulpits; They Will Be in the Congregation — Avoiding Attention, But Mightily Used!

A time is coming soon when there will be a spiritual famine such as the world has never seen. People are going to be starving spiritually on all sides. Yet the broken and famine-stricken will be taken one by one and told, "Come with me — I know someone full of Jesus. They've been tested, they've been through the fire, and they're full of the Holy Spirit. They will have a true word of deliverance for you!"

Beloved, already I see this happening! I know a number of the Joseph Company by name, because I've talked to them. They are able to give out the Bread of Life to the starving — because they have the keys to God's storehouse. They know the ways of the Lord, because they have come through their tests and trials with a grip on God. Something powerful is being revealed in them — and that is a heart fully persuaded that God answers prayer!

How are you responding to God's mysterious dealings with you? Are you fully persuaded that God is at work in all things, fulfilling His promises to you? Can you say, "It's enough right now that I know Jesus is with me — and He's prospering my spirit"?

Hold on in faith! Don't be afraid — because you are in Christ's school. Everything is under His control. Suddenly, the hour will come when your battle will end and your victory will be made real. You'll come out of the fire a vessel of honor — to do His will as part of the Joseph Company!

The Test of a "Good Hearer"

Recently, the Lord opened my eyes to an incredible truth about patience — something I'd never seen before. It appears in Jesus' explanation of the parable of the sower:

> Now the parable is this: The seed is the word of God. Those by the way side are they that hear; then cometh the devil, and taketh away the word out of their hearts, lest they should believe and be saved. They on the rock are they, which, when they hear, receive the word with joy; and these have no root, which for a while believe, and in time of temptation fall away. And that which fell among thorns are they, which, when they have heard, go forth, and are choked with cares and riches and pleasures of this life, and bring no fruit to perfection. But that on the good ground are they, which in an honest and good heart, having heard the word, keep it, and bring forth fruit with patience *(Luke 8:11-15)*.

This parable is all about patience! I don't mean patience toward people — but patience toward God. Jesus is speaking here of patience in our walk with God, patience in doing His work, patience in His working in us. I believe that once you see what God is saying here, you will understand more clearly why so many Christians are backsliding and falling away. And you'll also better understand the working of the Lord in your own heart.

The "good ground" Jesus mentions indicates those who heard the Word and eventually brought forth fruit "with patience." The other hearers brought forth a measure of fruit too — but only for a time. Why? It is because they were impatient with the Lord and His working in their life — and they fell away.

I pray that as we explore this parable, you'll see each of these hearers in a whole new light. I believe there is a fresh word here for you from the Lord.

1. First, Consider the "Wayside Hearer."

"Those by the way side are they that hear..." *(Luke 8:12)*. This hearer had the Word of God planted in his heart. And he heard it like any interested hearer: He sat, listened and didn't turn it off. He was not a mocker, but he had respect for the Word.

Yet, Jesus says, "...then cometh the devil, and taketh away the word out of their hearts, lest they should believe and be saved" *(verse 12)*. I have always had a difficult time with this verse. Am I to believe I can preach to a congregation, drive out the powers of hell, command the devil to leave — and yet Satan can come in promiscuously and rob a person of the Word he or she has just heard? Can the enemy hover over a believer, wait for the Word to fall on that person's heart, then freely pluck it up?

That, to me, seems like throwing the Word of God straight into the devil's mouth. I just can't accept it. Instead, I believe we have to ask: Is this wayside hearer simply an innocent, childlike person, anxiously hearing the Word? Is it true that, through no fault of the hearer, the devil can swoop down, rob him of the preached Word and blind him spiritually, so that he won't turn to the Lord? No — never! We don't serve a God who's like that. And that isn't the gospel we preach. We have to understand Jesus is saying something much deeper here.

You see, the wayside hearer has a heart that is "trodden down": "A sower went out to sow his seed: and as he sowed, some fell by the way side; and it was trodden down, and the fowls of the air devoured it" *(verse 5)*. Here is our clue: Jesus is describing the kind of heart this wayside hearer has. And the phrase He uses here is "trodden down." In other words, this person has "heard" often. In fact, he is a "professional hearer" — an expert at it. His heart has been trodden down, made hard like a well-walked road, by years of hearing without ever heeding!

This wayside hearer is described in Isaiah 5. The prophet tells Israel how God is going to turn them into a trodden-down vineyard — because they have heard so much reproof and rejected it all:

"...I will tell you what I will do to my vineyard: I will take away the hedge thereof, and it shall be eaten up; and break down the wall thereof, and it shall be trodden down: And I will lay it waste..." *(Isaiah 5:5-6)*.

Jesus quotes from this same passage to introduce the parable of the sower: "...Unto you it is given to know the mysteries of the kingdom of God: but to others in parables; that seeing they might not see, and hearing they might not understand" *(Luke 8:10)*. You see, God had instructed Isaiah: "...Go, and tell this people, Hear ye indeed, but understand not; and see ye indeed, but perceive not. Make the heart of this people fat, and make their ears heavy, and shut their eyes; lest they see with their eyes, and hear with their ears, and understand with their heart, and convert, and be healed" *(Isaiah 6:9-10)*. What Isaiah describes here is the condition of the wayside hearer!

The Wayside Hearer Is Hard and Trodden Down Because He Has Rejected the Word So Often.

Luke uses a Greek word for "trodden down" that means "rejection with disdain; an attitude of superiority." The wayside hearer has been reproved so often and for so long, he now smirks at the gospel. He laughs at it, mocks it. Nothing touches him anymore.

I think of a young Jewish man who came to Times Square Church during our first two years here. He was homeless, and the congregation adopted him. Almost everyone shared the gospel with him. Loving people gave him money and took him out for meals. Jesus Christ was made very plain to him. And that young man came to the altar at least twice. Both times I saw him standing there with his hands folded — and wearing a devilish grin on his face! I used to look up in the balcony and see him sleeping through the sermons. I prayed that at least one message would pierce the trodden-down soil of his heart.

It never happened. Eventually he became so vile, disruptive and explosive we had to ban him from the church. He had become hard — a man with a trodden-down heart. No person in New York heard more of the gospel. No one received so much love. No one was more prayed for. But he had hardened his heart and shut his ears.

Beloved, that is when the enemy comes in — when the heart is hardened! Satan swoops down and steals the seed that has been distributed, before there is a chance of even a tiny crack opening in the ground. The devil doesn't promiscuously have access to any heart that hears the gospel. Not at all! Rather, he steals from those who have been reproved — yet who smirk in disdain at God's Word!

This "trodden down" hearer is the most impatient of all people. He does not want to deal with his problems. He'd rather drown them in pleasure — alcohol, drugs, sex, anything — to calm down his terrible feelings of guilt. You speak to him of having heaven some day — but he wants it all now! He longs only for good times — no problems, no self-denial, no hardships. "Taking up a cross? Enduring suffering? No will of my own? Waiting forever for God to work character in me? You've got to be crazy!"

Indeed, multitudes of Americans are in a big hurry to prosper — to "get theirs" while the getting is good. That's what motivated Ivan Boesky, Michael Milken and so many other greedy Wall Streeters. They all thought the economy was headed for collapse, so they tried to make a quick fortune they could hide in a Swiss bank account.

How sad it is now that this spirit is creeping into the church. Many Christians have no patience for being tested or tried. They have no time for waiting on God, for bearing fruit with patience, as Jesus described. Instead, they want a full, blessed, painless, prosperous lifestyle with no waiting, no preparation, no reproof. And, sadly, they have teachers and a gospel to back them up!

These believers hate any preaching of obedience, separation, holiness, repentance. They call it all "doomsday preaching." Why such resistance, such spite? It is because they are trodden down with the urge to "get it all now." They want to be entertained, blessed — to go to church, feel happy and leave in the same condition as when they entered. They don't want the Holy Spirit to prod them, to dig deeply, to do the slow work of faith. They'd rather go to a charismatic circus!

2. Consider the "Rootless Hearer."

"...which, when they hear, receive the word with joy; and these have no root, which for a while believe, and in time of temptation fall away" *(Luke 8:13)*.

These hearers make the best-looking converts you've ever seen. They're happy, full of joy, vibrant. They testify to Christ's work in their lives. And theirs is a true conversion. They want to go on with the Lord — convicted by the Word, repentant, living in His joy.

Yet I ask every new convert reading this message right now to pay careful attention: If you ever fall away from the Lord, it will be because you are in this category — a "rootless hearer"!

You've been saved, filled with God's peace, and you're praising the Lord. You sing, you worship, you have joy. But one problem remains: You still battle a powerful temptation! It is like a snake, coiled and hissing, ready to strike at you with its poison. You hate this besetting sin that once controlled your life. And now you're on your knees, crying, "Oh Jesus, deliver me! I don't want this old lust haranguing me. I want to be free, clean. Help me. It has hold of my heart!"

Jesus says rootless hearers "...in time of temptation fall away" (*verse 13*). This does not mean the temptation is so overwhelming it sweeps them away. It doesn't mean they fall because of an overwhelming desire for drugs, a sexual urge, a thirst for alcohol. No — it all has to do with being impatient with the work of God! If you look back at a time when you fell or failed God, what would you say happened? You got mad at God for not answering your prayer! You didn't believe He would honor His Word to keep and deliver you. And in time of temptation, you fell away because you were impatient with His work in you.

A woman in our church has a sister who fell from grace back to drugs. This backslidden woman is tormented by her addiction. Yet she is like an evangelist, telling converts who struggle with impatience: "Stay in church — stay with the Lord! Look at what's happened to me. It's so hard to get back!" I'm sure if you sat down with her, she'd probably tell you, "I prayed — but I was overwhelmed. My preacher told me Jesus was my deliverer — that He would keep me from the power of sin. I cried, I prayed, I wept. But nothing happened!" No! Her sin was impatience!

Oh, what agonizing cries the rootless hearer sends up in time of temptation: "Lord, set me free! Take away my desires, the old sins. When will You ever deliver me, so I will never have to be afraid anymore?" Yet when the rootless hearer comes into a time of temptation, he falls — because he is not patient enough to put down roots!

You see, it is not enough to repent — to simply say "yes" to God. You have to put down roots in the Lord — and that takes patience. You can't simply drop a seed into the ground, stand over it and command, "Grow roots!" No — it's a natural process that takes time. It is a sovereign work of God.

Yet, as a young believer, you were surprised whenever you fell. You immediately condemned yourself. And after repeated failures, you told yourself it was no use trying. Then the devil whispered to you, "You're no good. You're too wicked. You can't make it. You might as well quit!" But you had forgotten that God always judges you with great compassion! He knew you had not had time to put down roots. And that is the very reason you fell: You hadn't had time to grow roots!

This may sound like an excuse, but it isn't. It is a valid explanation for what happens in our walk with the Lord. And the answer to it all is: Go back! Pray, dig in. Ask the Lord for roots. And ask Him for patience until they come.

But, you ask, what about mature Christians who once had roots — people who were grounded in Christ, yet still fell into sin? You know Christians who have been saved for years, who seemed to have deep roots — but who took a terrible fall. The Bible says, "...their root is dried up, they shall bear no fruit..." *(Hosea 9:16).* Such believers didn't stay close to Jesus! They had roots at one time — but they drifted away, and those roots dried up. The winds of false doctrine blew them away, because they allowed their roots to dry.

God Tests Us to See If We Will Patiently Wait for Him to Deliver Us.

God knows that our impatience is totally destructive. Consider Israel's impatience: Moses went up to the mountain, and God delayed him there. So what happened below? The people lost patience! After forty days, they rose up to play, dance and carouse in a drunken orgy. Finally, they melted all their jewelry and made a golden calf to worship. I picture these Israelites saying, "Where is Moses? Where is our God, our help? What kind of deliverance is this? God has let us down! He saved us only to turn us over to this awful desert. Now we're going to do our own thing!"

Yet at that moment, Moses was on his way down the mountain, with God's Word in his hands. Indeed, God is always on His way. He's always right at the door!

Consider what happened to Saul. Samuel told Saul to wait for him at Gilgal before fighting the Philistines. He warned him not to go into battle until Samuel had returned and could offer sacrifices to the Lord. Samuel said, "It may take me six, seven, eight days. But I'll be there."

So Saul gathered with Israel at Gilgal. But after five days, the Israelites grew impatient. The Philistine army had been gathering and building strength — and Saul's people began fleeing left and right. Soon the king had only a handful of soldiers left. Finally, on the seventh day, he grew very impatient: "Where is that prophet? Where is the burnt offering? We need it now!"

What Saul didn't know was that God had delayed Samuel — because He wanted to see what was in Saul's heart. God wanted to know if he would hold onto his faith while everything looked bad — if he would say,

"I'll die trusting God if I have to. I'm going to stand on His Word to me!"

Instead, Saul took matters into his own hands. He said, "Bring me the lamb." And he laid it out and offered the sacrifice himself (which was against Israel's law!). Then suddenly, Scripture says, "...it came to pass, that as soon as he had made an end of offering the burnt offering, behold, Samuel came..." *(1 Samuel 13:10)*. Here came Saul's answer, his deliverance. But he had already acted in impatience. He hadn't been willing to stake his future on God's Word. The answer had been at the door all along — but he lost it all!

Perhaps this is true of you as well: Your deliverance was close at hand. But you fell because you could not hold on just a little while longer. You lost heart — and you fainted too soon!

David is another man who grew tired of waiting. He complained, "For I said in my haste, I am cut off from before Thine eyes: nevertheless Thou heardest the voice of my supplications when I cried unto thee" *(Psalm 31:22)*. David was looking back and saying, "In my impatience I accused the Lord of not answering my cry. I accused Him of abandoning me in my temptation and trial. But all the while, He heard me and preserved me. I stand here today preserved by Him!"

3. There Is Also the "Thorny Hearer."

"And that which fell among thorns are they, which, when they have heard, go forth, and are choked with cares and riches and pleasures of this life, and bring no fruit to perfection" *(Luke 8:14)*. Jesus tells us this hearer didn't fall. He didn't go back to the world. No, he kept going on. But he didn't bear any fruit!

This "thorny hearer" goes to church, listens to the preaching, reads his Bible, hangs around God's people. He goes through all the motions — but he bears no fruit to fullness! He makes a lot of promises to God but never fulfills them. He's simply there — spiritually empty, just a body filling a pew.

Jesus says the thorny hearer "goes forth." In other words, once he hears the Word, he goes on with his life. Oh, he prays a little every day, talks the Christian talk, witnesses to others on occasion. But he's preoccupied, busy — with cares, pleasures, business!

How did he become so bogged down with the cares of the world? Through riches! The Bible says this type of hearer is drawn into lustful pleasures by his desire for wealth: "But they that will be rich fall into temptation and a snare, and into many foolish and hurtful lusts, which drown men in destruction and perdition" *(1 Timothy 6:9)*.

I believe the thorny hearer is more impatient than anyone else in this parable. I picture him as high-powered, active, entrepreneurial, a person of action — kind, charitable, not selfish. But a terrible kind of impatience has gripped him: It is an impatience with the high-cost demand of the cross of Christ! The thorny hearer cannot fully embrace self-denial. He cannot tolerate the idea of forsaking all to follow Jesus. He "chokes" *(Luke 8:14)* on the demand to come out of the world and be separate and clean. And he chokes on the call to make his career secondary — to give his life to God's interests.

I know very few rich people who embrace self-denial. They're used to providing everything for themselves, catering to their flesh. They are like the thorny hearer, who has never been weaned from the things of the world. This hearer knows nothing of the spirit that was in Moses, who "(Chose) rather to suffer affliction with the people of God, than to enjoy the passing pleasures of sin for a season" *(Hebrews 11:25)*.

Thank God, there are some wealthy Christians who are able to do this. But, as the Bible makes clear, most rich people spend their time, their energy and all their waking thoughts on investments, cares, pleasures. And they "go forth" content with a fruitless walk!

A Pentecostal minister once made a pitiful confession to me. He said he went to visit his parents in their tiny trailer home. His elderly father was a retired minister and was very poor, with no insurance. As the son looked at his parents' meager surroundings, Satan whispered to him, "See this? If you give your whole life to the gospel, you'll end up in poverty! Think of all the missionaries who spend their lives for God. They all come home with nothing!"

Something came over that son. At that moment, he decided he would never be poor! He determined to make all the money he could, so he could retire in style. This man was an official in his denomination and was very well-known and respected. But he started "wheeling and dealing" with his finances. All his tithes went toward investments. He "went forth" with his life, involved in ministry — but his preoccupation with wealth began to choke out his love for Jesus.

Eventually, all of his investments went sour. But, sadly, there has not been any repentance or change in him. He still ministers, often preaching at conventions. But he is still wheeling and dealing on the side, trying to build himself a nest egg. Unlike his father, he may retire someday with a lot of money. But his father is going to go out in glory! I believe the Lord will always provide for that elderly minister and his wife. They may not be rich, but they'll always have food on the table. And when that father dies, he'll go to the Lord in peace and rest — home to receive his new body, a mansion and all that goes with it.

But the son will be bogged down with the cares of this life. If he ever does secure his future, he'll never be able to enjoy it. Why? It is because he will live and die with no fruit to perfection!

4. Finally, There Is the "Good Ground Hearer."

"But that on the good ground are they, which in an honest and good heart, having heard the word, keep it, and bring forth fruit with patience" *(Luke 8:15)*. These hearers have a "good, honest heart." Yet, what does this phrase mean? The answer is found in 2 Thessalonians: "And the Lord direct your hearts into the love of God, and into the patient waiting for Christ" *(3:5)*.

This verse contains the two distinguishing marks of a "good-ground" hearer: 1. a heart that is set on loving God, and 2. one that is convinced Jesus will always deliver on time. These two characteristics are necessary for a heart that produces lasting fruit.

Now, the good-ground hearer is just like everybody else. He endures great afflictions, fiery trials and tests that seem strange to him. His body grows weary. Sometimes he gets depressed. Sometimes he's seduced by the flesh, and his passions are unruly. Sometimes his thoughts are disorderly and have to be brought into obedience to the Lord. Sometimes his love for Christ is tested, and he has long dry spells. Sometimes he is troubled by a distressed conscience. But his heart has a definite direction! In every circumstance, he directs himself first into the love of God, and then into the patient waiting for Jesus Christ.

Now, waiting patiently on Christ has a dual meaning: It means, first of all, anticipating Jesus' Second Coming. But it also means waiting for Jesus to come suddenly in answer to your prayers, to deliver or bless you. The good and honest heart says, "Jesus, I know I'm not perfect. I know my heart is black without Your cleansing blood. But I also know I love You with all my heart, and I am set on obeying You. I want to walk pleasing before You. Yet I don't have the power to do anything of myself. You have promised to keep me. And I am going to wait for You to come with my deliverance!"

Jesus used a special word in referring to bearing fruit with patience:

"cheerful." This means, literally, "a hopeful endurance through all tests and trials." Indeed, God's Word is most productive in us when it produces a quiet, trustful rest in the Lord. Hebrews tells us: "For ye have need of patience, that, after ye have done the will of God, ye might receive the promise" *(10:36)*. Have you set your hope — your whole life — on this Word? Do you believe it will keep you throughout all the years of your walk with Him?

Take God's Word and settle it in your heart right now. Let it produce an honest, pure, good heart in you. You'll find that in every trial and temptation, it will always direct you immediately into His love and into patience — until Jesus comes with healing and victory!

13

Have You Felt Like Giving Up Lately?

Fighting the Fears Satan Tries to Plant In You

Is it possible for righteous, godly, Spirit-filled Christians to become so low and downcast, they feel they can't go on — and they come to the brink of giving up?

Think about it for a moment. I'm talking now about believers who are close to Jesus — who know His heart and mind, have done battle in prayer, have experienced His miracles, have seen victory after victory in their lives. Such people are dedicated to the Lord's work. They present themselves daily as living sacrifices. Tell me: Is it possible for such Christians to be so pressed down and troubled, to be in such despair and despondency, that they become convinced they're not going to make it?

Absolutely — yes!

Consider Holy Job — a Man Whom God Himself Called "Perfect and Upright"!

Scripture says of Job, ". . . that man was perfect and upright, and one that feared God, and eschewed evil" *(Job 1:1)*. This man feared God alone. He shunned evil and ran from all compromise. But now Job faced the crisis of his life: He had lost his entire family, all his possessions, everything. And his body was covered with boils from head to toe. He had come to a place where he could not take any more suffering. He cried out:

"For the arrows of the Almighty are within me, the poison whereof drinketh up my spirit: the terrors of God do set themselves in array against me . . . . Oh that I might have my request; and that God would grant me the thing that I long for! Even that it would please God to destroy me; that he would let loose his hand, and cut me off!" *(6:4, 8-9)*. Job was saying, "I have only one request — to die! I've had it, God. Cut me off!"

Do these sound like the words of a totally righteous man? The fact is, Scripture testifies that Job had no known sin in his life. He stood as perfect as any man could be before God. And yet God allowed him to go through such despair that his life became unbearable: "...wearisome nights are appointed to me. When I lie down, I say, When shall I arise, and the night be gone? And I am full of tossings to and fro unto the dawning of the day" *(7:3-4)*.

Finally, in total despair, Job cried out: "...my soul chooseth strangling, and death rather than my life. I loathe it; I would not live alway: let me alone; for my days are vanity....I am a burden to myself" *(verses 15-16, 20)*. Job was in anguish because his problems were unsolvable. He couldn't reason his way out of them. He was completely at wit's end!

About that time, three of Job's friends came along — so-called "comforters" — and tried to figure out why Job was suffering. They couldn't understand why God would allow any righteous man to become as mentally, spiritually and physically afflicted as Job was.

Beloved, this is the perennial dilemma in the church — and also in the eyes of the world: It seems that when you give your life to the Lord, all you get is suffering in return! No one, within the church or without, has ever understood how a loving God could allow those who have given their all for Him to go through such times of trouble and despair.

So, Job's friends kept lecturing him, "God does not afflict the righteous. You must be in sin!" "If iniquity be in thine hand, put it far away, and let not wickedness dwell in thy tabernacles" *(11:14)*.

I ask you: How would you feel if you heard such words from close friends, when you were trying your best to understand your suffering? These supposed men of God told Job, "You've got some hidden sin in your life. Out with it — confess! Only then will your troubles disappear."

But was God angry with Job? Not at all! Scripture makes it clear that wasn't Job's problem. And Job knew this. He said to God: "Do not condemn me; shew me wherefore thou contendest with me....Thou knowest that I am not wicked...My soul is weary of my life..." *(10:7, 2, 1)*.

Let me list several of Job's other complaints before the Lord. As you read them, ask yourself if you've ever had similar thoughts:

● "Hast thou not poured me out as milk, and curdled me like cheese? ...I am full of confusion..." *(verses 10-15)*. In other words: "Lord, You've stirred up my life, and I'm going sour. I'm totally confused!"

● "Wherefore hidest thou thy face, and holdest me for thine enemy?" *(13:24)*. "God, You've taken my children, everything I have. Why have You made Yourself my enemy?"

● "My face is foul with weeping, and on my eyelids is the shadow of death" *(16:16)*. "My eyes are red from crying. My face is like a dead man's!"

Have you ever come to such a point in your walk with Jesus?

Consider Holy Jeremiah — The Weeping Prophet!

Jeremiah had the fire of God burning in his bones. This holy man walked with God and was fearless before men. He had an ear attuned to heaven — a pipeline to God's throne — and spoke as the Lord's voice to his generation. No one could stand against his power and authority. He shook his listeners to the core!

Yet Jeremiah also came to a place of total despair. The Lord allowed him to experience a despondency few people have ever touched. And Jeremiah came to the brink of giving up!

The prophet was convinced he had fallen under some kind of deception. Satan had whispered to him that he was being rejected and mocked because he had been deceived by God: "O Lord, thou hast deceived me, and I was deceived...I am in derision daily, every one mocketh me" *(Jeremiah 20:7)*.

Consider these words of Jeremiah — the godly man who thundered prophecies to the nations: "Cursed be the day wherein I was born...Cursed be the man who brought tidings to my father, saying, A man child is born unto thee; making him very glad. And let that man be as the cities which the Lord overthrew...Because he slew me not from the womb; or that my mother might have been my grave, and her womb to be always great with me. Wherefore came I forth out of the womb to see labour and sorrow, that my days should be consumed with shame?" *(verses 14-18)*.

Do these sound like the words of a fearless prophet of God? Jeremiah was so overwhelmed by trouble and affliction, he wished he had died in his mother's womb! His cry echoes Job, who said, "Wherefore is light given to him that is in misery, and life unto the bitter in soul ... Which rejoice exceedingly, and are glad, when they can find the grave?" *(Job 3:20, 22)*. Job was saying, "God, why did You give me all of this light, only to turn it off suddenly? All I want is to lie down and die — to get out of this trouble I'm in!"

So It Was With the Godly Prophet Elijah!

Elijah knew the supernatural workings of God firsthand. He had brought a dead child back to life. And now, he stood before Ahab and prayed the very heavens shut. He told Ahab, "I've been on my knees before a holy God. And I tell you, it won't rain again until I say so!"

Talk about power — Elijah first shut the heavens, and then he opened them again. When he prayed later, rain fell on the land once more. But that's not all: Elijah then outran Ahab's chariot — and he was in his eighties at the time! He poured twelve barrels of water over the altar and called down fire from heaven to consume it. What a sight that must have been!

Elijah's greatest desire was to see revival in Israel. For years he had been saddened by the wickedness of God's people — and now he believed his prayers were being answered. He thought he was witnessing the start of a great reformation in Israel.

But Jezebel quickly stepped in and squashed the revival. Moreover, she threatened to kill Elijah. Suddenly, this once-fearless man was running for his life. He ended up in a desolate spot in the wilderness, where he sat down under a juniper tree, "...and he requested for himself that he might die..." *(1 Kings 19:4)*.

Elijah had literally given his life for revival, both in prayer and in action. Yet now he believed he was a total failure! He grew depressed, crying, "...It is enough; now, O Lord, take away my life; for I am not better than my fathers" *(same verse)*.

If you read between the lines in this passage, you can hear Elijah saying, "I gave my all, Lord — I laid down my life. I had no personal agenda. I wanted only to please You. And now it's all blown up in my face!"

This poor, dejected prophet shut down completely for forty days and nights. That meant forty nights of despair — of sleeplessness, waiting for the dawn, trying desperately to figure things out. It must have been one long nightmare of defeat, rejection, hopelessness. And during that time, Elijah lost all memory of every miracle God had ever done for him. Something simply had come over him — a dejection and despondency that brought down his soul. Now, not even the thought of past blessings could comfort him.

You might think, "Surely someone who has seen such miracles wouldn't have any doubts or depression. He would only have to recall the great wonders God has wrought. That would override all his fears." Not so! There comes a time when no past miracle or blessing can help you in your present trial.

I have counseled many Christians — ministers, evangelists, soul-winners who have been mightily used of God — who have experienced such a depth of despondency. These people were once powerful in ministry, preaching glorious revelations of God. But suddenly they grew weary. Troubles piled upon them. They were slandered and rejected. And they ended up feeling they'd spent their whole lives in vain. They told me, "There's no use going on. I don't feel I've done anything for the Lord. I'm a failure!"

I was appalled that any Christian could be so defeatist. I answered them almost indignantly: "Snap out of it! Have you forgotten all the miracles God has done for you? He hasn't forsaken you. Count your blessings!"

Theogically, I may have been correct. But often that theology simply doesn't work. It certainly didn't work for Elijah. That holy man ended up hiding in a cave — making his home in an utterly dark place of despair!

Have you ever dropped out for a while, as Elijah did? Have you ever gone into hiding — so hurt, so down, you didn't want to see or talk to anyone? Yours may be a cave of silence — a withdrawal from people and responsibilities. Or, maybe at this point you're still not convinced a Christian can experience such despair. You may say, "All these examples are from the Old Testament. But we live in a day of grace. Surely no Spirit-filled believer should live in fear. There shouldn't be any depression in God's house!"

Is This Merely an Old Testament Experience?

I ask you: Can New Testament saints who are full of God's Spirit go through times of deep despair — people who spend time on their knees, who give their lives in service to the Lord, who don't walk in sin but are wholly dedicated to Jesus?

Paul, the apostle, is quick to answer this. He surely was a New Testament saint — a godly, precious man who had given up the whole world that he might win Christ. He spent every breath in the cause of the Master. And this man had a revelation of Christ as did no other person on earth. Jesus had revealed Himself not just to Paul, but in him. And the Spirit took Paul into heaven and showed him unspeakable glories. Indeed, Paul was given the very mystery of the gospel. His epistles have instructed God's people throughout the centuries.

But the Bible says when Paul went to Asia to preach the gospel, he received only trouble: "For we would not, brethren, have you ignorant of our trouble which came to us in Asia..." *(2 Corinthians 1:8)*.

God had been using Paul mightily throughout Asia, and especially in Ephesus. A great revival had fallen on the city and lasted for two years: "So mightily grew the word of God and prevailed" *(Acts 19:20)*. During that time the Lord had worked great miracles: Demons were cast out. The lame and the sick were healed. And Paul was at the center of it all. He anointed handkerchiefs and aprons, which, when laid upon people, brought immediate healing and deliverance: "And God wrought special miracles by the hands of Paul: So that from his body were brought unto the sick handkerchiefs or aprons, and the diseases departed from them, and the evil spirits went out of them" *(verses 11-12)*.

The miracles were so great and the conviction so strong, the Ephesian converts gathered up all their occult books and curious arts — 50,000 pieces of silver's worth — and held a massive bonfire in the city square. Yet, this only enraged the satanic forces in Ephesus! After all, the goddess Diana was worshiped in that city. But now the citizens were no longer buying idols of Diana for worship. This stirred up a group of silversmiths, who made their living by selling the statues they shaped. The men rose up against Paul — riling up the crowds against him!

Suddenly, in the midst of this great revival, a massive riot broke out. The people dragged Paul into a theater, and the apostle had to defend himself before a raging mob. Eventually, he left Ephesus hearing the taunts and mockeries of the wicked.

Do you get the picture? Paul had given two years of his life to this revival. He had seen a mighty move of God. But then turmoil came into his life so heavily, he said: ". . . we were pressed out of measure, above strength, insomuch that we despaired even of life" *(2 Corinthians 1:8)*. In other words: "I thought, 'It's all over — I'm not going to make it. I won't come out of this alive. The sentence of death is on me!'"

I believe I know something of what Paul went through. Years ago, I was at a large meeting with sister Kathryn Kuhlman in Los Angeles. More than 5,000 people filled the place, with standing room only. At the time, my wife was going through a bout with cancer. And I was carrying the burden of Teen Challenge. I had been traveling and writing, and I'd grown weary and tired. Of course, that's always when the enemy comes to you — when you're physically low, with no strength left.

I was sitting on the stage, waiting to preach, as sister Kuhlman directed the worship. The place was full of God's Spirit, and marvelous things were happening. Yet, suddenly, the enemy came in and whispered to my heart:

"You are the biggest phony on the face of the earth! You're working with troubled people just to make a name for yourself. And now your wife is going to die. You say you've given your life for the Lord's ministry — but it's all vanity! You don't have the fire of God. You've lost your anointing. You can't preach tonight, because all your words will be fake!"

The voice was so loud, I couldn't quiet it. I kept trying to shake it off, but as I stepped up to the pulpit, it was still screaming in my ears. When I opened my mouth to preach, hardly anything came out. I tried for five minutes to speak — but I just couldn't. Finally, I motioned to sister Kuhlman to take over the service, and I turned and walked off the stage.

Backstage a pastor asked me, "David, what's wrong? What's the matter?" I could only shake my head. "I'm sorry," I said, "I can't go on. I can't preach tonight. I'm a phony!"

Like Jeremiah, it took me weeks to walk through my confusion and anguish of heart. Finally, God brought me out of it. But I discovered that such afflictions cannot be explained physically. Simply put, the enemy came in like a flood, with all the powers of hell arrayed against me. In just a few moments, I found myself in a pit — unable to explain it!

We don't know exactly what Paul spoke of when he said, "...our trouble which came to us in Asia..." *(same verse)*. Some scholars believe he was going through a great physical battle — that he was so sick he was near death. Yet I don't believe Paul's troubles were physical. I don't think he was talking about shipwrecks, stonings or beatings. Rather, I believe Paul was speaking of mental anguish — a deep, spiritual warfare that had left him wiped out!

You may ask, "How could this be? No godly, overcoming believer should ever be fearful or embattled by the flesh." Yet I, for one, am glad Paul spoke so truthfully about his feelings! Otherwise, I might think my own experiences with despair are strange, unique — not shared by other lovers of Jesus.

The fact is, many godly men and women throughout history have testified that Satan has attacked them in this way. He comes bringing lies, discouragement, hopelessness. One day a person can be rejoicing, secure in his salvation. But the next, an unexplainable feeling of worthlessness comes over him. Suddenly, for no reason, his peace is gone. He is plagued by restlessness. Despondency sets in. He feels undeserving, unholy, unacceptable to God.

This isn't just a physical sickness or a sense of rejection. Rather, it is an unexplainable mental anguish — something that can come upon you at any time. I don't know what to call it exactly. But women, especially, are plagued with it — and "experts" have tagged it with all kinds of names. One day, things just begin to pile up in your mind. You can't explain it. And nobody can reach you. Suddenly, you don't want to talk to anyone. All you want to do is hide.

Whatever happened to Paul in Asia, it overwhelmed him completely. He was brought so low, all his strength was gone. He wrote, "...we had the sentence of death in ourselves..." *(verse 9)*. In other words: "I couldn't see any way out. It wasn't humanly possible for me to make it through!"

You may wonder, "How could things get that bad for this great man of God? Did Paul really want his life to end?"

The fact is, Paul had taken upon himself the care of overseeing all the churches he had pionereed. He loved those new believers with all his heart. He grieved over their sins and compromises. And he corrected them with great anguish. This in itself was a tremendous burden for any man or woman of God to bear. Paul wrote: "For out of much affliction and anguish of heart I wrote unto you with many tears; not that ye should be grieved, but that ye might know the love which I have more abundantly unto you" *(2:4)*.

Paul's anguish at constantly having to correct and direct his flock afflicted him and made him weak. It was like giving birth to a child: It took a great toll on his physical body. Paul then wrote: "For, when we were come into Macedonia, our flesh had no rest, but we were troubled on every side; without were fightings, within were fears" *(7:5)*. You may be saying, "Do you mean Paul, the great apostle, had fear? Isn't this the same man who spoke so much about having victory over fear? Can this really be Paul talking?"

Yes — absolutely! That is Satan's design — to plant fears in us. He wants us to lose our confidence that God answers prayer — to think that all of our interceding, fasting and seeking Him have been in vain.

Notice what Paul adds to the verse he wrote about feeling "the sentence of death": "...that we should not trust in ourselves, but in God which raiseth the dead" *(1:9)*. It was all about faith! I strongly believe that God allows His people — and especially ministers of the gospel — to go through many difficult things so that their faith may be built from it. Then, when they share or preach, they no longer speak from theology — but from personal experience of God's delivering power. That is why Paul could say, "I don't want you to be ignorant of how the devil tried to overwhelm me in Asia. I want to share with you how God brought me out of it — so that you, too, can be healed and delivered!"

In recent years, Satan has tried to play the same "phony" trick on me — but he cannot succeed. Each time I have rebuked him, saying, "You broke the record last time, devil. I'll never play that one again. And you'll never convince me I'm a phony!"

I Believe I Am Speaking to a Number of Godly People
Who Love Jesus With All Their Heart —
And Who Are at a Point of Deep Despair!

Perhaps, like Paul, you are being pressed beyond measure — tested beyond your endurance. Your strength is nearly gone, and you are on the brink of giving up. You see no way out. You want to run, but there is no place to go. Now you say with Paul, "This is above my strength!"

So — how do you get out of it? What is the way to victory? All I can tell you is how God continues to bring me out. Here are four important truths He has given me:

1. Don't think you are experiencing some strange, unique battle. On the contrary — you are in good company! Recall Job, Jeremiah, Elijah, David, Paul — even me. What you are going through is common to believers throughout the centuries.

"Beloved, think it not strange concerning the fiery trial which is to try you, as though some strange thing happened unto you: But rejoice, inasmuch as ye are partakers of Christ's sufferings; that, when his glory shall be revealed, ye may be glad also with exceeding joy" *(1 Peter 4:12-13)*.

2. When you think you can't go on another hour — when everything looks absolutely hopeless — cry out to God with all that is in you, "Lord, help!" Consider the counsel of the psalmist:

● "As for me, I will call upon God; and the Lord shall save me. Evening, and morning, and at noon, will I pray, and cry aloud: and he shall hear my voice. He hath delivered my soul in peace from the battle that was against me: for there were many with me" *(Psalm 55:16-18)*.

● "I will love thee, O Lord, my strength. The Lord is my rock, and my fortress, and my deliverer; my God, my strength, in whom I will trust; my buckler, and the horn of my salvation, and my high tower. I will call upon the Lord, who is worthy to be praised: so shall I be saved from mine enemies. The sorrows of death compassed me, and the floods of ungodly men made me afraid. The sorrows of hell compassed me about: the snares of death prevented me. In my distress I called upon the Lord, and cried unto my God: he heard my voice out of his temple, and my cry came before him, even into his ears" *(18:1-6)*.

● "O Lord my God, I cried unto thee, and thou hast healed me. O Lord, thou hast brought up my soul from the grave: thou hast kept me alive, that I should not go down to the pit" *(30:2-3)*.

Here is a key verse: "For he shall deliver the needy when he crieth; the poor also, and him that hath no helper" *(72:12)*. Jesus has sent the Holy Ghost to be your helper. And He will not turn a deaf ear to your cry for help!

3. Dive into God's Word, lay hold of your special promise, take it into the secret prayer closet and hold God to it. Here are two of my favorite promises from the Bible. I hold these up to God whenever I cry out to Him:

● "Or what man is there of you, whom if his son ask bread, will he give him a stone? Or if he ask a fish, will he give him a serpent? If ye then, being evil, know how to give good gifts unto your children, how much more shall your Father which is in heaven give good things to them that ask him?" *(Matthew 7:9-11)*.

Ask the Lord for good things. He is waiting to give them to you! Ask Him to set you free, to take away all your shame, to remove all the stain of sin. He longs to do it for you!

● "Now unto him that is able to do exceeding abundantly above all that we ask or think, according to the power that worketh in us, unto him be glory in the church by Christ Jesus throughout all ages, world without end. Amen" *(Ephesians 3:20-21)*.

Take this promise to God every day, saying, "Father, You said You'd do well above everything I ask. Today, I'm asking You to over-answer my prayer." God is pleased by such faith.

4. Trust the Holy Ghost who abides in you. The Father has sent His Spirit to reside in your heart. But you have to acknowledge the Holy Spirit within you! You've got to believe that when you cry out, the Holy Ghost abiding in you will answer. God doesn't have to send an angel to speak to you; He has already put His resources within you — the Holy Ghost Himself!

That is the secret, plain and simple: As you face your present hour of suffering and confusion, turn everything over to the Holy Ghost. Say to Him, "Holy Spirit, You know the way out of this mess. I don't. It's completely beyond me. So, I'm resigning, right now. And I give up direction of my life to You. I know that what I'm going through is not uncommon to believers. And I'm going to call upon the Lord for help. I'll hold Him to His great and precious promises. And I will trust You to do the rest. You know the very mind of God!"

If you make this simple confession, you will know times of refreshing from the Lord. Even when you are ready to give up, He remains faithful to deliver you!

14

Turning Wimps Into Warriors

How to Stand Up to the Enemy

I was in fourth grade when I first heard someone use the word "wimp." That was the name kids called Big Tom, the biggest boy in our class. Tom could have beaten up anybody. He was strong, husky, muscular — and he could lift almost anything. But he simply refused to fight.

Even the smallest boys in our class poked fun at him. And as skinny and frail as I was, I ended up defending Tom! He and I became good friends. But it was awful to watch him take so much unnecessary harassment. And yet it all might have stopped if he would've stood up and said, "I've had enough! I don't want to fight — but if you jump on me one more time, I'm going to defend myself. I'm not your punching bag anymore!"

But Tom never did that. Whenever those smaller boys picked on him, he fell down like a limp rag. Up through the fifth or sixth grade he was still being called "wimp," "coward," "sissy," "powder puff." And the older he got, the worse the taunts became. My last memory of Tom was of a six-foot boy full of fear — always the brunt of some other boy's wrath.

You may be thinking, "It's good Tom wasn't a fighter. He must have been a peace-loving boy." I'm not suggesting Tom should have dared others to pick on him. But Tom's problem was that he truly was a coward!

Beloved, it's time we Christians faced up to a sad fact about ourselves as well — and that is, the church of Jesus Christ is full of wimps! When I use the term "wimp," I am not being sarcastic. I simply don't know another word to describe the spiritual cowardice sweeping through the church. I'm not talking about every Christian, of course. But the house of God today is filled with weaklings who are afraid of the devil and his wrath, who never stand up to him, and who are constantly abused by the powers of hell.

The Bible warns that in these last days Satan has come forth in great wrath because he knows his time is short. Indeed, he has brought his entire arsenal against God's people, trying to wear them down. He has sent legions of lying, demonic spirits to seduce and harass the church. And even now he is injecting into believers' minds all manner of lies, bringing guilt, condemnation, depression and fear.

So Few Believers Know How to Stand Up and Fight!

With all the talk going on in the church about spiritual warfare, Christians still have not learned how to stand up to the enemy. We are pushovers for the devil! Yet I don't believe every misfortune that befalls a Christian comes from the devil. We wrongly blame him for a lot of our own carelessness, disobedience and laziness:

• Your horrible nightmare was not of the devil if you went to bed with a bellyful of jalapeno peppers and a liter of Pepsi®. You may think, "The devil harassed me all night long! I saw a herd of buffalo stomping on my stomach, their beady eyes laughing at me. It was hellish." No — it was foolish! That wasn't the devil tormenting you — it was your own doing!

• If you stay up late watching sensual movies on your VCR, don't try to say the devil put that lust in your heart. You put it there yourself, by turning on the TV!

It's easy to blame the devil for our foolishness. That way, we don't have to deal with it. But there is a real devil present in our world today — and he is busy at work. How else can you explain what has happened to multitudes of Christians? Many are nothing like their Savior. They backbite, gossip and complain. They are jealous, unkind, unmerciful, fomenting strife and trouble. They live year after year in bitterness, hatred, carnality and covetousness.

I know people in churches everywhere who swear they love their pastors — yet they listen to vicious gossip about them! They know their shepherd is giving his very life for them, week after week. Still they let the gossip and half-truths rattle on and on — and they do nothing to shut it up. By their silence they approve everything that is said — and that poison becomes planted in their own spirits.

Let me tell you something of Satan's strategy: If he cannot pull the Almighty out of His throne, he will try to tear God's image out of you. He wants to turn worshipers into murmurers and blasphemers. And every bit of gossip you hear, every tale told about someone, comes right out of the pits of hell!

Just as he sought to get at Job and Peter, Satan begs God to get at you — to sift you as wheat. But there are two things every believer must know when Satan comes in like a roaring lion:

1. Satan cannot attack you at will. God has put a wall of fire around each of His children, and Satan cannot go beyond that wall without God's permission. God does allow the wall to come down at times — but under very limited parameters. He does this to produce unshakable faith in us, to train us in warfare and to prove His power and glory on earth. Yet with every trial we face comes this promise: "…God is faithful, who will not suffer you to be tempted above that ye are able; but will with the temptation also make a way to escape, that ye may be able to bear it" *(1 Corinthians 10:13)*.

2. Satan also cannot read a Christian's mind. Some people are afraid to pray because they think the devil eavesdrops on them. Others think the devil can read their every thought. Not so! Only God is omnipresent and omniscient: "I the Lord search the heart…" *(Jeremiah 17:10)*. "…I am he which searcheth the reins and hearts…" *(Revelation 2:23)*. "…all things are naked and opened unto the eyes of him with whom we have to do" *(Hebrews 4:13)*. Only the Lord can read our minds and thoughts!

But Satan doesn't need to read our minds — because he can read our actions. He watches our footsteps, noticing where we go and what we do. He knows when we slip away to do something we shouldn't. He sees our weaknesses — and he injects lies to suit our deeds. He hears our conversations about how frail and weak we are — and he tries to frighten us over our weaknesses.

Scripture commands us to stand up, be strong and do battle against the flesh and the devil: "Be on the alert, stand firm in the faith, act like men, be strong" *(1 Corinthians 16:13, NAS)*. "Brethren…be strong in the Lord, and in the power of his might" *(Ephesians 6:10, KJV)*. "…be strong in the grace that is in Christ Jesus" *(2 Timothy 2:1)*. "…young men…ye are strong, and the word of God abideth in you, and ye have overcome the wicked one" *(1 John 2:14)*.

In this last verse, the apostle John was not talking to eighty-year-old, seasoned men of God. He was addressing young warriors who were full of God's Word. John was telling them, "Because you took a stand and believed His Word to you, you have won the battle over the devil. You have overcome the wicked one in your life!"

Beloved, God's Word is not a "wimp Bible." And our message is not a "wimp gospel." God is looking for people who will be warriors rather than wimps. We are prophesied to win the battle — but only if we stand up and fight! Scripture says we are more than conquerors, totally victorious over all power of the enemy.

Old Testament warriors were mighty in battle against satanic forces. Scripture says they "subdued kingdoms, wrought righteousness, obtained promises, stopped the mouths of lions, quenched the violence of fire, escaped the edge of the sword, out of weakness were made strong, waxed valiant in fight, turned to flight the armies of aliens" *(Hebrews 11:33-34)*.

But something is terribly wrong today. Too many Christians are weak-kneed, powerless — easily victimized, manipulated, humiliated by Satan. God has put in me a holy indignation against this lack of resistance. And I believe it is time we became victorious warriors, not cowering wimps!

The story of Gideon tells how God turned a group of wimps into warriors. And I see in this story four steps to becoming a fearless warrior against Satan:

Step One: You Must Get Sick and Tired of Being Sick and Tired!

You have to become fed up with being held down by the devil — living low, depressed, joyless, empty, harassed.

The book of Judges tells us: "And the children of Israel did evil in the sight of the Lord: and the Lord delivered them into the hand of Midian seven years. And the hand of Midian prevailed against Israel..." *(Judges 6:1-2)*. Every year at harvest time, the Midianites moved over Israel's land with thousands of camels, sheep and cattle. These animals ate everything in sight, leaving Israel impoverished. "So Israel was brought very low because of Midian..." *(verse 6, NAS)*. Indeed, the Israelites were at their lowest point ever. They were driven to living in dark caves and damp dens, starving, scared and helpless.

Then something happened. It started with Gideon, and it spread throughout the whole camp: Israel got sick and tired of hiding in those dark caves! Gideon had grown weary, exasperated. After seven long years, he was tired of the Midianites prevailing over Israel. I picture him on a mountainside, looking down at all the bedouin tribes. He watched as warriors on horseback plundered Israel's villages, trying to kill everything in sight. Finally, Gideon said to himself, "How long should we put up with this? They go through our land with no opposition. Nobody stands up and does anything about it. We're told we have a God who moved for our fathers. But look at us now — we're stripped, helpless. We live in constant fear!"

Sadly, this is a picture of how most Christians live today. The enemy has come in and robbed them of all their peace and effectiveness. He plunders their lives and families at will — and they give no opposition. Instead, they hide in some dark cave of depression and bitterness. And they simply stand by as Satan brings more calamity upon their homes. They have been brought low — low in faith, low in hope, low in strength, low in attitude.

That is just where Israel was. Then something rose up within Gideon. And he said just what God was waiting to hear: "This has gone far enough! We serve a mighty, victorious God. Why do we go on, day after day, taking this abuse? For seven years we have hidden in these caves and let the Midianites roam freely over us, with no fight or resistance!"

I ask you — how low are you? How far down has the devil brought you? To the point of depression, bitterness, fear? When are you going to wake up and say, "Enough of this! Enough of allowing the devil to rob me and my family. I'm sick and tired of it, and I will not live this way! God never intended this for me. And I'm not going to let the devil take anything from me anymore. I've had enough!"

God will not do anything until you are throroughly disgusted — until you are sick and tired of being sick and tired!

Now, you may be saying, "Brother Dave, it was sin that brought the Midianites down on Israel. Israel was simply paying for their sin." That is true — they were suffering judgment for their idolatry. But Scripture also says the people then "cried unto the Lord" *(verse 6, KJV)*. And that's just what God wanted them to do!

You may be thinking, "I can't stand and fight the devil, because I'm paying for my sin. I sinned — I failed God. All these things are happening because the devil knows he's got me!" If that is true, then you have to do as Gideon did — cry out to the Lord! We serve the same God that Israel did. And if He heard Israel's cry in their idolatry, He will hear you in the depths of your failure.

The moment you cry out to God, something happens in the heavenlies. You may not be able to see it — but God already has begun to move on your behalf!

Step Two: Deal With Your Fears and Unbelief!

Israel had fallen into idolatry. But their root sin was still unbelief, resulting in all kinds of fears. And God sent them a prophet to expose their root sin: "When (they) cried unto the Lord because of the Midianites . . . the Lord sent a prophet unto the children of Israel, which said unto them, Thus saith the Lord God of Israel . . . I delivered you out of the hand of the Egyptians and out of the hand of all that oppressed you, and drave them out from before you, and gave you their land; and I said unto you, I am the Lord your God; fear not the gods of the Amorites, in whose land ye dwell: but ye have not obeyed my voice" *(verses 7-10)*.

God was saying, "I commanded you, 'Fear not' — but you disobeyed and feared. Now I cannot finish My work until you have dealt with your fears!"

The prophet told them, "Look at you — a bunch of wimps, hiding out, afraid to stand up and fight. You've already given up. But you have a history of God delivering! He gave your fathers great victories when they trusted Him. And He has promised to deliver you too — yet you don't believe Him! He brought you out of slavery and defeated all your past enemies. Why do you now act like helpless cowards?"

Moses had instructed Israel: ". . . be not afraid of them . . . let not your hearts faint, fear not, and do not tremble, neither be ye terrified . . ." *(Deuteronomy 20:1-3)*. He was saying, "God is with us. And because He is present, you have no reason to be terrified. You are never to be afraid that the enemy will make you fall!" Many Christians, however, are terrified the devil is going to destroy them. They're afraid they'll make a mistake or go back to their sin, and the devil will have his way. But that's a lie from the pit of hell! The Bible says you don't have to be terrified as you walk through this life.

When you hold onto fear, it becomes contagious. Everybody around you catches it. Moses sent home every warrior who was fearful: ". . . What man is there that is fearful and fainthearted? Let him go and return unto his house, lest his brethren's heart faint as well as his heart" *(verse 8)*. He was saying, "Just go home and take it easy. Otherwise, you'll destroy the victory for those who rise up to do battle!"

When Gideon gathered his army, God also told him to send home every fearful soldier: ". . . Whoever is fearful and afraid, let him return and depart. . . . And there returned of the people twenty and two thousand" *(Judges 7:3)*. Twenty-two thousand wimps went home — all quaking in their sandals, afraid of the forces of hell. But God had said to Gideon, "I must have men of faith and courage! Tell these to go home and pray until they've developed a backbone."

God is speaking the same word to His church today. He is asking,

"Why do you fear? Why do you sin by not trusting Me to bring victory to your life? I have promised to defeat every demonic power that comes against you!"

Yet some Christians will never change. They can't get along without their pet murmurings and complainings. They are hooked on misery! They sound like the worldly crowd — all their talk is of misery, misery, misery. It's all about divorce, cheating, family problems, job problems, heartache, sickness, who's in what hospital, whose kids are in jail, which husband is a drunken bum, which secretary ran off with which boss. Without their miseries, they have nothing to talk about!

Yet those who seek the Lord are built up in faith by hearing His Word to them: "So then faith cometh by hearing, and hearing by the word of God" *(Romans 10:17)*. And here is God's Word to all who call on His name: "Fear thou not; for I am with thee: be not dismayed; for I am thy God: I will strengthen thee; yea, I will help thee; yea, I will uphold thee with the right hand of my righteousness.... They that strive with thee shall perish.... They that war against thee shall be as nothing, and as a thing of nought" *(Isaiah 40:10-12)*. "Blessed be the Lord God of Israel .... To grant us that we, being delivered from the hand of our enemies, might serve him without fear, in holiness and righteousness before him all our days" *(Luke 1:68, 72-75 NAS)*.

God says you can live in victory and righteousness without fear — all the days of your life!

Step Three: Pull Down Your Besetting Sin!

"Now the same night ... the Lord said to him ... pull down the altar of Baal which belongs to your father, and cut down the Asherah that is beside it" *(Judges 6:25)*.

Gideon's father, Joash, had erected great statues of Baal and the goddess Asherah, made from huge stones. His reasoning was, "Baal has given Midian power over us. Maybe if we worship their god, he'll give us power." People came from miles around to worship there, including Midianites and Moabites. It was a powerful, demonic stronghold in Israel!

But God told Gideon, "I'm not going to deliver Israel until you get rid of this idol that stands between us. Lay it aside — cut it down!" So in the middle of the night Gideon "took ten men of his servants, and did as the Lord said unto him..." *(verse 27, KJV)*. He took an ox and used ropes to pull down Baal and Asherah!

God is giving His church today the same message He gave Gideon: "I want to help you — but I can't when you don't trust Me. You're full of fear. And before I bring deliverance, you're going to have to pull down this stronghold, this besetting sin!" "...lay aside every weight, and the sin which doth so easily beset (you)..." *(Hebrews 12:1)*. We are to pull down all strongholds of fear and sin!

Gideon pulled down demonic strongholds using a strong ox. But we have been given weapons far more powerful than his: "For the weapons of our warfare are not carnal, but mighty through God to the pulling down of strong holds ... casting down ... bringing into captivity ..." *(2 Corinthians 10:4-5)*.

There is only one way to bring down your besetting sin: "...building up yourselves on your most holy faith, praying in the Holy Ghost.... (He) is able to keep you from falling, and to present you faultless before the presence of his glory with exceeding joy" *(Jude 20, 24)*. All victory comes by praying in faith! This doesn't mean cold, empty prayer — but prayer in the Spirit, prayer that believes God to answer: "Praying always with all prayer and supplication in the Spirit..." *(Ephesians 6:18)*.

Beloved, God provides the victory for you as you pray! But you have to keep going back to Him again and again, praying in the Holy Ghost against your besetting sin. Every moment you spend in prayer brings down another stone from your idol. Soon you'll see it weakening, getting smaller. And one day you'll wake up and find your stronghold is dead, gone — cast down forever.

Step Four: Learn to Stand Up to Satan on Your Own!

You have to learn to fight your own battles. You can't depend on someone else for your deliverance!

Perhaps you have a prayer-warrior friend you can call and say, "I've got a battle before me. Will you pray for me? I know you have power with God." That is fine — but it is not God's complete will for you! God wants you to become a warrior! He wants you to be able to stand up against the devil.

God promised Gideon, "...Surely I will be with thee, and thou shalt smite the Midianites as one man" *(Judges 6:16)*. God told him, "I have sent you — I will be with you!"

But then the people of the city came looking for the one who tore down their idols: "...And when they inquired and asked, they said, Gideon the son of Joash hath done this thing. Then the men of the city said unto Joash, Bring out thy son, that he may die: because he hath cast down the altar of Baal, and because he hath cut down the grove that was by it" *(verses 29-30)*.

But where was Gideon? He was hiding — still unsure of God's promises, still wondering if God was with him. Gideon said: "…if the Lord be with us, why then is all this befallen us? and where be all his miracles which our fathers told us of … ?" *(verse 13)*.

And so it is with many of us! Jesus has promised us, "…I am with you always…" *(Matthew 28:20)*. And yet we have not learned to stand on His Word and fight! Instead, we look at all our weaknesses and think, "If God is truly with me, then where are His miracles? Where is the evidence I'm strong? I'm still plagued by lust. My home condition is still the same. God, if You are with me, why haven't things changed?" Things will begin to change — the moment you are fully persuaded that God is with you, that He speaks to you and that He will show you all you need to know!

Before Gideon went to battle, God gave him every necessary detail. He kept paring down Gideon's men until only 300 were left — 300 warriors out of 22,000 men! But those were all God needed. They came down upon their enemies from the hills, screaming, yelling, smashing pitchers and blowing trumpets. "…and all the host [of their enemies] ran, and cried, and fled" *(Judges 7:21)*.

God will show you how to get out of your problem. He will tell you how victory is going to come, and He'll provide you with every detail. But first, He says, "I'm going to wait until you're fully convinced I am with you. I'm going to wait until you put your trust in Me!"

And that is what a warrior does! He rejects defeat. He casts out every fear. He tears down his besetting sin through prayer. And, finally, he stands on God's Word — preparing his heart before the Lord to receive victory!

Dear saint, you are stronger than you think. Like Gideon, you may wonder, "How can I fight? I'm so weak, so inexperienced." But God told Gideon, "…Go in this thy might…" *(6:14)*. "What might?" you ask. "Gideon didn't have any might. He was a wimp!" Gideon's might was bound up in God's word to him: "Surely I will be with thee."

That same word — "I am with you" — is your strength. And you will receive that strength by believing this word is true — and by acting on it! As surely as you know anything else, you can know God is with you. You can know His Spirit is all about you. No matter what the devil brings against you, you can stand in His victory and power — because "God hath said." That is your strength!

The Gospel Of Grace

15

Knowing the Path to Victory

Therefore being justified by faith, we have peace with God through our Lord Jesus Christ: by whom also we have access by faith into this grace wherein we stand, and rejoice in hope of the glory of God....For if by one man's offence death reigned by one; much more they which receive abundance of grace and of the gift of righteousness shall reign in life by one, Jesus Christ" *(Romans 5:1-2, 17)*.

Do you remember what your life was like before you surrendered to Christ? You were an enemy of God living in blindness, a lost soul without hope. You were ungodly, guilty — and the wrath of God was "abiding on you" *(see John 3:36)*.

How did you find forgiveness and acceptance before God? How did you enter into the blessed assurance you were saved, rejoicing in the love of Jesus Christ? Was it because God saw something good in you? Did you possess some inherent righteousness that attracted Him to you? Did you earn His favor with obedience and kindness?

No — absolutely not! No one is ever saved by his own works or merit. Scripture says, "But we are all as an unclean thing, and all our righteousnesses are as filthy rags..." *(Isaiah 64:6)*. All our sins are blotted out and we are reconciled to God by faith in the shed blood of Jesus Christ. It is by grace alone we are saved — and not by anything we have done.

The theological definition of grace is "the unearned pardon, mercy and favor of God." Scripture says: "But of him are ye in Christ Jesus, who of God is made unto us wisdom, and righteousness [which is justification], and sanctification, and redemption" *(1 Corinthians 1:30)*.

Please don't be put off by all the terms in this verse. Simply put, the goal of the gospel is redemption — and God's grace includes everything He has done for us through Christ to redeem us from the power of the devil and bring us into the kingdom of His glorious light.

Justification is the cornerstone of grace. To be justified by God means to be "acquitted" — forgiven of all sin and guilt — and to be considered holy and righteous before Him. No one is justified — that is, he cannot become holy or righteous — by his own works, obedience or faithfulness. Rather, these things are all the result of a justifying faith in the power of Christ's blood to make us acceptable in God's sight: "For by grace are ye saved through faith; and that not of yourselves: it is the gift of God: not of works, lest any man should boast" *(Ephesians 2:8-9).* "…even we have believed in Jesus Christ, that we might be justified by the faith of Christ, and not by the works of the law; for by the works of the law shall no flesh be justified" *(Galatians 2:16).*

Here is the foundation of all faith, which every believer must fully understand. Your entire walk with God depends on it: You cannot have peace with God if you do not know how you are made right before Him. You must be fully convinced you are clear before God, not by your own diligence or works — but by believing and trusting in the victory of the Cross of Jesus!

The apostle Paul did not want to be found standing before Christ in his own righteousness. Here was a good man — a Pharisee who had diligently kept all the numerous rules and regulations of the law. He paid tithes faithfully. He loved God with all his heart. He attended all the functions of the synagogue. He studied the Word of God endlessly. He loved his fellow man and went about doing good. According to the law, Paul was a perfect man.

But all that became as rubbish to Paul — he counted it all as loss — when he came into the revelation of the righteousness of Christ: "But what things were gain to me, those I counted loss for Christ.…and do count them but dung, that I may win Christ, and be found in him, not having mine own righteousness, which is of the law, but that which is through the faith of Christ, the righteousness which is of God by faith" *(Philippians 3:7-9).*

To Be Made Righteous by Faith Is the Hardest Thing for the Flesh to Accept!

There are many sincere believers today who have not yet submitted to the righteousness of Christ. They still go about trying to please God by their good deeds. They accept salvation by faith — but then they want to take over from there.

There is something in our flesh that rebels against a faith-walk. We want to earn our salvation — to help God out. We don't mind being saved by faith; but we don't want to live by faith. Our flesh cries out, "All my obedience, all my hard work to please God — it has to count for something!" Yes, it is worth something — but not in meriting forgiveness and pardon.

We don't want to accept that we are made right before God simply by believing. We would rather "bite the bullet" — and when temptation overwhelms us, we say through gritted teeth, "Bless God, I'll get victory if it kills me!" (And it will kill you!)

But that is not the path to victory. Obedience and faithfulness come as a result of standing steadfast on the rock of justification by faith alone. Paul said this of a certain people: "…they have a zeal of God, but not according to knowledge. For they being ignorant of God's righteousness, and going about to establish their own righteousness, have not submitted themselves unto the righteousness of God. For Christ is the end of the law for righteousness to every one that believeth" *(Romans 10:2-4)*.

These people were trying "to establish their own righteousness." We know that process by another name: legalism! Legalism is misunderstood by most Christians. Even most ministers don't know what it is. I used to believe legalism had to do with manmade rules and regulations designed by sincere, God-loving people who were trying to lead holy lives. I thought it was all about observing dress-code restrictions and other do's and don't's. No — legalism is much more subtle than rules and regulations. It goes far beyond that!

When I was a boy, I heard evangelists thunder against the sins of the day. They preached against bobbed hair, women's "open-toe" shoes, makeup and fancy dresses. This was called "holiness" preaching — but the standards kept changing with the new fads. And I thought that was legalism!

When I first came to New York City more than thirty years ago, I was shocked by all the rigid rules in Hispanic Pentecostal churches. Our workers would go to the streets, pray with drug addicts and try to get them into local churches. But if a newly saved girl was wearing jeans or makeup, the pastor would rush out and say, "You can't come in here dressed like that!" One minister told a young girl, "Go home and dress like a woman — then come back. We don't allow worldliness in this church!" I thought that was legalism, too.

A young couple in England who received our newsletters began listening to tapes of our services at Times Square Church. They grew to love the messages of holiness. So they came to visit — but when I met them after a service, they looked hurt, crushed, their eyes filled with tears. They told me they were upset because the women in our church did not wear head coverings! They said, "How can the Holy Spirit be at work here, when you don't obey the command to cover a woman's head?" I thought that was legalism as well.

I hear from prayer groups all across the country who are tossed, turned and left confused by all kinds of new rules brought in by passing teachers. One tells them, "You must kneel to pray. God hears only those who kneel." Another teacher comes along and says, "You must sit in His presence. You need not kneel. That is Catholic!" Someone else says, "You must stand when the Bible is read. You dishonor God when you sit during the reading of the Word!" Yet another tells them, "That is bondage! Jesus made the people sit when He preached the Word."

I thought all this talk was pure legalism.

All of this is indeed all rules and regulations. But it is all only a part of legalism; it is not the heart of the matter. No, legalism is far worse than all these things. In fact, all of us have a bit of its leaven in our hearts — because legalism is based on pride!

Legalism Is an Outward Show, a Facade — a Pretense of Holiness to Impress People, Not God!

At its heart, legalism is a desire to appear holy. It is trying to be justified before men and not God. Legalism is wanting to be known as a prophet, a man of prayer, a woman of intercession — and feeding and fostering such an image!

The legalist is not out to earn justification. He is more interested in appearances — in convincing other Christians that he is devoted, pious, serious, all-out for God. He says, "I am deeply religious — and everybody ought to see it!"

We see this in the Jewish Talmudic writers' list of seven classes of Pharisees. Among these classes were:

• The Shechemites. These Pharisees said long prayers in public to be considered holy — but on the side they robbed widows of their estates!

• The Stumblers. These were so mock-humble they wouldn't dare lift their feet before a holy God. Instead, they shuffled along with a "poor, humble, insignificant me" attitude.

• The Bleeders. This group would not lift their eyes from the ground, lest they look at something evil. They got their name from constantly walking into walls; the more they bled, the holier they thought they were!

Beloved, these types are in every church! They have a sad, serious, "holy" look. Some of them dare not raise their hands to praise God — nor clap and be happy or joyful. They think of themselves as "shut in with God," holy, above everybody else. They sit in "deep meditation," their lips moving, lost in the Spirit. Yet "all their works they do for to be seen of men…" *(Matthew 23:5)*.

God Has Lovingly Reminded Me of Some of My Legalistic Games!

Last year, Gwen and I spent a vacation at a Florida hotel with some dear friends, a couple from Texas, Dr. and Mrs. Rice. We all had spent the week seeing Disney World, and now we just wanted to relax. As we stood in the lobby of the hotel, Gwen suggested we go to the Rices' room to play dominoes.

Now, I know the Rices have always considered me to be a righteous man — and I figured I didn't want to blow it! I realized that during the week our friends hadn't once seen me retreat to pray. I thought, "How am I supposed to be holy in front of these people if I don't go pray?"

So I told them, "I'm sorry, I can't play dominoes. I need to go in my room and touch God. You all go ahead and play." But do you know what I was really saying? "I don't have time to waste, like you poor earthlings. You worldly minded ones go and tinkle around with dominoes. This prophet is going to shut himself in with God!" (I ask you: How can you relax at playing dominoes when you know that someone like that is nearby, "pleading with God"?)

When I got to our room it was about eight o'clock. I thought, "I'll watch just a half hour of CNN News — then I'll pray." One hour of news later, CNN announced an upcoming documentary on the rise and fall of Hitler. I quickly reasoned, "That has to do with prophecy. I have to see it!"

At a quarter to ten, I'd already seen Hitler rise and fall — when I heard Gwen coming down the hall! I jumped up, ran to the TV, shut it off, turned out the light — and fell on my face in the dark at the foot of the bed!

When Gwen walked in she saw her devoted prophet-husband getting up slowly from his holy position — piously acting as if he had been in prayer for two hours. I looked up meekly, rubbing my eyes, and said to Gwen, "Oh, honey, isn't the Lord good?"

I hope you can laugh at this as loudly as our congregation did when I shared it in my sermon. But, more importantly, I hope you laugh at it hard enough to drive the truth down into your soul: We all play games, trying to maintain a facade of holiness before people! I had to maintain my image of a holy man — and that is legalism at its worst.

The fact is, people who truly have the righteousness of the Lord don't have to put on airs. They are common, ordinary folks who know how to weep and laugh and enjoy Jesus and the fellowship of the saints. They are involved in other people's burdens and needs — and they're not always "shut away," trying to maintain an image.

We all look at appearances — but God sees the heart! We each need to come down from our high horse of pretended holiness — to be honest and real, the way we know God sees us. That is the only way to enjoy true fellowship with Him and with each other!

Beyond Legalism Is the Perversion of the Gospel of Grace!

Grace as it is preached in many churches today is producing a class of Christians who are still pleasure-lovers, deeply involved in sin. Multitudes today live like the devil, yet claim, "I am the righteousness of Christ by faith!" Beloved, that is a lie from the pit of hell. They are deceived!

A few years ago, on my Sundays off between crusades, I used to drive by a certain church that preached what is called "the grace message." (This isn't a Baptist, Presbyterian or Pentecostal doctrine; the gospel of grace is indeed the gospel of Jesus Christ.) As I drove by, the deacons stood outside smoking, several of them shaking off a hangover from Saturday night. Some of these men were known adulterers, some wife-beaters. Still others were known around town as cheats in their business. Yet, because of the "grace message" they heard, they were convinced they were justified, no matter how they lived — that they were made the righteousness of God in Christ.

I knew the pastor of this church to be a righteous man. But there was something wrong with his message: He didn't preach the entire gospel! He once told me, "David, I really believe in righteousness. And if you have the righteousness of Christ, it will produce a desire to be pure and holy." But I thought to myself, "Wait a minute — you've been preaching to these people for eight years. After all that time, where is the evidence among them of a pure walk with God? Why hasn't your 'grace message' produced a truly godly congregation who are separated from worldliness?

Why is there still so much divorce, and so many illegitimate babies born to your teenagers? Many of your people still live for the devil. They're dying and going to hell — and you know it!"

I preach without reservation that justification and righteousness come by faith alone. I am saved by faith, made righteous by faith and kept by faith in Christ's blood. That is the very foundation of the gospel and of true grace preaching. But not all faith is justifying faith! The Bible clearly speaks of two kinds of faith: one that justifies, and another that is of no value — a faith that even the devils exercise!

Scripture says many people "believed (in Jesus)...when they saw the miracles which he did. But Jesus did not commit himself unto them...for he knew what was in a man" *(John 2:23-25)*. These people had a belief in Christ — but it wasn't the faith of those who receive "power to become the sons of God..." *(1:12)*.

Justifying faith is more than a faith of assent; it does more than just acknowledge God. James argued: "Thou believest that there is one God; thou doest well: the devils also believe, and tremble" *(James 2:19)*. James was talking about a dead, temporary faith — not an eternal one. And Jesus warned about this kind of faith, saying some believe "for a while...(but) have no root...and in time of temptation fall away" *(Luke 8:13)*.

But there is a justifying faith — one that "purifies the heart" *(see Acts 15:9)* and "believeth unto righteousness" *(Romans 10:10)*. The great Puritan writer John Owen said it well: "We absolutely deny that we are justified by that faith alone which can be alone — that is, without a principle of life and obedience in all things, at all times....For we recognize no faith to be of the sanctifying kind, but that which virtually and radically contains in it an obedience at all times — yea, we acknowledge no faith to be justifying, which is not itself a spiritually vital principle of obedience and good works."

For faith to be justifying, there has to be an accompanying desire to obey and be faithful to God. This kind of faith contains a vital force — a principle of total, everlasting obedience and love for God. Anything short of that is a dead, temporary faith. It does not produce the true benefits of grace — but instead it mocks grace!

Many "Grace" Preachers Do Away With the Law Before It Can Do Its Work of Convicting of Sin!

We are not saved by the law — but we are convinced and convicted of our sin by the law; "for by the law is the knowledge of sin" *(Romans 3:20)*. The law was sent "that every mouth may be stopped, and all the world may become guilty before God" *(verse 19)*. "The law was our schoolmaster to bring us unto Christ, that we might be justified by faith" *(Galatians 3:24)*.

"The law is holy...and just, and good. Was then that which is good made death unto me? God forbid. But sin, that it might appear sin, working death in me by that which is good; that sin by the commandment might become exceeding sinful" *(Romans 7:12-13)*. Paul was saying, "I couldn't really confess my sins until I knew they were sins! I couldn't seek after the holiness of God until I saw how far from Him I was. The law hit home to me, destroying my nonchalance about sin. When I saw God's holiness by His commandments, sin became utterly sinful to me!"

That is the conviction that drives you straight to the arms of Christ, crying, "Mercy, Lord! I can't save myself; I can't fulfill Your law. I've seen the sin of my heart!" Faith has been defined as "the flight of a convicted, repentant sinner unto the mercy of God in Christ Jesus." Only the person who has been convicted of his sins by the law of God will "flee to Christ" for refuge.

On the day of Pentecost, Peter stood and offered the crowds the gospel of God's grace. But first he put them under the blazing light of the law. He pointed his finger and said, "Ye have taken, and by wicked hands have crucified and slain (Jesus)" both Lord and Christ *(Acts 2:23)*. The people were pricked in their hearts — so utterly convicted by the Word of God they cried out, "What shall we do?" *(verse 37)*.

Adam was given the gospel of grace — after his "eyes were opened" *(see Genesis 3:7)*. It was only after he had seen his pitiful condition and the consequences of his sin that God brought to him the message of mercy and hope. Yet this is why modern-day grace preaching is not changing sinful hearts: because it does not open the eyes of the sinful! There is no guilt, no shame, no sorrow for sin.

Indeed, pardon for sin is being offered to people who do not even admit they are sinful. They are offered justification for sins they have never felt guilty of committing, deliverance when they do not even know they are bound, righteousness for which they do not hunger or thirst, freedom from a holy wrath they do not know rests upon them!

There Is a Spirit of Lawlessness in the Land!

The sinner calls it "rights": The right to practice homosexuality. The right to abort. The right between consenting adults to do with their bodies whatever they choose. In short, the right to do whatever they please! Sinners want all these rights — but they do not want to pay any penalties and consequences. That is a spirit of lawlessness!

This spirit is now creeping into the church: "Give me free pardon and everlasting life — without any cost. Free me from all guilt and condemnation. Promise me a justification I can never lose. But don't disturb me by asking me to lay anything down! Let me have it my way — without giving up my personal freedom, without any call to obedience!" This may not be what is actually said — but it is what is lived. And now we have invented a queasy "grace message" with no foundation on which to build a holy life — a gospel that appeases the spirit of lawlessness in our land.

You may be saying, "I don't understand all these Bible doctrines — grace, justification, sanctification. It's all too confusing."

But God gives us something very simple, which we all can understand: "…God resisteth the proud, but giveth grace unto the humble" *(James 4:6)*. If you have any pride in you — especially in thinking you are more spiritual than others — then you can be sure God will bring you down. He says He will resist you!

But God pours out His grace to the humble. You don't have to figure out how to get this grace. James 4:6 says He will give it to you! "Humble" as used here means "broken in spirit, repentant." It is a sense of emptiness, helplessness, need. You don't have to understand any doctrine to be humble before God; you don't have to wonder if you are doing everything right. God says, "Just stay broken — stay needy, hungry and thirsty. And I will supply all the grace you need."

"Submit yourselves therefore to God…" *(verse 7)*. While this ungodly world cries, "Give me my rights, let me do it my way" — God's people submit to Him. We cry, "Not my will or my rights — only Yours, Lord!"

If your heart is pricked in any way by this message, it is a good sign God is dealing with some pride in you. Can you laugh at your own games of hypocrisy and legalism? If so, you can laugh the devil right out of your soul! Can you say the following right now: "All my righteousness and goodness are filthy rags in God's sight, without the blood of Christ. But because of the blood, all my works, obedience and faithfulness are received as a sweet-smelling savor unto the Lord." That is true zeal for God!

16   The Witness of The Spirit

Living by the "Principle of Peace"

"And it is the Spirit that beareth witness, because the Spirit is truth" (1 John 5:6).

Several years ago I was invited to attend a revival meeting in a suburban church just outside of New York City. People had been raving about a "successful crusade" being held there by two young male evangelists. Finally, I went to one of their services, and I was seated up front with the ministry team. Little did I know, I was about to endure a terrible experience!

People had been calling this pair a "powerful evangelistic team." One preached, and the other sang and played the organ. But as the service began and I watched these two young men, something deep inside me began to twitch. I felt a strange uneasiness.

Before the young preacher began his message, he hyped up the audience. He had a beautiful set of boxed gifts he gave out each night to the person who brought the most visitors. There were toasters, radios, mixers — even a bicycle for the closing night! His preaching was nothing but one exciting story after another. The crowd loved it — but I got nauseated! Now the uneasiness inside me spoke loud and clear: "This is not of God — it's all flesh! There is something evil going on. The Holy Spirit is not here. Those two evangelists are gay — and they're fooling everyone!"

I was sick that night, grieved beyond words — but it was all because the witness of the Spirit was working in me! The pastor was so excited about the big crowds that he'd shaken off all discernment. And the people loved this flesh-show because they had blinded themselves spiritually. They were simply following the pastor!

A few years later, I saw those two young evangelists in an airport. This time the Spirit's witness told me to confront them. We greeted one another, and then — with no malice in my voice — I said, "I know what you two boys are — you're homosexuals. Please, quit mocking the Lord! Go out and get another job. God won't let you get away with this charade. I don't want to have to expose you!"

My warning didn't seem to bother either of them. A few years later I was in northern Canada for a crusade. Late after a service one night I was hungry, so my host drove me to a remote restaurant a half-hour away. As we walked in, who did we see sitting at a table nearby, entertaining two very effeminate men? It was the two young evangelists! How shocked they were when I passed their table. They knew they'd been caught!

Not long after that they were exposed and left the ministry. The Holy Spirit confirmed what He had shown me years earlier. Yet what frightened me most about the ordeal was that all the pastors of large churches who invited these young men to speak never discerned what they were. No one had the witness of the Spirit to expose it all!

On another occasion I was invited to hear a so-called "powerful evangelist" who was holding his sixth week of meetings at a large Pentecostal church in a Southern city. This time my wife, Gwen, and I slipped into the balcony unnoticed — and what a show we saw! The evangelist came out dressed like a nightclub performer, wearing a red plaid, sequined jacket. The crowd applauded when he was introduced. I was startled by it all — and immediately I turned to Gwen and said, "Honey, that's the biggest phony who has ever stepped into a pulpit!"

For the first five minutes he merely pranced about the stage, joking and flattering the crowd. Then he stepped down into the audience and kissed a few women, imploring their husbands not to be jealous. I thought to myself, "He's a showman. He doesn't know God at all!"

His preaching, too, consisted of one incredible story after another — and the crowd was awestruck. He said, "I was sitting in a barbershop when the Vice President came in and sat in the chair next to mine. He turned to me and, to my surprise, he knew my name. He said, 'Brother Billy Bob, the President and I have heard all about your great meetings. Please stop in next time you're in the Capitol.'"

I turned to Gwen and said, "Honey, he's lying! He's telling great, big fibs!" But everyone was clapping and going crazy. The gray-haired pastor was eating it all up. And the big crowd was feasting on all the outrageous lies!

Gwen and I left — and all the way to the car I had to hold my stomach. It was not a physical pain; rather, it was a deep, inner groaning, an unexplainable hurt. It was the witness of the Spirit again — showing me the difference between the holy and the profane!

God had given that pastor what he coveted: a packed house and big crowds. But it had cost him the witness of the Spirit! He was blinded — he'd lost all discernment. Every Spirit-filled person who lived a holy life in that church recognized the sham in the first five minutes — and they walked out. These had the inner witness of the Spirit — and they could not stand to be in that man's presence!

Sometimes the Holy Ghost Won't Let You Sit Still!

There are times when the Holy Ghost's inner witness will not allow me to keep quiet. The Spirit rises within me and I have to speak up, loudly exposing the flesh and the devil. On one occasion, a "Christian" rock group begged me to attend their outdoor concert. I went, and most of what I heard was merely okay; it was all loud drums and unintelligible music. Then, toward the end of the concert, the smoke machines went on and lights began to flash — and the crowd went into a frenzy!

As I looked up, my spiritual eyes saw hordes of demons flying off the stage and hovering above the whole congregation. At that point, I fell backward to the ground, literally stricken by the Holy Spirit. The witness within me was saying, "This is Ichabod. The glory of the Lord has departed!" Suddenly, the Holy Ghost took over my voice. I got up and ran throughout the whole place, knocking over chairs and crying out, "Ichabod! Stop it — it's the devil!" But nobody cared. When I got home, I fell on the living room floor, doubled up, groaning and weeping. I couldn't catch my breath. When Gwen saw me she was hysterical. "Dave, what's wrong? Where do you hurt? Speak to me!" I couldn't even talk. Never had I felt such grief! Finally, I blurted out, "Honey, it's the grief of God! There's a blindness in that ministry. They don't understand it was all satanic. Everyone was clapping — but they should have been weeping!"

I will never forget that night. Into the wee hours I cried, "Oh God, there were all those preachers, staffers, parents, teenagers — and none of them could see it! No one knew it was flesh, that Satan was manifesting himself. Oh Lord, am I the crazy one? Why was I so stirred? Why did I run through that crowd like a fool?"

It was the Holy Ghost within me — bearing witness to truth! "Even the Spirit of truth; whom the world cannot receive, because it seeth him not, neither knoweth him: but ye know him; for he dwelleth with you, and shall be in you" *(John 14:17)*.

The Holy Spirit abides in us to reveal to us what is true and what is false. He speaks with a still, small voice, deep within the heart. Many of our holy forefathers believed in this operation of the Spirit in believers. They preached much about "having the witness." But I don't hear this truth being preached anymore. In fact, the witness of the Spirit is virtually unheard of in most churches today.

Yet the fact is, believers need the Spirit's witness like never before. And we're going to need it more and more as the day of the Lord draws near. Satan has come brazenly as an angel of light to deceive, if it were possible, the very elect of God. His evil seductions are going to flourish: false doctrines, false teachers, false gospels. Even now, multitudes are being swept away by false gospels — captivated by wicked false prophets and corrupt teachers.

But you can have the Holy Ghost's witness in you — to help you know whether what you're hearing is right or wrong, truth or lies. With His witness at work in your heart, you can listen to any teaching tape, go to any meeting, read any book — and know beyond a shadow of a doubt what's pure and what's unholy. You can walk in the assurance that you will not be deceived by any wickedness!

You see, the Spirit's inner witness operates on the "principle of peace." The peace of God is the greatest thing you can have. And when your peace is disturbed, you can be sure the Holy Ghost is speaking to you. When there is a troubling in your spirit — a shaking and a turmoil deep inside — God is telling you that something is false. You will feel His embarrassment — His grief and anger!

You may say, "I already have the Holy Spirit living in me. But I want His witness in my heart. How can I get it?"

1. The Holy Ghost's Witness Can Operate Only in A Humble, Pure Vessel in Which the Peace of God Reigns!

"And let the peace of God rule in your hearts…" *(Colossians 3:15)*. Sin brings turmoil to the heart. And any hidden, unrepented sin will rob a believer of his precious peace! His heart will be torn by guilt, condemnation and fear — and the Spirit will speak only two words to him: "Repent! Flee!"

Yes, the Spirit will speak to you to correct you; He will deal with you about sin, righteousness and judgment. But when it comes to giving you direction — that is, the still, small voice which tells you what to do and where to go — He will not operate in an unclean vessel! If you persist in sin — if you do not confess it or deal with it — your heart will feed you a steady stream of lies. You'll hear teachings that make you at ease in your sin. You'll think, "My problem couldn't be that bad. I don't feel convicted." But you will be totally led astray!

Isaiah spoke of a people who went about claiming to desire the true counsel of God. They said: "Let him make speed, and hasten his work, that we may see it: and let the counsel of the Holy One of Israel draw nigh and come, that we may know it!" *(Isaiah 5:19)*. But these people had deceit in their hearts — and they ended up perverted in all their counsel! Sin had perverted their judgment. As a result, they weren't able to discern evil. And the things that were holy and pure, they called unrighteous. Isaiah said of them, "Woe unto them that call evil good, and good evil; that put darkness for light, and light for darkness; that put bitter for sweet, and sweet for bitter!" *(verse 20)*.

Some time ago a minister acquaintance of mine warned me not to listen to a certain Bible teacher. He told me, "That man is preaching the worst false doctrine. Stay away from him, or it will destroy you. He's dangerous!" This man was full of anger toward that teacher. But when I heard the teacher on tape, my heart leaped within me. Peace flooded my soul! I kept waiting to hear the "dangerous" part — but the message was all about walking in holiness and having a pure heart. So I got another tape, then another — and each one was sweeter than the first. I thought, "How could anybody say this is dangerous or evil?"

But that accusing preacher had really believed what he'd told me. I believe a voice had spoken to him — but it wasn't the voice of God! It was the voice of his own flesh crying out, because he was being convicted of his sins. The messages on holiness and purity had touched something deep within him and made him angry. And an inner voice was telling him that this good teaching was evil. He had totally misjudged it. Why? Because sin had blinded him! He had compromised somehow, and the spirit of the world had crept into him. Jesus said those who are of this world cannot hear the voice the Spirit, "whom the world cannot receive, because it seeth him not, neither knoweth him…" *(John 14:17)*.

Beloved, be very careful not to be influenced by someone else's so-called witness! Whenever somebody tells me something evil or reproachful about another person, I want to meet the accused. Often it is that person's pure devotion to God that provokes the sinner's heart!

2. There Can Be No Inner Voice of the
Spirit in a Proud Believer!

Let me distinguish clearly between pride and humility:

● A humble person is not one who thinks little of himself, hangs his head and says, "I'm nothing." Rather, he is one who depends wholly on the Lord for everything, in every circumstance. He knows the Lord has to direct him, empower him and quicken him — and that he's dead without that. He says, "I won't do anything until I get the mind of God. I will not act until He commands!"

● A proud person, on the other hand, is one who may love God in a fashion, but he acts and thinks on his own. At its root, pride is simply independence from God. And the proud person makes decisions based on his own reasoning, skills and abilities. He says, "God gave me a good mind, and He expects me to use it. It's silly to ask Him for direction in every detail of life."

This person is unteachable because he already "knows it all." He might listen to someone who is higher in authority or better known than himself — but not to someone he thinks is inferior. I know this to be true; at one time it described me!

I was a high-flying young evangelist, known all over the world. I would have listened to some well-known man of God. But I seldom listened to an unknown, uneducated person. Whenever some young preacher came into my office to try to tell me something, he got five minutes of my time before he was pleasantly escorted out. I reasoned, "I've got all this experience. I've been through such deep waters. Unless they have been equally experienced, they have nothing to say to me."

In recent years, I've thought God had dealt a death-blow to this attitude in me long ago. Then something happened several weeks ago that made me see I may still have some of it. Someone on our mailing list sent me a teaching tape by a man I'd never heard of. I took the tape home and listened for about fifteen minutes, and I realized this unknown man was speaking truth. The witness of the Spirit told me I was listening to a truly holy, humble man. Then the preacher spoke of having no education. He hadn't studied any books; only the Spirit had taught him. He explained in his Southern, monotone drawl that the only book he'd studied for the last fifteen years was his Bible.

For a fleeting moment I thought, "This man can't teach me anything. I'm an avid reader — and I've read entire volumes of the Puritans and all the great missionaries' lives. But he sounds like he's never read a book!" So I shut off the tape.

Then the Spirit's witness spoke to me clearly: "Turn it back on. He has much to teach you!" Now I've ordered six more of his tapes and his book — and I've been greatly blessed. My blinding pride could have robbed me of something God had meant for my growth!

You Can Easily Know a Proud Person by His Fruits!

Not one word a proud person receives is of God! It is impossible for him to judge righteous judgment — impossible to speak God's mind — because the Holy Spirit is not present in him to bear witness to truth. "There is a way which seemeth right unto a man, but the end thereof are the ways of death" *(Proverbs 14:12)*.

You may wonder, "How can a person who is filled with the Holy Ghost hear strange voices instead of the Spirit's?" Consider King Saul — a prime example of pride — a man who insisted on doing things his own way. He couldn't wait for God to act. So when the prophet Samuel was slow in arriving to make the sacrifice before battle, Saul played priest and offered up his own sacrifice. It was an act of pure self-will, independence, impatience with God's ways!

God also had commanded Saul to slay all the Amalekites. But again Saul did things his way: When the battle was over, he spared King Agag. Samuel rebuked Saul for this, asking, "Why did you not obey God and kill him?" Saul answered, "Because I feared the people." Again — human wisdom!

The Bible says, "But the Spirit of the Lord departed from Saul, and an evil spirit from the Lord troubled him. And Saul's servants said unto him, Behold now, an evil spirit from God troubleth thee" *(1 Samuel 16:14-15)*. Saul was troubled; he had no peace. Everybody could see it in him: He had a troubled look, an angry spirit. Another spirit had begun speaking to his inner man — and it was a witness from hell!

Saul constantly heard voices imitating God. They told him to kill David. They said his own son was a traitor. They convinced him he was being betrayed by his own bodyguards. "No one loves you. Everybody is against you!" Saul became full of envy, hatred, anxiety, fear.

Can a Holy Ghost-empowered person lose the Spirit, be given over to an evil spirit, and yet continue preaching and prophesying? Yes! Saul had been Spirit-empowered: "And the Spirit of God came upon Saul..." *(1 Samuel 11:6)*. Then we read that "the Spirit of the Lord departed from   Saul..." *(16:14)*. And, finally, "...it came to pass...that the evil spirit from God came upon Saul, and he prophesied in the midst of the house: and David played..." *(18:10)*.

Saul was still prophesying — even though there was an evil spirit in him! You can be sure that what came out of this man was not of God. It may have sounded right — but everything he spoke was another gospel. Even though this man at one time had been chosen of God and anointed of the Holy Ghost, he was speaking straight from the flesh.

Right now, thousands of Christians are exchanging tapes and books — but much of it is full of poison! You might not recognize the error at first; but if you have the witness of the Spirit, just keep listening awhile, and He will expose it. The proud teacher or preacher — under the direction of an evil spirit — eventually will say something that makes you uneasy. You may hear an entire hour of good-sounding gospel before you hear the five minutes of gross error.

But only the witness of the Spirit can reveal it to you!

3. One Night During a Prayer Meeting, God Told Me Something About Our Church I Was Not Expecting to Hear!

The Lord whispered to me, "This church needs shock treatment! Too many have grown satisfied and complacent. You feel safe and secure from all the winds and waves of false doctrines sweeping over the land — but you are not prepared for what is coming!"

Beloved, this chapter on having the Spirit's witness functioning in you is not a request — it is a matter of life and death! If you don't have the witness of the Holy Ghost in these last days, you're not going to make it. You'll give in to the coming spirit of the Antichrist!

Here's an example: In President Clinton's health plan, there is a provision for a national health identification card — and, eventually, a state-of-the-art, tamper-proof numbering system. This probably means an implantation device in the head, arm or somewhere on the body. No one will receive health coverage without a number.

We also are headed for a cashless society — first by credit card, and later by a laser implantation beneath the skin. The European Community has already planned for this. We may be on the very brink of the mark of the beast! And if you don't have discernment, you'll become an accessory to a murderous government system that takes your tax dollars for abortion.

Tragically, some Christians are not going to recognize these antichrist setups. That is why you need the Holy Spirit witness every day — on your job, at work, at school. You'll need to rightly judge politicians and leaders so you'll not suddenly be sucked into the Antichrist system.

Wake up, beloved! This is what Jesus was trying to tell us about the foolish virgins who ran out of oil for their lamps! They had a supply of the Holy Ghost — but they didn't have His witness at the final moment. And if you haven't made provision to have a functioning, Holy Ghost witness in these last days, you'll run out of oil at the last hour.

Don't end up a foolish virgin! If you are running out of oil — trusting your church or your pastor to keep your soul — then repent! Humble yourself and search your heart! Cry out to God to rid your soul of all anger and bitterness. Confess your sins and forsake them. And depend on God once again for everything!

Get the peace of God in your heart, so you can have a Holy Ghost witness. And ask the Father for a greater enduement of the Spirit. Invite Him to be your guide and your witness in everything. You don't have to be afraid in these days. He is anxious to become your witness!

Don't Run From Jezebel!

17

Listening to the Lord's Still, Small Voice

God intends for every believer to be in full control of his or her life — through the power and might of the Holy **Ghost!** The Bible makes it clear that our walk is to be ordered by the Lord. David testified, "Those who trust in the Lord will not be confounded" *(see Psalm 22:5)*.

Your life is not under control, however, if you are being victimized by a spirit of fear, lust, despondency or depression. If you are constantly bombarded with feelings of worthlessness or thoughts of giving up — your life is simply not under control. If any of this describes you, I pray that the Holy Ghost will use this message to grip your soul — and to put some fight back in you. God wants you to stand up against the devil — to reclaim all the territory you've given up to him!

I want to show you how one of the most powerful, godly men in all of the Bible lost control of his life for a season — and how he got back in control. It is the story of Elijah. God told this mighty prophet to call together the 450 priests of Baal and the 400 prophets of Asherah at the top of Mount Carmel. God was going to have a contest — a showdown with the devil! It was all about who would be worthy of worship — the pagan gods, or Jehovah God.

You remember that Holy Ghost fire came down from heaven, consuming the sacrifice on Elijah's altar and licking up the twelve barrels of water. When the middle-of-the-road believers saw this, they all fell on their faces and worshiped the Lord. Then these people fell into a holy rage — because they had been fooled! Their exposure to the worthless idolatry had kept them under bondage in captivity. So they took those 850 heathen priests and slew them all.

Meanwhile, Elijah told King Ahab, "Get ready for rain!" And the prophet went up on the mountain and prayed down a mighty thunderstorm, ending the drought. Then the Spirit of God fell upon him — and

Elijah outran Ahab's chariot for sixteen miles, back to the palace in Jezreel.

Scripture says, "And the hand of the Lord was on Elijah…" *(1 Kings 18:46)*. Indeed, no man could do any of this without the Spirit of God resting upon him mightily!

Elijah's Personal Battle Began at the Gate of Jezreel.

When Elijah came to Jezreel, he stopped outside the city gate and wouldn't go in. He represents where many of us are right now — outside the gate of evil, separated from sin, beyond the reach of all enemies.

Up to this point, Elijah was very much in control of his life. He was uplifted, fearless, zealous for God and hating idolatry. His prayers prevailed; none of his words fell to the ground. And God had just used him in the greatest manner of all his ministry. Elijah single-handedly had shaken the very powers of hell!

We don't know what Elijah was thinking as he sat outside the city gate. But we do know he "was a man subject to like passions as we are…" *(James 5:17)*. He was fully human, in spite of all he had just accomplished. I believe Elijah greatly expected God to finish the work He had begun — to bring down all idolatry in the land. He probably thought, "Perhaps those righteous ones who saw the fire fall will rise up and cast Jezebel out of her palace. Surely she's fearful. She's probably packing her bags and ordering a chariot right now. There could be riots in the streets. And the people are going to need a prophetic voice when everything erupts. I've got to be here!"

As he waited outside the city in anticipation of God's move, Elijah felt very important, very needed — and mighty in God. But, beloved, you can experience something like Elijah did on Mount Carmel — pulling down strongholds, prevailing in prayer, rescuing souls from Satan's clutches — and yet immediately experience a great fall!

The most vulnerable point in your life as a Christian is right after you've experienced a mighty victory. Many pastors, evangelists and laypeople who have been greatly used of God have fallen because they became careless and smug in their hour of power. They thought they'd come to a place in God where they were above being attacked — that they could handle anything without any trouble. But an angry devil moved in at the first sign of their smugness. He injected into their minds a spiritual pride — and they fell because they were not prepared!

That same pride was in Elijah. The true contents of his heart came out later as he hid in a cave on Mount Horeb: "…I have been very jealous for the Lord God of hosts: for the children of Israel have forsaken thy covenant, thrown down thine altars, and slain thy prophets with the sword; and I, even I only, am left; and they seek my life, to take it away" *(1 Kings 19:10)*. Elijah was saying, "I'm one of a kind, Lord. I'm the only one left In Israel who is fighting for You!"

There Are Two Battles in This Story!

The battle on Mount Carmel never was between Elijah and Jezebel — it was between God and the devil! Elijah was full of God's Spirit, and Jezebel was possessed by Satan. It was a battle between the powers of hell and God's corporate body on earth.

This is the kind of warfare most of us are engaged in right now. It is a battle over morals, between the church of Jesus Christ and the workers of iniquity — abortionists, drug pushers, flaunted homosexuals, pornographers, godless politicians.

Yet we also see in Elijah's story a personal battle unfolding. This one is between the devil and Elijah alone! Satan is saying, "I may have lost the battle for the church. But I'm going after God's man!"

Jezebel represents Satan in this story. Everything she did was directed by the devil. She was his tool to bring confusion, disorder and turmoil to Israel. Listen to how God's Word describes her: "I have a few things against thee, because thou sufferest that woman Jezebel, which calleth herself a prophetess, to teach and to seduce my servants to commit fornication….And I gave her space to repent of her fornication; and she repented not. Behold, I will cast her into a bed, and them that commit adultery with her into great tribulation, except they repent of their deeds" *(Revelation 2:20-22)*.

Jezebel is a type of the devil — reprobate, past repentance. She represents a seducing spirit that is at work in the world right now, desiring to bring mixture into God's house. This spirit's aim is to rob the church of all holy worship given to the Father. It seeks to sidetrack believers out of worshiping God from a pure heart!

"And Ahab told Jezebel all that Elijah had done, and withal how he had slain all the prophets with the sword" *(1 Kings 19:1)*. Jezebel listened as Ahab told how the miraculous fire fell on Elijah's altar…how the people fell to the ground in awe and fear of God…and how they slew her 450 Baal priests and the 400 prophets of Asherah!

Suddenly, Jezebel's face turned red with anger. (It was the devil rising up in her.) She said, "I may have lost all my priests. I may have lost the affection and worship that I expected from the people of God. This is a crippling blow to all my plans. But now I'm going after Elijah! I'm focusing all my attention on this servant of God who has caused such havoc in my kingdom. I don't care what else happens — I'm going to get this man!"

At this point Elijah was sitting outside the city, minding God's business — blameless, victorious, not an unholy thought in his mind. Then suddenly, seemingly out of nowhere, a messenger of Satan appeared with a message from hell: "Then Jezebel sent a messenger unto Elijah, saying, So let the gods do to me, and more also, if I make not thy life as the life of one of them by tomorrow about this time" *(verse 2)*.

Satan was threatening: "Elijah, you're as good as dead! You've gone too far — and now the battle is between you and me. You've had it — you're a dead man!"

God allowed this personal challenge for a reason. And it's the same reason every godly, dedicated believer must experience the same battle. You see, it's one thing to stand up against the workers of iniquity. When you see the forces of evil at work in America — judges ruling God's name out of school, doctors killing babies, lesbians preaching from church pulpits — you know that Satan is working against the whole body of Christ. And that is a corporate battle.

Yet it is another thing entirely when you come face to face with an angry devil — and he's out to get you personally. He comes after you as an individual, because you've made an impact in the kingdom of God — you've shaken hell!

It Was a Lie That Jezebel Would Kill Elijah!

The devil uses lies and fear to try to take control of believers' lives. And he did it with Elijah. First, Jezebel swore her oath by gods that already had been exposed as powerless. Elijah had nothing to fear from those gods. Furthermore, God had put a wall of fire around Elijah. He had surrounded His servant with chariots of fire and a host of angels. The prophet wasn't in any danger!

But Elijah wasn't thinking about those chariots. Nor was he thinking about the God who was with him on Mount Carmel — the One who could help him through his personal battle as well. No — Elijah panicked! Scripture says, "he arose, and went for his life..." *(verse 3)*. In just a few hours he went from holy boldness, assurance and authority — to fear, despair and confusion!

You must understand, the devil could not kill Elijah. Only God holds the keys to life and death. And besides, Satan didn't want to kill Elijah — because he knew death would only propel him into God's presence and out of his reach. Nevertheless, just twenty-four hours after Elijah's great victory, the prophet was sitting in the desert under a juniper tree, moaning, "I've had enough! I can't take any more. I want to die!" "He himself went a day's journey into the wilderness, and came and sat down under a juniper tree: and he requested for himself that he might die…" *(verse 4)*.

I ask you — are you under the juniper tree? Are you worn out, confused, your life out of control? Is all power gone? Are all victories fading fast, with fear and despair setting in? Have you ever said, "Enough, Lord — I want to die!"

Jeremiah Experienced the Same Great Battle!

The prophet Jeremiah was another holy man of God. He was righteous, blameless, without an unclean spot in his life. This man sounded so in control: "The Lord is with me as a mighty terrible one: therefore my persecutors shall stumble, and they shall not prevail: they shall be greatly ashamed; for they shall not prosper: their everlasting confusion shall never be forgotten….Sing unto the Lord, praise ye the Lord: for he hath delivered the soul of the poor from the hand of evildoers" *(Jeremiah 20:11-13)*.

This sounds like a man who is full of faith and victory. Yet suddenly we hear the groaning of a confused, dismayed, dejected prophet! Jeremiah sounds like he too is sitting under the juniper tree: "Cursed be the day wherein I was born: let not the day wherein my mother bare me be blessed. Cursed be the man who brought tidings to my father, saying, A man child is born unto thee; making him very glad….Let that man be as the cities which the Lord overthrew, and repented not…because he slew me not from the womb; or that my mother might have been my grave, and her womb to be always great with me" *(verses 14-17)*. This holy man of God was saying, "Why didn't they kill me when I was born? If only I had died in the womb!"

What had happened to make his attitude change so quickly? The devil had come directly against him — through Pashur, the chief governor, who beat him and cast him into prison! Jeremiah fell into confusion: "O Lord, thou hast deceived me, and I was deceived: thou art stronger than I, and hast prevailed: I am in derision daily, every one mocketh me" *(verse 7)*. He was saying, "I have to do Your will, Lord, because You're stronger than I am. But whenever You tell me to prophesy, nothing comes to pass. Everybody mocks me!"

I ask you — do you walk holy and righteous before God? Is your heart set on obeying and loving Him? Are you hungry for God — walking according to His power with all the light you've been given? Let me warn you — it is possible for you to have a season when things spin out of control! The enemy will come at you in the your time of greatest blessing — because of what you have done to his kingdom!

We all know that addicts, alcoholics and ungodly people live their days out of control. But many godly people also go through seasons of running from the devil, their lives out of control. Few of us, in fact, can say with Nehemiah: "...Should such a man as I flee?...I will not (run)" *(Nehemiah 6:11)*. Most of us have already run, like Elijah!

Perhaps you're under attack right now — and you're sitting under the juniper tree, dazed and confused. You're saying within your heart, "Lord, I've had enough. Take me home!" But I want to show you how to take back control of your life from the devil — how to reclaim the ground you've lost to him!

Here are three things the Holy Spirit spoke to my heart on this matter:

1. You Must Keep in Mind That God Is With You — Even in Your Running!

God is with you during every attack of the enemy. He never leaves you nor forsakes you. Elijah was in utter despair — totally confused, fearful, wanting to give up. But God looked upon him in his despondency and sent him a private angel — to be a butler and a cook for him!

Scripture says: "As he lay and slept under a juniper tree, behold, then an angel touched him, and said unto him, Arise and eat. And he looked, and, behold, there was a cake baken on the coals, and a cruse of water at his head. And he did eat and drink, and laid him down again. And the angel of the Lord came again the second time, and touched him, and said, Arise and eat; because the journey is too great for thee. And he arose, and did eat and drink, and went in the strength of that meat forty days and forty nights..." *(1 Kings 19:5-8)*. Have you ever been served a meal so nutritious, it lasted forty days? That had to be some meal!

Here is what I believe the Lord said to the angel before sending him to

Elijah: "Be patient with him! He's hurting, confused, full of questions. He thinks he wants to die, but he really wants to live. He feels useless, at the end of his rope. But I still love him! I've got much more work for him to do in My kingdom. Soon I'm going to awaken his spirit. But, meanwhile, feed him well — refresh him! And tell him the journey is too great for him. He can't make it without eating the food I supply!"

Thank God the angel said that to Elijah! It is true — the journey is too great for all of us. We can't handle it. That is why God has given us this Word — and it's better than any angel. He says, "Go to My Word — eat and drink. There you will find all the strength you need to go through this trial."

2. Taking Back Control Requires Dealing With the Lord's Still, Small Voice!

The voice of the Spirit will ask you the same thing He asked Elijah: "What are you doing here, Elijah?" *(1 Kings 19:9, NAS)*. God was saying to his servant, "How long will you allow the devil to lie to you? When will you wake up and say, 'Enough of this foolishness!' It's time to take a stand, to fight back — to take control!"

Perhaps the Lord is saying the same thing to you right now: "Why are you hiding here, living in this fear and depression? How long will you let this go on? You don't need to fear — I have never left you. Get up! Your work for Me is not done. Get out of this cave of sadness and guilt!"

God had to put this question to Elijah twice. At first, Elijah answered that his holiness and zeal had gotten him in trouble: "Lord, they've slain all Your prophets. I'm the only one left — and they're trying to kill me!" But God asked the question again — because Elijah hadn't told the whole truth. You see, God was after what was deep in Elijah's heart — the real reason his spirit and soul were down and out. It was this:

"God, you let the devil get to me! You let him harass me, take away my joy, put fear in me. And I did not deserve such treatment! I have been holy, obedient, doing all You told me to do. Yet after all my praying, preaching and obedience, I ended up with the biggest battle of my life!"

Does this describe your spirit as well? You've tried your best to do God's will and work, giving Jesus your whole heart and energy — and yet you've fallen under attack from the devil! The Lord is coming to you now, asking, "Why are you so down — why so panicky? Let's get to the heart of this. What's the real problem behind it all?" He wants you to admit what is really in your heart: "God, I didn't deserve this attack from the enemy, when I was trying so hard to please You!"

Perhaps you already have poured out your heart to God in this way. But have you told Him the rest of what's deep inside? "I'm tired of all the lessons, Lord! I don't want to learn anymore. I'm here simply to do Your will — to win victories for You, to save souls. Just let me do that and then go home to glory!"

This is the whole issue, the whole problem: We're tired of learning God's ways! We think, "Is there never a time when I can sit back and know the devil is defeated? Won't my battles ever end?" No — God has a different plan! And it is this: "When you learn how to resist the devil, he will flee from you!" *(see James 4:7)*.

You may say, "I already know that!" But many Christians think resisting the devil means railing at him — yelling, trying to scare him away. But that is of no effect. God is talking about something entirely different here. He is saying: "How can you learn to resist Satan until I have let him come at you, roaring and threatening? He is not a figment of your imagination — he is a real devil. And you have to learn to give opposition to him!"

Professional snake handlers — those who draw poison from rattle-snakes for medicinal purposes — get their training by going straight into the snake pit. It is the only way they can rid themselves of fear. And it is the only way to learn snakes' devices — how they move and operate.

Beloved, God wants to take you into the pit — to stand face to face with the devil! He wants you to hear the enemy's crafty lying and roaring, so you can learn how to resist him. He wants to teach you to stand firmly — to quietly withstand all of Satan's empty rattling!

Scripture says of Michael the archangel: "Yet Michael the archangel, when contending with the devil he disputed about the body of Moses, durst not bring against him a railing accusation, but said, The Lord rebuke thee" *(Jude 9)*. Michael was saying, without fear: "I don't have time to play games with you, devil. I have work to do. The Lord will take care of you!"

3. You Regain Control When You Begin to Understand Why God Has Allowed You to Endure Such a Personal, Grievous Battle!

First, God allows your trial because He wants to make you "devil-proof." That doesn't mean you won't be attacked again. But you will be trained to stand! It is all part of His preparing you for greater service, greater anointing, expanded usefulness in His kingdom.

Furthermore, the Lord is trying to strengthen you against the devil's wiles. He is raising up a body of believers who have faced the devil, who have been strengthened against him — and who know his devices and are not afraid of him. God is saying, "Once you understand why you're going through this, you will have taken back all the ground you've lost. You will be in control again — by the power of the Holy Ghost!"

Once Elijah's trial was over, he would never run again. He now had a sense of direction — he was reassured in his spirit. You see, God was about to send him to nations to raise up kings, leaders and prophets! God told him: "Go, return on thy way...anoint Hazael to be king over Syria... and Jehu...to be king over Israel...and Elisha...to be prophet in thy room" *(1 Kings 19:15-16)*. Elijah had been given fresh anointing power. He was in control again! "So he departed thence..." *(verse 19)*. Elijah came out of the cave to do God's will. He didn't have to shed a river of tears. No — he simply had heard the Word of the Lord!

Beloved, the only hold the devil can have on you is fear. And you've got to shake it off in faith. You have to say, "I'm not going down. God is going to give me a fresh anointing from heaven. He's going to use me!"

Do you believe that God is not finished with you — that He is teaching and training you for better things? He wants to speak to you in your cave of despondency. He wants to tell you what to do and where to go — and He wants to bring you out. So, get up out of your despair. Shake off the bondage of fear and depression. Depart from your cave. You'll discover that the moment you get up and walk out, the anointing will flow!

18

The Power of a Blameless Life

Discovering God's Favor

Ye are witnesses, and God also, how holily and justly and unblameably we behaved ourselves among you that believe" *(1 Thessalonians 2:10).*

That's a pretty powerful statement to make — to call on God as a witness to your holiness! Yet, without flinching, Paul boasted to the believers in Thessalonica: "I and my coworkers lived blamelessly before you and before God. Our conduct was righteous and pure. God is witness to our holy behavior — yet you also are witnesses. You saw that we walked holy and blameless before God and men!"

Paul was an effective preacher. And he knew the secret to his effectiveness in moving people toward God. He could stand boldly before every living soul, every principality and testify: "I live daily under the gaze of a holy God. I walk always as if His holy eyes are upon me. And you all are witnesses to my blameless life!"

The apostle desired every believer to have the same power he had in moving people toward God. And he prayed night and day that all of God's children would be established holy and unblamable before God: "To the end he may stablish your hearts unblameable in holiness before God...at the coming of our Lord Jesus Christ with all his saints" *(3:13).*

Let me share with you Paul's description of a blameless life — and about the power such a life releases:

Paul Clearly Explains What a Blameless Life Is.

Here is the kind of behavior required of the holy, just, unblamable believer, according to Paul:

1. To be blameless is to have no deceit of any kind. "For our exhortation was not of deceit..." *(2:3).* A blameless Christian is one without any deceit in his heart! Paul said, "I was not a fraud, preaching one thing to you and yet living another. My behavior was an open book!"

He warned the Corinthians, however, that certain men were going about claiming to be apostles. He said, "They boast that they walk as I do, in blamelessness. They say, 'I'm an apostle, appointed of God...'" "(But) such are false apostles, deceitful workers, transforming themselves into the apostles of Christ" *(2 Corinthians 11:13)*. Paul said, "You can't fake a blameless walk. My message goes right to the conscience of men — because I live the truth I preach!" *(see 4:2)*.

2. To be blameless is to touch nothing unclean. "Our exhortation was not...of uncleanness..." *(1 Thessalonians 2:3)*.

Paul's emphasis here is on sensuality, lust. He's saying, "Not an unclean word came out of my mouth. My conversation was pure, coming forth from a clean heart." This man had his body under control. No fleshly passion drove him; no spirit of lust or fornication possessed his mind. He was a free man!

Show me any minister — or any believer — who tells dirty jokes, makes sexual innuendos or has roving eyes, and I'll show you someone whose heart has not been cleansed! You may sit in church thinking you worship God from a pure heart. Yet if you go to your job and a stream of unclean talk springs out of you — or if you even give ear to dirty jokes — then you give credence to filth!

God says, "I won't have it! If you are going to walk blameless before Me, you're going to have clean ears, a clean heart and a clean tongue!"

3. To be blameless is to be without guile. "Our exhortation was not ...in guile" *(verse 3)*.

The Christian without guile is not clever, crafty or manipulative. He has no hidden sin or hidden agenda. He is totally honest and open. Yet the church today is filled with manipulators — in both pulpit and pew! These people work to have their own way — not through the power or leading of the Holy Spirit, but through the cleverness of their minds.

Paul said, "I didn't manipulate you into the kingdom of God. I didn't use clever words or try to play on your feelings. I gave the gospel to you straight!" The apostle never played word games; he never used psychology to get people to like him. Can you imagine Paul going around to people in the congregation, hugging them and putting on a forced smile, wanting to be admired and accepted? Never!

Paul said, "We were gentle among you, even as a nurse cherisheth her children" *(verse 7)*. But when sin came in, he rebuked it with thunder from out of heaven! He didn't desire or need the approval of any man, yet he loved people with all his heart.

"Neither at any time used we flattering words, as ye know, nor a cloke of covetousness...Nor of men sought we glory, neither of you, nor yet of others..." *(verses 5-6)*. Paul didn't seek personal recognition from any person. Rather, he was always mindful that God was watching him and checking his motives. So he abstained even from any "appearance of evil" *(5:22)*. He lived as if Jesus were coming within the hour!

Now, to be sure, there are many sinners who could meet all of these standards of behavior. No matter how wicked this generation is, there are still people who don't manipulate and aren't driven by sensuality. Their language and morals are clean; they are without guile and deceit. They possess a moral power, because their goodness creates a dignity and strength of character. Often these people are exalted by others. But the fact remains — they have no power with God!

For example, the rich young ruler who came to Jesus measured up to these standards. He had been good from his youth upward. And that won him the love and respect of Jesus. But something was lacking. And that one thing made all the difference!

Paul said, "All of the good qualities in my life — all of these godly characteristics — are based on one rock-solid purpose in me. It is what keeps me from sin, corruption and deceit." Beloved, if you don't have this same purpose operating in all you say and do, you can never be blameless before God and man: "That the name of our Lord Jesus Christ may be glorified in (me)..." *(2 Thessalonians 1:12)*.

Here is what motivated Paul to live a blameless life: He was jealous for the glory and name of Jesus! He knew everything had to be built on that foundation — because all human goodness is as filthy rags!

Indeed, this is what distinguishes the blameless walk: a consuming desire to honor the name of Jesus before all men! Such believers would rather die than do or say anything that would bring reproach on the Lord. They are not perfect — they still battle the flesh — but now they are pursuing the righteousness of Christ by faith.

Perhaps you've already said to your heavenly Father, "Lord, I lay down my sin — I lay down all iniquity and sensuality. I want only to walk blameless before You. I want to please You and bring glory to Your name."

If so, here are three things you can expect to happen in your life:

1. The First Thing That Happens to a Blameless Believer Is He Gains the Favor of God.

The bride in Song of Solomon was consumed by love for her beloved. And because of this, she said, "I was in his eyes as one that found favour" *(Song of Solomon 8:10)*.

Indeed, God promises wonderful favor to the blameless believer: "...keep my commandments...let not mercy and truth forsake thee: bind them about thy neck; write them upon the table of thine heart: So shalt thou find favour and good understanding in the sight of God and men" *(Proverbs 3:1-4)*. God is saying, "If you set your sights to walk blameless before Me, you'll walk in My favor. You will be pleasing unto Me!"

Oh, the greatest joy you could ever have as a Christian is to go through life knowing you're pleasing to God. The Lord won't have to hide His face from you or shed a tear over you — because you do not bring shame or reproach to His holy name. Instead, you bring glory to Him — and He is pleased!

But that's not all. God's favor also includes power. Paul said, "For our gospel came not unto you in word only, but also in power, and in the Holy Ghost, and in much assurance..." *(1 Thessalonians 1:5)*. His favor brings the power of the Holy Ghost to all you say and do. Your words will not fall to the ground — because they will have Holy Ghost power! *(see 2:1)*.

Paul said those Holy Ghost-empowered words produce great results: "And ye became followers of us, and of the Lord, having received the word in much affliction, with joy of the Holy Ghost" *(verse 6)*. Why were Paul's words so powerful, so effective? Because, he says, "(We) were ensamples to all that believe..." *(verse 7)*. It was not Paul's preaching nor his praying alone that won people to the Lord. It was his exemplary life! God had in Paul a clean heart — one He could favor with the power of the Holy Ghost.

God's divine favor also brings high esteem among men. It is written of David: "David behaved himself more wisely than all the servants of Saul. So his name was highly esteemed" *(1 Samuel 18:30, NAS)*. "And the fame of David went out into all lands; and the Lord brought the fear [respect] of him upon all nations" *(1 Chronicles 14:17)*.

The man who protects the name of Jesus by living holy before others will be given a good name before them — by God Himself!

I have heard some Christians say, "I don't care about my name. It doesn't matter what people think of me. I just want to be an unknown, a nobody. Let the Lord have all the glory." That may sound humble — but it is not, according to Scripture! The Bible says, "A good name is rather to be chosen than great riches, and loving favour rather than silver and gold" *(Proverbs 22:1)*.

A good reputation is a coin to be spent for God's glory. It is to be used to influence people and nations. And God gives the righteous a good name so they can use it to glorify Him in greater measure!

2. The Favor and Blessing God Pours Upon a Holy Life Results in a Disturbing, Repelling Power.

When you set your heart to walk blamelessly before God — laying down your besetting sins, living in a way that's pleasing to the Lord — you will be feared and despised by those who have lost the favor and blessing of God. Lukewarm or compromised Christians will be absolutely disturbed and repelled by your life.

We see this illustrated vividly in 1 Samuel: "And Saul was afraid of David, because the Lord was with him, and was departed from Saul.... And David behaved himself wisely in all his ways; and the Lord was with him. Wherefore when Saul saw that he behaved himself very wisely, he was afraid of him" *(1 Samuel 18:12-15)*.

David's blameless behavior struck fear in Saul's heart. Whenever Saul was around David, he remembered the time he had enjoyed the favor of God and the high esteem of men. But disobedience, envy, pride and self-will had cost Saul every bit of power with God. And it robbed him of all respect of the people. Now Saul had come face to face with a younger man — a less experienced, probably less articulate man — who exuded the power and integrity of holiness. He was pure in heart, full of the Holy Ghost. And Saul was afraid of him!

Keep in mind, this was no idolatrous Canaanite who was afraid of David. No — Saul was a man who had known the power of the Holy Spirit. He stood head and shoulders above David. And he had been God's anointed. He once was a mighty man, chosen of God.

Sadly, Saul represents the compromised church today — those Christians who have compromised and lost the anointing of God. He is a type of believer who once was full of the Holy Ghost, baptized, on fire for God. But disobedience, pride and lust robbed him of everything he once knew of God. Now, David was simply living a clean life — and God was pouring out favor upon him: "All Israel and Judah loved David, because he went out and came in before them" *(verse 16)*. David walked before the people as a defender of God's holy name. They remembered his battle cry when he slew Goliath: "I come to thee in the name of the Lord!" *(see 17:45)*.

But Saul didn't want to be around David. Scripture says, "Therefore Saul removed him from him…" *(18:13)*. He became so disturbed and envious of David's closeness to God, he threw a javelin at him. Saul even used his own backslidden daughter to try to ensnare David. He became consumed with a passion to destroy David and his good name!

I tell you, there is nothing scarier to a compromised Christian than a holy, blameless life. And the more your life lines up with the Lord's will and His holiness, the more repelling you will become to backslidden believers. Indeed, your worst opposition will come from within the church of Jesus Christ — from compromised people who have secret sins they don't want to give up. They will call you legalistic, unbalanced, strange. They will attempt to disgrace you, to destroy your name and your blameless walk before God.

These are Christians who no longer walk in God's favor. They have no power of the Spirit on them. Their words are like feathers — weightless, bearing no spiritual authority. Nothing they say has any impact, because they have lost the power and presence of Jesus. And your holy walk will disturb and repel them. You won't have to say anything to them. They'll simply see your blameless walk with the Lord, and it will be as a prophet's holy finger, pointing to their heart. They will fear, envy and hate you!

You may say, "I haven't experienced such rejection. My church is full of saints who highly esteem me and stand with me. Is it because I'm not living a blameless life?" No — it is probably because you are sitting among other blameless believers! But go back to your old, dead church — and tell them how Jesus has become real to you. Wait till they discover you don't sit in front of a TV and pollute your soul…you don't engage in filthy conversation…you love to go to every church service — you pray, worship and soak in God's Word. They will give you the "good-bye" hand of fellowship! They will be repelled by you; they will despise you. And when you leave, they'll look at each other knowingly and say, "Boy, has he gone off the deep end. What a fanatic! He's no fun — he's too spaced out." "…they shall separate you from their company" *(Luke 6:22)*. Why? Because your life will have convicted them of what they once had — and what they now have lost!

Paul experienced this kind of rejection because of his uncompromising walk with God. He wrote to Timothy: "…all they which are in Asia be turned away from me..." *(2 Timothy 1:15)*. He wrote to the Colossians from prison that he could name only two or three who were a comfort to him: "...These only are my fellow workers unto the kingdom of God, which have been a comfort unto me" *(Colossians 4:11)*. And in another letter to Timothy, he wrote, "...no man stood with me, but all men forsook me..." *(2 Timothy 4:16)*.

I ask you — are you willing to pay that kind of price to have the favor of God in your life? Yet, if you do choose to live a blameless life, even the ungodly will esteem you highly. They'll point to your life and say, "That's what Christianity ought to be." And likewise, the truly righteous ones in the church will flock to you. They'll say, "I like being around you. There is something comforting and refreshing about you. God is with you!"

3. Finally, God Favors the Blameless Believer With a Power of Proper Focus.

Once you enter into a blameless walk with the Lord — living above reproach, holy and unblamable — the Holy Ghost bestows on you what I call "the power of proper focus."

Paul's blameless life brought him into a spiritual focus such as God desires for every member of His body. In a letter to the Thessalonians, Paul makes one of the most powerful statements in all his writings: "For now we live, if ye stand fast in the Lord" *(1 Thessalonians 3:8)*. Do you know what Paul is saying? He's claiming, "I get my joy, my life, my greatest blessing, from seeing you grow in Christ!"

At one time, if I were asked about my spiritual focus, I would have answered, "I really live — I really get my joy — when I walk in victory. When I know I'm living an overcoming life, standing fast in the Lord, then I'm happy. I rejoice in knowing I'm not in sin!" But that isn't what Paul said. He had already worked through all of that. He didn't live his life focused on some sin or problem.

Yet most Christians today spend their entire saved lives focused on their own sin. Many have battled lust, perversion, fornication or addictions for years. They have victory in every area of their lives but one or two. And they are literally consumed by those remaining few. They are spiritual cripples — powerless, full of guilt, living as a slave to their sin. And they have narrowed their focus to one question, one concern: "How will I ever become free of this?" Such Christians derive their greatest joy and peace from gaining victories in their personal walk. But they have no vision for the church, the lost or the eternal purposes of Jesus Christ.

Paul said he "always labour(ed) fervently for you in prayers, that ye may stand perfect and complete in all the will of God" *(Colossians 4:12)*. He wasn't interceding for himself or his own needs. He said, "Night and day I labor in prayer for you. I want you to stand complete in the will of God!"

Dear saint, complete victory is yours if you really want it. God does want you finally free — free to live for others, to minister to others, to help others into blamelessness — to rejoice over the work of the Spirit in the whole body of Christ, and not just in yourself.

Paul believed that a blameless life changed a person's focus — from always looking inward, to looking instead to the needs of Christ's church and the world. I ask you — when you sit in church and see someone you've been witnessing or testifying to, can you rejoice because you see victory coming into that person's life? Is your whole joy focused on that one lost soul? On that suffering elderly person? On Cuba, China, Mongolia?

God has fully provided for us in the sacrifice of His Son, so that we are able to say: "By grace, God has put His fear in my heart. I have forsaken all my iniquities. I am blameless before the Lord. God is my witness!"

Such a thing is possible — for every believer! Paul could say, "Sin no longer has dominance over me. I have laid aside every weight, every besetting sin. I have died to this world, and I die daily to my flesh." And that is why he did not spend his time groaning over his sins. They were all forsaken! He could now groan over his lost brethren. And he groaned that Christ would come forth in His church: "For what is our hope, or joy, or crown of rejoicing? Are not even ye in the presence of our Lord Jesus Christ at his coming? For ye are our glory and joy" *(1 Thessalonians 2:19-20)*.

God did not intend for you to spend the rest of your life fighting some perversion, addiction, adultery or secret sin. No — He wants you to fix your eyes on Jesus! He wants you to say, "Lord, I'm going to turn my eyes away from my own need and pray for others — even though I'm not yet where I want to be." Victory will come when you start giving yourself to others — interceding for other believers, and reaching out to the lost.

A Blameless Life Is Possible — But You Must Desire It With All That Is in You!

First, you must face the utter reality of your condition: "If I continue in my sinful ways, I'll grow increasingly weak and powerless. I'll no longer enjoy God's favor. I won't be pleasing to Him. And I'll never get the focus

He wants to give me. I'll end up like Saul — dead inside, full of hate and envy. I'll go into eternity crying, 'God no longer is with me!'"

You've got to get that honest before God. I cried out to Him, "Lord, send Your Word! Convict me and heal me. Show me how to walk away from all sin!" And God sent this word to me: "...behold, now is the day of salvation. Giving no offence in any thing, that the ministry be not blamed" *(2 Corinthians 6:2-3)*.

God says, "You can be free now. You don't have to wait!" When He told Israel to sanctify themselves before going into battle, they didn't have to wait a week, a month or a year before they got clean before Him. They had to begin now, that very day!

"Giving no offence in any thing, that the ministry be not blamed" *(verse 3)*. Let me ask you: Are you involved in anything that might bring reproach on the name of Jesus? Can you say with Paul, "I also do my best to maintain always a blameless conscience both before God and before men" *(see Acts 24:16)*?

Set your heart to be blameless now — today! Desire it with everything in you. Soon you will discover God's favor upon your life. Your words and actions will have an impact on others, with Holy Ghost power. And you will find yourself focused totally on Jesus and His desires. That is blameless living!

Hatred
For Sin

19

Is Your Hatred for Sin
Tempered With Mercy?

I **want to tell you about an anointed servant of God who
hated sin as few people ever have**. His hatred for evil was so
passionate, so intense, he was ready to kill all transgressors. I am speaking of Saul, the first king of Israel! No person in the Old Testament
expressed a greater hatred for sin than did Saul.

The Philistines invaded Israel, perhaps to test the resolve of the newly
appointed king. They came at Israel in three separate companies, attack-
ing on three different flanks. A cowardice spread among the Israelite
soldiers, and they began fleeing to caves, dens and rocks to hide from the
enemy. Saul was left with only six hundred fighters. And they were badly
outnumbered and poorly armed: "...there was neither sword nor spear
found in the hand of any of the people that were with Saul and Jonathan:
but with Saul and with Jonathan his son was there found [weapons]"
(1 Samuel 13:22).

Saul and his motley army sat under some trees, wondering what to do.
But, meanwhile, Jonathan and his armor-bearer slipped away from the
camp to plan their own strategy. This young son of Saul was a godly man,
full of faith. He told his helper: "...there is no restraint (limitation) to the
Lord to save by many or by few" *(14:6)*.

The pair sneaked off to a place near Michmash, where they saw a
company of Philistine soldiers on a ridge above them. Jonathan stood up,
exposing himself to the soldiers, and they dared him to come up. Somehow, he and his armor-bearer climbed up the steep rock ledge and
surprised the enemy soldiers. Almost immediately, they slew twenty
Philistines!

When the slaughter was accomplished, the rest of the Philistine soldiers panicked. Evidently, there was a narrow passageway out of that
battlefield, and the soldiers got bottled up in it. Scripture says they
trembled and shook, and even began to fight with one another: "And

there was trembling in the host...and they went on beating down one another" *(verses 15-16)*.

One of Saul's sentries heard the commotion. Looking down into the valley, he saw two men putting the Philistines to chase. He called out to Saul, who came and looked upon the scene. Saul couldn't figure out who the two soldiers were. So he ordered his officers, "See who among us is missing." A head count was made, and a soldier reported back to Saul: "Jonathan and his armor-bearer are gone!"

When Saul heard this, he and his army joined the battle. Suddenly, all the deserting Israelites emerged from the dens, rocks and cave hideouts. And they ended up chasing the Philistines away!

In the heat of battle, however, Saul gave a rash command. He said to his soldiers: "...Cursed be the man that eateth any food until evening, that I may be avenged on mine enemies. So none of the people tasted any food" *(verse 24)*. He had commanded, "Let no one stop to eat until this battle is finished!" It was a foolish statement to make.

Of course, Jonathan hadn't heard the command. And while he was fighting in a wooded area, he came upon some trees where a supply of honey was dripping to the ground. He poked his rod into one of the honeywells and enjoyed a refreshing mouthful. Immediately, his eyes brightened, and he was energized for battle.

That evening, after the battle, the ravenous Israelite army dove into the spoils. They slew sheep and oxen on the ground, and they chomped on meat that still had blood in it. Both of these actions were contrary to the law. Someone saw this happening and reported it to Saul, and the king was horrified. He knew that the law required animals to be killed off the ground and their blood to be drained. Suddenly, an indignation and rage filled him. He commanded everyone to gather around him, and he roared: "...Ye have transgressed: roll a great stone unto me this day" *(verse 33)*. (The phrase "this day" in Hebrew actually means, "This very moment — immediately!")

Saul was saying, "God is offended! You have grieved Him! This is outright, blatant sin. Quick — there is no time to lose! Bring me a large stone. And every one of you, bring your cattle and slay them on the stone. Let the blood drain from the animals, and don't eat any meat with blood in it. Do it right!"

I can visualize the scene: Saul stands indignantly by the altar he erected, while the Israelites come forward, shame-faced and sheepish. He shakes his head and says to his captains, "How could they do such a thing? Are they really that stupid? I can't allow the wrath of God to fall on this nation. This has to be made right." He was outraged!

That night the soldiers were weary, traumatized from the battle. They wanted to go home. But they hadn't done a major mop-up of the Philistines. They had won only a partial victory. So Saul demanded they return to battle and chase the Philistines all night. He said, "We're not sleeping tonight. We're going to fight until I'm avenged of my enemies!"

But the priest suggested, "Let's consult the Lord first." The Bible says, "And Saul asked counsel of God, Shall I go down after the Philistines? Wilt thou deliver them into the hand of Israel? But he answered him not that day" *(verse 37)*.

Once more, Saul's hatred for sin was aroused. He raged, "God isn't speaking because He's mad at us! Somebody has sinned — and I'm going to find out who it is. I will not allow sin to go on among God's people. Line up, everybody — Israel on one side, and my son and me on the other."

Scripture says they cast lots, and the lot fell to Saul and Jonathan. "…And Saul and Jonathan were taken…" *(verse 41)*. The king and his son had been isolated. So Saul turned to Jonathan and said, "So, it's you!" "…Tell me what thou hast done…" *(verse 43)*. "What did you do, Jonathan? How have you sinned?"

Now, Saul already had told the people, "So help me God, even if the guilty party is my own son, he will die!" I ask you — how's that for a rage against sin? Jonathan looked at his father incredulously and asked, "You mean, you want to kill me because I tasted a little honey?" But Saul was unbending. He stood strong in his hatred for sin and cried out, "…thou shalt surely die, Jonathan" *(verse 44)*. He commanded his officers to take Jonathan out and kill him. But the soldiers stepped in and rescued him.

Beloved, here is a picture of an anointed servant of God, expressing an uncompromising hatred for sin. But there is something tragically wrong here! You see, Saul hated sin in the congregation. And he hated sin in his family. Yet he excused the awful sin in his own heart. He hated only the sins of others!

Saul should have been in mourning over his own sins. He had just had an encounter with the prophet Samuel, who had exposed his sinfulness. The prophet had rebuked him for his foolishness, disobedience, impatience and rebellion. At this point Saul should have said, "If anyone needs judging, it's me!" But he still had a rage for the holiness of God — and against the unrighteousness of the people.

I want to tell you what's behind the "kingdom dominion" gospel in America today. The driving force behind the doctrines of these "Reconstructionists" — those who want to revert to Old Testament laws — is an intense hatred for the corporate sins of America! The key leaders of Reconstructionism say our society is rotting, decaying, out of control — and the only way back to sanity is to return to the law. They literally want to bring back Moses' commands: "Stone abortionists. And stone any girl who's had an abortion. Do as the Muslims do — cut off the hands of those who steal. Forty stripes on the bare backs of abusers. Death to all drug pushers and rapists. No mercy — no compassion for transgressors!"

Talk about a rage against sin. Yet, tellingly, there is no mention of punishment for one's own personal sins!

One of Reconstructionism's major writers took exception to the prophecies I wrote in my book **Set the Trumpet to Thy Mouth**. He wrote me several venomous letters about it. When I read them, I could hardly believe he was a Christian.

This man writes book after book raging against sin in America — and yet he smokes and drinks! He says he feels the "burden to cleanse modern society" — but he won't cleanse himself of his own sinful habits.

I call this the Saul Syndrome. It is characterized by a hatred for the sins of society, the sins of the church, the sins of others — but no grief over one's own sins!

Even the Most Righteous Among Us Has a Tendency to Hate Others' Sins While Being Blind to His Own.

David was a man of God who hated sin with everything in him. He said, "...I hate every false way" *(Psalm 119:104)*. "Ye that love the Lord, hate evil..." *(97:10)*. Yet this same man committed adultery with Bathsheba. And he sent her husband to his death in battle.

The Bible says Bathsheba "...mourned for her husband" *(2 Samuel 11:26)*. Think of the hurt and guilt this poor woman must have carried. She had cheated on her husband, and now she was without him. I don't think she had any idea that her secret lover, David, had plotted her husband's death.

David's sin had "displeased the Lord" *(verse 27)*. He had seduced Bathsheba, planned her husband's death, and then deceived her by acting as if he was doing the right thing (that is, marrying her after he'd impregnated her). So, ten months after the affair, God sent Nathan the prophet to deal with David's sin *(see 2 Samuel 12)*.

Nathan came to David's court pretending to represent a poor man who had been terribly misused. He told the king, "There's a man in this kingdom who is very wealthy. And a friend of his came to visit him. The friend was hungry after his journey and needed something to eat. Now, this wealthy man had a lot of sheep. His neighbor, on the other hand, had only one little lamb. And it was the family pet. That little lamb ate and slept with the family. They loved it. But, rather than send out one of his servants to fetch one of his own sheep, this rich man went over and stole his neighbor's little pet lamb. And he killed it and fed it to his visiting friend."

David was enraged. He told Nathan, "So help me, that man is dead! He's going to die!" (The Hebrew here reads, "He is worthy of death.") Then David added, "That man is also going to restore the lamb fourfold!" He raged against this awful sin. Oh, how he hated it!

Yet, beloved, do you see how unconfessed sin in a child of God produces an unrighteous, unholy indignation against sin in others? If you have hidden sin, as David did, you'll feel an indignation against others' sins. Hidden sin begets a "religious spirit" — that is, a judging spirit.

Years ago, during a repentance conference our ministry held, a pastor's wife came to us. She confided, "My husband is quite well-known in holiness churches as a powerful holiness preacher. He thunders against makeup on women, going to movies, improper dress. But he's a big phony. He's hooked on pornography. He never faces his own sin!" This man preaches legalism to cover up his own vicious, hidden sin.

Jesus said, "...why beholdest thou the mote that is in thy brother's eye, but considerest not the beam that is in thine own eye? Or how wilt thou say to thy brother, Let me pull out the mote out of thine eye; and, behold, a beam is in thine own eye? Thou hypocrite, first cast out the beam out of thine own eye; and then shalt thou see clearly to cast out the mote out of thy brother's eye" *(Matthew 7:2-5)*.

Paul wrote, "Thou therefore which teachest another, teachest thou not thyself? Thou that preachest a man should not steal, dost thou steal? Thou that sayest a man should not commit adultery, dost thou commit adultery? Thou that abhorrest idols, dost thou commit sacrilege?" *(Romans 2:21-22)*.

I believe all godly saints must have a genuine hatred for sin. And all true shepherds must cry out against sin and compromise. But a pure hatred for sin must come out of a heart that has been probed, searched and judged itself.

David cried out against sin and compromise: "Do I not hate them, O Lord, that hate thee? And am not I grieved with those that rise up against thee? I hate them with perfect hatred: I count them mine enemies" *(Psalm 139:21-22)*. This bold statement came out of a repentant, broken spirit — because David had already examined his own heart. In the next verse he says, "Search me, O God, and know my heart: try me, and know my thoughts: And see if there be any wicked way in me..." *(verses 23-24)*.

We are so unlike Jesus in venting our hatred for sin in others. We want judgment to fall on them, but God wants mercy. We want to call down fire from heaven on transgressors — but God wants to forgive and reconcile all sinners. I never could have been a prophet who preached mercy to King Manasseh. He filled Jerusalem with blood by sending thousands of screaming babies to the belly of Molech. If God had sent me to that wretched man to encourage and reconcile him, I would have thundered at him instead!

Yet, the Bible says Manasseh repented. Even so, I wouldn't have believed his tears. All I would have heard were the screams of the babies. And all I would have thought about was what he'd done to corrupt that society. But I wouldn't have known about all his sleepless nights. I wouldn't have seen the terror in his eyes or heard his haunting cries. I wouldn't have believed that God could still love and forgive such a vile sinner. But He did. And Scripture says He had mercy on Manasseh.

Nathan the Prophet Shows Us God's Way of Dealing With Fallen, Sinful Saints.

Nathan knew David had sinned. He knew David was involved in murder, lies, cover-up, deception. Yet, Nathan loved David. He wasn't anxious to expose him. He wanted to save him! Nathan didn't go around David's court, whispering to his associates and servants, "We need to pray for the king. A woman is trying to seduce him, and he's caught in her trap. I've got such a burden for David!"

Don't be fooled: This kind of talk is plain, outright gossip! And it is made worse by being clothed in pious words such as "prayer," "concern" and "love." May God have mercy on those who spread this kind of talk. I wouldn't want to be in their shoes!

I believe Nathan spent months praying for David. He truly hated David's sin. He knew the Lord does not wink at sin, and that sin has consequences. And he knew David was living a lie — that he had disregarded the name of the Lord. Nathan also knew of David's fear. David had refused to go to battle; he hid in the palace instead. He had lost all his fight. He was afraid an enemy arrow might strike him — and he'd have to face God with unconfessed sin!

I want to make an important point here: God made the first move toward David. He initiated the first step toward reconciliation. You see, when we believers sin against the Lord, we tend to hide from Him. We feel unworthy, as if we'll never measure up to His holy standard. So we hide, just as Adam and Eve hid when they sinned. But God went after Adam and Eve. He tenderly asked them, "Why do you hide from Me?" In other words, "Why are you trying to destroy our fellowship, our communion?"

Likewise, God sent Nathan to David. He missed the intimate fellowship He had had with His servant. But David was hiding from God because of guilt, fear and condemnation. So God waited and waited — until finally He said, "If he won't come to Me, then I'll go to him." So He sent Nathan. And it is in God's approach to David that we discover His heart toward all fallen saints.

I used to preach about Nathan's exposure of David in an entirely different way. I have the sermon on tape — but I cringe when I listen to it now, because I delivered it in the wrong spirit. I had a rage against sin that wasn't tempered by the mercy of God!

I used to thunder, "There sits David, thinking he has gotten away with sin. He goes on with business as usual — sporting around with his stolen wife, as if nothing is wrong. But here comes that mighty man of God, Nathan, full of holy zeal! He marches in and tells David the story of the stolen lamb. Then he looks David in the eye, points a bony finger in his face and thunders, 'You are the man! You have transgressed God's law and brought shame on His name. It's all over, David — your sin has found you out. Shame on you! Repent!'"

Isn't this the way you might have exposed David? "Praise God — sin has to be exposed. Our leaders have to be pure, spotless!" But that is not how it happened with David — because that is not how God deals with His fallen, beloved servants. Rather, God had already told Nathan that David was forgiven. He told the prophet to go to him with a message of reconciliation: "When you tell David what I've told you, he'll think he's going to die on the spot. But you've got to tell him he's forgiven — that he's not going to die. Tell him also that I will walk with him through everything that comes upon him because of his sin."

I believe Nathan spoke to David in a spirit of reconciliation — soft-spoken and respectful — as he told the story of the stolen lamb. He hoped David would see himself as the man in the story, bow his head and admit, "Oh, Nathan — you're talking about me."

Instead, David raged with indignation. And now I see Nathan walking slowly to a window, his heart broken. He turns sadly and says with grief in his quivering voice, "David — you're the man. You're the one who took another man's pet lamb. Look at all that God has done for you — all the blessings He's given you. The Lord was ready to give you all your heart's desires. But you've killed an innocent man — and you've taken his wife as your own. You have despised the Lord, David. And the enemies of God are rejoicing over what you did.

"I'm sorry to tell you this — but the sword is not going to leave your home. Your wives will be taken from you. And God will do all of this before Israel. You will be judged publicly. There are consequences to your sin."

God, in His love, had to make David see the utter horribleness of his sin. Then, suddenly, all of David's pent-up feelings poured out of him. He prayed out all the guilt, fears and sorrows of those ten long months: "Oh, Nathan, I've sinned against God!" It wasn't the prophet who was screaming — it was David. He felt wrath falling upon him — because God had exposed everything!

David never thought he'd gotten away with sin. On the contrary, he was a very troubled, guilt-ridden man. As you read Psalm 51, you hear him praying out all the fears he'd carried in his heart. He had witnessed what sin had done to Saul — and he was afraid it was happening to him!

• "...take not thy holy spirit from me" *(Psalm 51:11)*. David was afraid God had left him — just as He'd left Saul!

• "...renew a right spirit within me" *(verse 10)*. He knew an evil spirit had come upon Saul, and he didn't want that to happen to him.

• "Restore unto me... joy..." *(verse 12)*. David had lost all his joy and peace.

• "Cast me not away from thy presence..." *(verse 11)*. He had been hiding, afraid to come to the Lord's presence. He felt cast away completely!

David faced all of his fears. And now Nathan brought to him the message from God's heart: "...The Lord also hath put away thy sin; thou shalt not die" *(2 Samuel 12:13)*. It was time to be reconciled. The Lord missed David's fellowship and wanted him back!

God sees the terrible agony that sin brings to fallen people. He grieves over the way we run from Him when we're under sin's guilt. He knows all about our fear of being cast away — of being lost, of never being right again. And He gets no pleasure from seeing us writhe in agony over our sin. He doesn't sit by and say, "Let him suffer a little more. When he really feels the pain, then I'll come rushing in."

No! The Lord has been waiting all along for you to come back to Him and be forgiven. And after so long a time, He will no longer wait; He will make the first move. He will send somebody after you, who will come not to rebuke you but to reconcile you to God's heart. The Lord will tell you, "Yes, you hurt Me, you despised Me. You were impatient and ungrateful. But I want to forgive you. I want you back in My arms!"

Nathan told the king, "David, I've got good news for you. The Lord has forgiven you." David must have wondered, "But — how can I stand before a holy God?" The prophet answered, "You're not going to die. You're going to live."

"For thou, Lord, art good, and ready to forgive; and plenteous in mercy unto all them that call upon thee" *(Psalm 86:5)*. I don't pretend to understand the mercy and grace of God. It is completely beyond me. David was forgiven and restored — and Bathsheba bore him a son, whom God named Solomon: "...and the Lord loved him" *(2 Samuel 12:24)*. I ask you: How could this be? Who can comprehend such mercy?

The next thing we see is that David regained all his lost courage. He got his fight back. He responded to Joab's call to come against the city of Rabbah, and Israel won a great victory there. King David returned to Jerusalem in great honor. God had restored him completely!

Don't be mistaken: David suffered greatly. He paid a grave price. You see, he ended up paying those four lambs that he himself had set as restitution. Those lambs were Bathsheba's baby and three other sons — Ammon, Absalom and Adonijah. All of them died.

Yet, even as David suffered these judgments as the consequence of his sins, the Lord comforted him in his sorrow. When he reaped what he'd sown, the Spirit of God helped him through it all. After each trial, he was comforted.

When you repent of your sin and are broken before the Lord, He sees you through every step of the painful consequences. His mercy, grace and goodness enable you to bear it all with hope.

Two Final Questions for You:

1. How do you hate sin? In what tone of voice do you express your hatred for it? And is that hatred tempered with mercy?

2. Are you as tough on yourself as you are on others? "For he shall have judgment without mercy, that hath shewed no mercy; and mercy rejoiceth against judgment" *(James 2:13)*. If you have shown no mercy to others, you will be shown no mercy!

I realize that Jesus called the Pharisees snakes and vipers. And, yes, John the Baptist pointed out Herod's sin and called him a fox. The apostle Paul publicly rebuked sorcerers, and he named proud sinners by name. I agree that prophets must cry aloud, spare not, and show God's people their iniquities. But these words were spoken to people who didn't have repentant hearts — who had pharisaical attitudes and fierce pride.

This message, on the other hand, is about how God deals with sin and failure in those who are sorry, broken, repentant: "... Ye... have seen the end of the Lord; that the Lord is very pitiful, and of tender mercy" *(5:11)*.

If you've fallen, yet you have a repentant, broken spirit — it doesn't matter how badly you've failed God. He will come after you to reconcile you, because He sees your broken heart. "The sacrifices of God are a broken spirit: a broken and a contrite heart, O God, thou wilt not despise" *(Psalm 51:17)*. That is the difference!

Heavenly Father, help us all to recognize when the heart of a fallen brother or sister is repentant. And help us to forgive as You do — to seek full reconciliation and restoration for all of Your saints.

The Pain
Of God

20

God's Grief in Meting Out Justice

According to Scripture, we are never to think of God as a cold, unfeeling Father. Our God feels deeply! He is touchable. His heart can be moved upon. In fact, He is touched with the feelings of our infirmities *(see Hebrews 4:15)*.

God not only feels pain, but grieves as well. You remember that Jesus wept at Lazarus' tomb. Here is a picture of God in flesh weeping! It shows us that the Lord feels with us and weeps with us. After all, Jesus said, "...he that hath seen me hath seen the Father..." *(John 14:9)*.

We catch another clear glimpse of God's pain in the Garden of Gethsemane. Just hours before the guards came to deliver Jesus to the high priest, He wept so profusely and so deeply that blood was mixed with His tears. God was in pain over the sins of humankind!

Have you ever wondered why Jesus wept in the garden — why He had such pain in His heart? It wasn't because of the pain He would face on the Cross. No, Jesus wasn't longing to reject the cup. Rather, I believe Jesus was looking down all the years of humankind to the Second Coming. And as He looked through those years, He saw the unthinkable. He saw multitudes of people rejecting His free offer of full, complete salvation. And He saw the pain and suffering they faced as a result of their rejecting Him.

Jesus didn't wail, "I'm about to shed My blood and go through such pain — but you're going to reject Me. I'll get even with you on the Judgment Day. You'll have a payday coming!" No! Jesus was weeping over the multiplied millions yet to come — those who would know of His free offer of salvation, favor, blessing, unction, anointing — and yet would not avail themselves of any of it. Christ was weeping that so many were going to be lost, despite having a remedy so available to them.

This is the pain of God! It's the pain that humankind brings upon itself. Jesus didn't just carry our sins to the Cross. He also carried the pain of the whole world!

Here in New York City, we meet people everywhere who are nervous and depressed. We meet drug addicts, alcoholics and homeless people who sit outside the doors of our church. All these people have the gospel freely preached to them — and yet many reject it! In the garden, Jesus was picturing in His God-eyes the great masses of humanity and all their pain. And in that moment, it all was heaped upon Him — your pain, my pain, the pain of every person who rejects Him at any time.

Yet I also believe Jesus had sorrow of heart for another reason. He knew that people were going to mock Him, ridicule Him, make Him the song of drunkards. And He was pained because of the justice that would have to be meted out to all who denied His sacrifice!

When Christ said to His disciples, "...could ye not watch with me one hour?" *(Matthew 26:40)*, I believe it was out of pain. He wasn't rebuking them. Rather, He was pained because He knew their flesh was weak. And He knew what their weakness would bring down upon them. In the very next verse, Jesus says, "...the spirit indeed is willing, but the flesh is weak" *(verse 41)*. In His all-knowing eyes, Jesus foresaw the disciples forsaking Him and fleeing. He foresaw their emptiness and pain after rejecting Him, and their return to their former lives as fishermen. He knew that the events to follow would bring Peter to a denial of Him. Jesus saw this once-bold disciple running to the hills, crying, "How could I have denied Jesus? How could I have done such a horrible thing?"

So, when Jesus said to these men, "Could you not watch with Me?", He wasn't saying, "I need a pal during My trying times." No — He was God! He didn't need someone to stand by Him and encourage Him. Rather, Jesus was in pain for His disciples. He was saying, in essence, "If you don't watch with Me, you won't be prepared. You won't be able to handle what's coming!" He knew the apostasy that would spring up in their hearts because they were too lazy to gird themselves up. And the thought of their consequent suffering brought great pain to His heart.

Don't think for a moment that Jesus did not grieve over Judas. Nothing in His heart could simply dismiss that man, saying, "Oh, devil, go do your work." Rather, I believe Jesus wept inside as Judas walked out of the Upper Room to betray Him. Christ's all-knowing eyes foresaw that disciple casting thirty pieces of silver to the ground, crying, "I've betrayed the living God!" And surely Jesus felt Judas' grief as that tormented man went out to hang himself.

I want to share with you something the Lord recently revealed to my heart:

God Takes No Pleasure in Meting Out Justice!

Every time we sin against God, His justice demands that He chasten His children. Yet this is God's most painful work — to bring judgment upon those who break His laws! "For I have no pleasure in the death of him that dieth, saith the Lord God: wherefore turn yourselves, and live ye" *(Ezekiel 18:32)*. God says, "Do you think I receive pleasure when people die — even wicked people? Never! I get no pleasure from the downfall of any sinner."

Jesus took no pleasure in Judas' death. He didn't gloat, saying, "See what happens to traitors!" Nor does the Lord receive any pleasure from the death or destruction of drug pushers, abortion doctors, even murderers. He is not happy when anyone dies in sin. Yet how different we are from the Lord in this matter! We clasp our hands and say, "Thank You, Lord. You dealt with that evil." We feel none of God's pain when a sinner falls!

You may ask, "But doesn't God say in Proverbs 1:26, 'I also will laugh at your calamity'?" No! The context of this passage begins in verse 20. It reads, "Wisdom crieth without; she uttereth her voice in the streets ... saying, How long, ye simple ones, will ye love simplicty?..." *(verses 20-22)*. Wisdom is still speaking in verse 26, which reads, "I also will laugh at your calamity..."

It is wisdom — not God — that mocks the sinner. This passage is addressing those who cast aside all wisdom and mock its counsel. You see, there's a law involved — a fixed principle of God — that we call wisdom. If you cross the street when the light is red and are hit by a car, the wisdom present in that streetlight mocks your calamity. God could never laugh at the calamity of even the most wicked person. He cannot mock those who are being destroyed by their sins. On the contrary, He tells us He receives no pleasure from the death of any sinner.

Yet His wisdom cries out to everyone. It is crying out right now on the streets just outside Times Square Church. Those who should be hearing the voice of God — who instead are mocking that wisdom — will be mocked by wisdom on Judgment Day. At that time, wisdom will cry out, "How foolish you've been!" "Then they shall call upon me, but I will not answer; they shall seek me early, but they shall not find me" *(verse 28)*.

This same chapter in Proverbs also offers hope. It reveals God's heart in the final verse: "But whoso hearkeneth unto me shall dwell safely, and shall be quiet from fear of evil" *(verse 33)*.

We See Another Picture of God's Pain When Jesus Wept Over the City of Jerusalem.

"And when he was come near, he beheld the city, and wept over it, saying, If thou hadst known, even thou, at least in this thy day, the things which belong unto thy peace! But now they are hid from thine eyes. For the days shall come upon thee, that thine enemies shall cast a trench about thee, and compass thee round, and keep thee in on every side, and shall lay thee even with the ground, and thy children within thee; and they shall not leave in thee one stone upon another; because thou knewest not the time of thy visitation" *(Luke 19:41-44)*.

Who is weeping here? It's Jesus — God in flesh! He wasn't standing on some soapbox, pointing His finger and shouting, "One day an army will come and kill your wives and children!" No — Jesus was weeping as He prophesied. He was looking forty years ahead, to the time when Titus' army would invade Jerusalem, rape the city and destroy the temple. It would be a holocaust beyond all holocausts. And as Jesus foresaw this happening, He wept.

The inhabitants of Jerusalem shortly were going to reject Him — spit on Him, mock Him, rail against Him, curse His name, crucify Him. Yet here He was, weeping in pain over them — because God's justice demanded judgment! Justice was going to bring a heathen army into their streets — and men, women and children were going to be slain without mercy.

Yet I believe Jesus also was weeping over what Jerusalem could have experienced: a visitation of God. They could have had blessings, forgiveness, a new heart. But they rejected it all!

The next verse tells us why Jesus' pain was so great: "And he went into the temple, and began to cast them out that sold therein, and them that bought; saying unto them, It is written, My house is the house of prayer: but ye have made it a den of thieves" *(verses 45-46)*. Jesus went into the temple with a whip and drove out all the money changers. Why this serious scourging? He did it because He knew these were the very sins that were hastening the coming judgment!

Jesus was feeling the pain of that horrible future scene. He was hearing all the cries of the women who would have a knife stuck into their bellies. He was hearing all the screams of the children who would be trampled underfoot by Titus' army. And He was grieving as He saw stone after stone being pulled down from the temple. Jesus foresaw all of this and said, "Don't you money changers understand? What you're doing here is bringing down God's judgment!" God was in pain over His chosen people — because their sin was going to destroy them!

There had to be tears in Jesus' eyes as He snapped that whip. I don't believe a single stroke touched anyone in that temple. Instead, it struck tables and carts, snapping in the wind. He used the whip as a rod of love. It was His way of saying, "Wake up! You're forcing God to bring down on you what pains Him most."

Let me show you another glimpse of God's pain: "And the Lord said unto Moses...thy people, which thou broughtest out of the land of Egypt, have corrupted themselves...they have made them a molten calf, and have worshipped it, and have sacrificed thereunto...I have seen this people, and, behold, it is a stiffnecked people: Now therefore let me alone, that my wrath may wax hot against them, and that I may consume them...

"And Moses besought the Lord his God, and said, Lord, why doth thy wrath wax hot against thy people, which thou hast brought forth out of the land of Egypt with great power, and with a mighty hand? Wherefore should the Egyptians speak, and say, For mischief did he bring them out, to slay them in the mountains, and to consume them from the face of the earth? Turn from thy fierce wrath, and repent of this evil against thy people....And the Lord repented [changed His mind] of the evil which he thought to do unto his people" *(Exodus 32:7-14)*.

In reading this passage, many Christians mistakenly attribute more grace and mercy to Moses than to God. They think, "Moses is pleading for great mercy upon Israel, while God is ready to destroy them." Nothing could be further from the truth! There was only one reason Moses could pray as he did here: It was because He knew God's heart of mercy!

God was speaking here out of His justice — and justice demanded that the people be consumed. But Moses knew it would pain God too much to destroy His children. He knew God loved these people. So he pled, "Lord, I know that Your justice is crying out, and You have to proclaim it. These stiffnecked people should be wiped out. But I know something else, too, Lord. It's that You wouldn't be able to stand the pain if You did it! You may destroy 10,000 or 12,000 — but the more You destroy, the more pain You'll have. I know Your heart, God — and I know You can't destroy Israel, because You love her!"

The Bible says God "repented" — which means, He changed His mind about how He would judge Israel. He wasn't going to destroy them. Instead, the people would waste away in the wilderness. Yet God never removed His mercy from them. Although the people would continue to pain His heart for thirty-eight more years with their unbelief, the Lord would still protect them, lead them, feed them and clothe them to their dying day.

When I Think of What Job Went Through, I See How God's Heart Must Have Been Pained.

I wonder how many times the Lord saw Job and longed to say, "Enough! I can't let My servant undergo any more of this horrible pain. I've got to stop it!"

If you think Job suffered, you have to know how much God suffered with him. I imagine God saying, "Just make it through, Job, and I'll give back all you lost. Just hold steady, and I'll increase you one-and-a-half times." Finally, when Job's suffering was over, God said, "I'm going to double everything for you, Job. I'll give you twice as much as you had before!"

We see God's pain also when He had to mete out justice upon David for numbering Israel. God had commanded David not to number the people, so he would never be tempted to rely on the arm of the flesh. Yet David did just what the Lord had forbidden. And it pained God's heart: "And God was displeased with this thing; therefore he smote Israel" (1 *Chronicles 21:7*).

God had to judge David. The king had prided himself on having an abundance of mighty fighting men. So the Lord sent an angel to mete out His justice by slaying Israel by pestilence. Soon the proud people were dying like flies. David listened as messengers brought him awful reports — 10,000 dead in Hebron; 5,000 dead in Benjamin; 6,000 dead in Judah. The death toll just kept rising.

Before long, 70,000 Israelites were dead. The death angel had gone up and down the land, slaying people left and right. And now he was standing over Jerusalem, with his sword drawn, ready to strike. The remainder of David's mighty fighting men were on the brink of total destruction!

God was striking at the very heart of David's pride. He was trying to save this man — to rescue him from the enemy of his soul. And, Scripture tells us: "...Then David and the elders of Israel, who were clothed in sackcloth, fell upon their faces" *(verse 16)*. When David heard about all the deaths in Israel, he fell on his knees in repentance. He wailed, "Oh God, it's my fault! These people are guiltless. Please, Lord, spare them. Put Your judgment on me!"

God couldn't stand to feel David's pain any longer. Finally, He cried to the angel: "Enough! Put away your sword. The pain is too much for Me!" "And the Lord commanded the angel; and he put up his sword again into the sheath thereof" *(verse 27)*. It was as if God were saying, "If I allow justice to continue, I won't be able to stand David's awful pain. He'll die of a broken heart!"

Here is an incredible picture of God's heart of pain. David had grieved Him, and God's justice demanded chastening. But God didn't stand over David, gloating, "Have you learned your lesson yet?" No — David's tears had reached God's tender heart! The Lord was feeling David's pain, touched by the feeling of his infirmity. And He said, "Enough!"

When We Force God to Chasten Us and Judge Us for the Sins We Commit, We Cause Him a "Double Pain."

The first part of God's terrible "double pain" is when we sin in His presence, against His light and love. Yet it isn't just the sin itself that grieves God. It's that He knows the consequences of our sin will soon follow. God knows the price we're going to pay: Our sin is going to drive us to grief and misery! And that pains His heart greatly.

The second part of God's "double pain" is that our sin causes Him to keep His Word in judging us. He has to stand by like a loving Father and listen to our cries of anguish as He chastens us — all for the purpose of producing godly character in us.

Not long ago, I came to a crisis — to the end of my rope. I had been hearing slanderous things said about me and about an associate pastor who ministers with us at Times Square Church. It was awful, hurtful gossip. I couldn't believe people were saying some of the things they did. It all hurt me so badly.

After this had gone on for some time, I began to remind God of His Word: "A false witness shall not be unpunished, and he that speaketh lies shall perish" *(Proverbs 19:9)*. "...a liar giveth ear to a naughty [gossiping] tongue" *(17:4)*. "A talebearer revealeth secrets: but he that is of a faithful spirit concealeth the matter" *(11:13)*. "Whose hatred is covered by deceit, his wickedness shall be shewed before the whole congregation" *(26:26)*.

After some time, I cried out in despair: "Oh God, how long will You let this go on? The lies keep changing so much, I don't even know what they are from day to day. I can't fight it. You're my defender, Lord — and You say You will avenge Your people. But I don't see Your justice being meted out. Please, Lord — how much more must I take before You'll move?"

As I thought of all the slander coming against me, I began to think of other beleaguered pastors and servants. There are so many saints today — holy, righteous people — who are having to endure awful trials because evil words are being spoken against them by coworkers, family, even friends. "Why, Lord?" I prayed. "Where are Your righteous judgments? Why do You continue allowing Your people to be hurt? Why do You wait so long to bring about justice?"

The Lord answered, "David, I am merciful, long-suffering and slow to anger because it pains Me to mete out My justice. If you could feel My pain, you would never, ever, desire to see My judgment fall. You would understand why I wait so long to bring it down!" Then God showed me a frightful picture of the judgments He must send on those who sin against His Word. Awful things will befall those who continue in their sin of gossip and slander.

Yet the thought of divine retribution — of judgment falling on anyone — overwhelmed me. I cried out, "Oh, Lord, don't judge for my sake! Please, don't do this, even to those who have hurt me. Don't do it to justify me!" I was feeling God's pain — His reluctance to judge. And that pain continued in my heart for perhaps fifteen minutes.

Then the Lord spoke to me: "David, you know how painful it is to discipline your children, because you love them. It's the same for Me. It pains Me to mete out My judgment and chastening on those I love!"

Finally, God Allowed Me to See the Pain He Endured All the Times He Had to Chasten Me!

I can remember vividly four or five instances of very heavy chastening from the Lord. In those times I would say, "Oh, God, this is painful! I don't ever want to go through anything like this again."

And now God was saying to me, "David, I didn't want to go through it again, either. It pained Me to stand by and allow you to hurt. I did it all unwillingly. I took no pleasure in it. It was a grief to My heart. And yet it had to be done — because I love you!"

God has shown me the hard way that I am never to rejoice over anyone's chastening. Yet may the Lord have mercy on those Christians who rejoice in the chastening of another: "Rejoice not when thy enemy falleth, and let not thine heart be glad when he stumbleth" *(Proverbs 24:17)*.

Not only must you never be glad when you see God meting out His judgments. You also must feel God's pain as He metes it out! You simply cannot rejoice in the presence of a Master who weeps while He whips, before a Christ who's heartbroken. God's judgments on others ought to break your heart. Seeing it ought to make you cry out, "Oh God, enough! Please — have Your angel put up his sword."

"Now no chastening for the present seemeth to be joyous, but grievous: nevertheless afterward it yieldeth the peaceable fruit of righteousness unto them which are exercised thereby" *(Hebrews 12:11)*. God is talking about His own heart here, as well as ours. His chastenings are not joyous to Him, but grievous and painful.

Yet when God moves in to judge, He hovers over His children as He chastens them. As He brings one lash after another, He waits to see if the last lash brought a tear. He looks for even the slightest sign of sorrow or repentance. And He lets up at the first inkling of one! He longs to say, "Enough — no more! It pains Me too much."

Beloved, you must come to grips with this matter of God's pain. You have to chasten yourself — to bring your thoughts into captivity, and say, "Oh, Lord, let me pray for my enemies — for those who are trying to hurt me!" God loves the most wicked, vile sinner on the street. And if He loves that person, how much more does He love the Christian who hurts you and has made himself your enemy?

Perhaps you have an idea by now of how far we are from the heart of God. We have so much yet to learn of His heart. No, He does not delight in judgment. He takes no pleasure in the destruction of the wicked, nor in His chastening of His children. On the contrary, it pains Him awfully.

Let me tell you what the Lord delights in: "Who is a God like unto thee, that pardoneth iniquity, and passeth by the transgression of the remnant of his heritage? He retaineth not his anger for ever, because he delighteth in mercy. He will turn again, he will have compassion on us; he will subdue our iniquities; and thou wilt cast all their sins into the depths of the sea" *(Micah 7:18-19)*.

Thank God for His great compassion, available to all. He delights in mercy!

21 Seven Women Shall Lay Hold of One Man

The Glory of God in His Church in the Last Days

According to the prophet Isaiah, two kinds of churches will exist in the last days. And I believe these two types of churches are already in existence. We do not have to speculate about what they will be like — because Isaiah gives us a very clear, prophetic description of both.

Isaiah 4 opens with a concise and tragic description of what I call "the church of forgiveness only": "And in that day seven women shall take hold of one man, saying, We will eat our own bread, and wear our own apparel: only let us be called by thy name, to take away our reproach" *(Isaiah 4:1)*.

This is one of the most misunderstood verses in all the Bible. Some commentators suggest this happened during the reign of King Ahaz, when enemy armies came in and slew 120,000 men. But that is only speculation. There is no evidence that this verse has ever been fulfilled at any time in history. There is nothing to suggest that, even in Ahaz' time, seven women "took hold of one man."

Then the Holy Spirit spoke something to me concerning this passage. To my knowledge, you won't find what I have to say in any commentary. Yet, I see this entire chapter in Isaiah as one of the clearest, most unmistakable prophecies about how the church will look just prior to the coming of the Lord.

Like many Christians, I believe without a doubt we are living in the last days. Jesus' life, death and resurrection instituted the beginning of this period. On the day of Pentecost, Peter stood up and said, "...this is that which was spoken by the prophet Joel; and it shall come to pass that in the last days, saith God, I shall pour out of my Spirit upon all flesh..." *(Acts 2:16-17)*. Peter was saying, "These are the last days. God's outpoured Spirit is proof of it!"

Likewise, the apostle Paul wrote, "Now all these things happened unto them for ensamples: and they are written for our admonition, upon whom the ends of the world are come" *(1 Corinthians 10:11)*. Paul knew he was living in the last days. And to me, there is no question that we are living in the very last of the last days!

In Revelation 1, John sees Jesus standing in the midst of seven golden candlesticks: "...and his eyes were as a flame of fire; and his feet like unto fine brass, as if they burned in a furnace..." *(Revelation 1:14-15)*. John was smitten by this frightful sight — and he fell on his face in fear! Remember, this was the same John who once leaned his head on Jesus' bosom. And now, as he sees the Lord in this state, he is utterly stricken.

Scripture makes it very clear that these seven candlesticks represent seven churches — that is, the entire religious body of believers in the last days, all that we call "the church." And Jesus walks among these seven candlesticks, His piercing eyes searching the seven churches.

Scripture Always Refers to the Church in the Feminine Gender, in Many Cases as a Bride.

The seven would-be brides Isaiah mentions are clearly a type of the characteristics of many in the last-days church. Dispensationalists would say the seven churches of Revelation represent seven church ages. I am saying that I believe you will find the characteristics of all seven churches in all churches through the ages. Even in "blessed" churches that are complimented by the Lord — such as those of the spirit of Smyrna or Philadelphia — you will find mixture and characteristics that God hates.

These seven would-be brides are seeking to lay hold of one man, whom I take to be Christ. Yet these brides are not interested in loving Him. On the contrary, they have only one thing on their minds — the removal of their reproach! "...We will eat our own bread, and wear our own apparel: only let us be called by thy name, to take away our reproach" *(Isaiah 4:1)*.

I see here seven women approaching a man and saying, "You don't have to provide food for us. We'll take care of our own bread. And you don't have to provide any clothes for us. We'll provide our own robes." You don't have to be very deep spiritually to see the significance here. After all, "...sin is a reproach to any people" *(Proverbs 14:34)* — reproach of guilt! Sure, these women want to be the bride of Christ — but only on their own terms. They want an arrangement without intimacy, love or devotion.

The number seven is used in regard to these brides to remind us that in every church system there are such people. They attempt to "take hold of one man" — Christ — only to get relief from the guilt and condemnation of their sin. They don't want intimacy with Him. They want nothing more than forgiveness — to have the reproach of sin removed. I call this "the church of forgiveness only."

Please understand — I believe in justification by faith. It is by faith alone in Jesus Christ that we are saved. We are justified by His finished work on the Cross. And because of this we can live without guilt, fear or condemnation. This is the great meaning of the gospel. But if that is all you ever want of Jesus — if you don't want to be intimate with Him, to live on Him as the bread from heaven, and to come under His fiery gaze, which searches and convicts — then merely being forgiven is your entire focus.

I was in a town some time ago to speak at a meeting, and I passed a big amphitheatre advertising a Christian rock concert. I stopped to watch the kids set up their equipment for the show. Unbelievably, some of them wore T-shirts with a message that included a four-letter word. It read: " — Guilt!" I can't even quote the word to you here — and these were so-called Christians. Apparently, all they wanted was to get rid of guilt.

Many pastors and evangelists today preach a "forgiveness only" message — and that's all they preach. They cry, "Come, accept Jesus and enjoy a life without guilt, fear or condemnation. Just believe and confess, and you will be His bride. You can walk your own walk and talk your own talk!"

I do not believe we are saved by the law — but the law has a purpose. It is a mirror that holds up before us the commands and demands of God. And when we see we can't fulfill those commands, we are driven to Jesus. But God help us if we don't hear this kind of preaching!

Many churches have replaced the Word with ten-minute skits that contain no convicting gospel at all. There is no preaching of holiness, no word of separation from the world, nothing about sanctification or dealing with besetting sins. Yet the leaders defend themselves by saying, "People don't want to hear a hard gospel. We're simply giving what they need to cope in these troubled times."

Indeed, the Bible says of those who attend such churches, "...after their own lusts shall they heap to themselves teachers, having itching ears" (*2 Timothy 4:3*). These churchgoers are saying, "You don't have to feed us, Jesus. We can provide our own bread. We have our own gospel!"

All across America churches are feeding their sheep the same pabulum — a cotton-candy, "feel-good" gospel. These places are packed with thousands who have merely repeated a sinner's prayer, saying, "I believe." But the Bible says even the demons believe — and they tremble at the very thought of God!

Few of these people have been provoked to deny self and embrace the Cross — to die to all self and ungodliness. They don't want the burden of the Lord. They don't weep over the sins of Zion. They don't feel God's brokenness over the wickedness and compromise in these last days. Instead, they say, "...We will eat our own bread..." *(Isaiah 4:1)*. They don't want the bread that comes down from heaven — that is, Jesus Christ crucified, resurrected and seated at the right hand of the Father. He is the bread of separation — of holiness, purity, self-denial. But these say, "We will provide our own bread" — usually a gospel of permissive love, with no reproof, no smiting conviction.

Beloved, the Bible says their bread is defiled! The prophet Hosea called it "...the bread of mourners; all that eat thereof shall be polluted: for their bread for their soul shall not come into the house of the Lord" *(Hosea 9:4)*.

Yet the true house of God — the holy remnant church — will have nothing to do with this man-made bread. They know that most of it is pop psychology, with a few verses of Scripture sprinkled in to make it sound religious. It sounds good — but it leaves the sheep starving.

"...We will...wear our own apparel..." *(Isaiah 4:1)*. The "church of forgiveness only" says, "Listen, Lord, you don't have to provide us with clothes. We'll make our own and clothe ourselves." There are no robes of righteousness for this people — no holiness preaching, no reproof, nothing "negative." There is no separation from the world, no forsaking of all others, no cleaving to their husband. Instead, they say, "We will dress as we please!"

These would-be brides have no desire to submit to the authority of a husband. They don't want to live under the same roof with him. Nor are they interested in his needs. They don't want to know his heart or care about his concerns. They are totally consumed with self — with having their reproach removed!

So they have as little contact with him as possible — maybe one hour a week. Is there any intimacy, love, companionship, submission in this arrangement? No! Is there any clinging to Him? No! Do they desire to spend hours in His presence — in secret, sharing His very heart? No — they spend most of their time with "other loves," such as sports, TV, theater, pleasures of all kinds.

Without exception, such Christians always turn to a self-centered gospel. A man who was visiting our church recently from a large southern city approached me before one of our services. He said, "Brother David, I just had to leave my church. We sent a whole delegation across the country to a congregation where a 'great revival' was supposedly taking place. Everyone came back excited about it all — but something didn't sit right in my spirit. I didn't feel I could be a part of this 'new thing.' So I had to leave. Tell me — what is happening to our church? Where is the discernment? Why isn't our pastor intimate with Jesus? Why doesn't anyone seem to know God's heart? Why this sudden introduction of an 'imported' revival?"

Indeed, it is out of intimacy with Jesus that we receive discernment, direction, a knowing of what is right and wrong, of what is holy and pure. Intimacy with Christ gives us a firmness wherein we are not tossed to and fro by every wind and wave of doctrine. Yet right now there is such foolishness going on, with no discernment at all. It is man-made bread — it is not of God — and it grieves His heart!

Now, let me move on to the other church of which Isaiah speaks:

The Next Church Isaiah Saw Emerging in the Last Days Is Called the Church of God's Glory.

"In that day shall the branch of the Lord be beautiful and glorious, and the fruit of the earth shall be excellent and comely for them that are escaped of Israel" *(Isaiah 4:2)*. Who is the branch being spoken of here? All through the Old Testament, the branch that is mentioned as coming forth is none other than Jesus Christ, the Lord of glory.

According to Isaiah, there will be a church to whom He will appear beautiful and glorious, excellent and comely. Their motive toward Him will not be one of simply having a reproach removed. No — they will be passionately in love with a Man whom they see as desirous, glorious, excellent.

Right now, there is on the earth a remnant church that desires nothing but Christ. This remnant is but a small portion, perhaps a tenth, of what we think of as the church. I don't believe that the church which will please God in these last days has to be one of multiple thousands of believers. On the contrary, much of what we see taking place in megachurches today does not represent God's heart at all. No — the heart of the Lord is in those churches where Jesus is the center of attention — where everything is based upon the preaching of the Cross and built around the presence and character of Christ. God's heart is revealed to those churches that are in love with His Son — where people focus their all on Him!

These are the ones Isaiah refers to as being "...escaped of Israel" *(same verse)*. He says of them: "When the Lord shall have washed away the filth of the daughters of Zion, and shall have purged the blood of Jerusalem from the midst thereof by the spirit of judgment, and by the spirit of burning" *(verse 4)*. God has sent His Spirit into the world in these last days to reprove of sin and ungodliness. Many who hear His burning, judging, convicting Word will flee into Babylon — that is, into worldliness — and will be carried away into bondage. Only a remnant will remain. And Isaiah is saying here that God will bring these few through "...the spirit of judgment, and...the spirit of burning" *(same verse)*.

Indeed, the last-day church that will be filled with God's glory is more than just a forgiven church. It is a holy church — one that has been purged by the consuming fire of God's convicting Word. Holiness and purity characterize its people. Isaiah adds, "...left in Zion...shall be called holy, even every one that is written among the living in Jerusalem" *(verse 3)*.

You may say, "But, Brother Dave, it's clear this refers only to ancient Israel. Jerusalem and Zion are named here — and that pinpoints this prophecy to the Jewish population of Jerusalem at a certain time in history." No! It is much more than that. Consider what the Bible says elsewhere: "But Jerusalem which is above is free, which is the mother of us all" *(Galatians 4:26)*. "But ye are come unto mount Sion, and unto the city of the living God, the heavenly Jerusalem, and to an innumerable company of angels" *(Hebrews 12:22)*.

There is a new, heavenly Jerusalem — a spiritual city that is the mother of all believers: "...the city of my God, which is new Jerusalem, which cometh down out of heaven from my God..." *(Revelation 3:12)*. This is what the prophet Isaiah is talking about — a heavenly-minded remnant whom the Lord will bring through His consuming fire! When you believe on the Lord Jesus Christ, you are born into Zion. Your name is recorded there. And those who have fully given their heart to Jesus — who are intimate with Him and belong to Him — are known in Zion as sons and daughters of God.

The best evidence here that Isaiah is referring to the last-days church is found in verse 5: "And the Lord will create upon every dwelling place of mount Zion, and upon her assemblies, a cloud and smoke by day, and the shining of a flaming fire by night: for upon all the glory shall be a defence"

(Isaiah 4:5). Isaiah is predicting God will create a new pillar and cloud to cover His people!

Now, we know that when Isaiah prophesied this, the pillar and cloud in the wilderness had already passed away. Obviously, this was something that had yet to be created — a new thing. This cloud has to do with direction and comfort — with preservation from all evil and terror, and with guidance. And this means God's last-days, holy remnant people will have clear direction. They will not be confused. When everything around them is spinning in different directions and falling apart, they will have a cloud and a pillar of fire to lead them!

Israel had but one tabernacle — and they had one cloud and one pillar of fire. But today we all are tabernacles of the Holy Spirit — and God has provided a cloud and a pillar of fire for every one of us. Every individual — and every repentant, holy congregation — has the cloud of the Spirit to lead them by day and a pillar of Spirit-fire to lead them by night.

God is saying, in other words, "I'm going to see you through, no matter what your situation. Even in the worst storm of your life, you'll have clear direction from Me. I will give you a pillar of fire to lead you — as surely as I did Israel in the wilderness!"

Yet right now in America, there is a raging storm of confusion in the church. So many people are confused. There is little discernment — and yet there is much false doctrine, foolishness and flesh. Our ministry receives calls and letters from people all over the country who say, "What's going on? I can't figure it out. Our pastor is bringing in strange teachings, and it's tearing our church in two. Is this of God or not? Please tell us. We don't know what to believe anymore!"

My son Gary, who pastors a church in Denver, called me recently. He said, "Dad, I went to a meeting recently where things just went crazy. It almost frightened the leaders. They had to get up and say, 'All right, let's bring this all back to Jesus.' At the beginning they'd said it was a move of the Holy Ghost. But then they had to say, 'Let's bring it all back to Jesus.' Well, where had they been, if they had to bring everything back to Jesus?"

Beloved, this kind of thing is frightening. The focus in that meeting never should have been anywhere but on Jesus!

Often people come to me and say, "Brother Wilkerson, you've got to go with us. A great revival has broken out in such-and-such a church. It's marvelous. People are falling down left and right."

Now, I'm not against manifestations. I worked for five years with

Kathryn Kuhlman, and I saw people in her meetings fall under the power of the Holy Ghost in a way that was absolutely awesome. There was no manipulation involved; it was a genuine work of the Spirit. But if people want to tell me a great move of God is going on somewhere today, my first question will be: "Is God's Word being preached there with consuming fire? Are people falling under conviction for sin? Is the cry of the people there for the purging of the spirit of this world? Is holiness the result? Is there a strong message of reproof? Does it drive people to Jesus? Does everything focus on Him? Is Christ the sum of it all? Is there a new compassion for lost souls? Are hardened sinners repenting?"

That is the work of the Holy Ghost! He comes to reprove the world of sin, righteousness and judgment. So, if you're going to tell me the Holy Ghost has come down, then these things had better be happening. If not, then judge it for what it is — flesh!

The Holy Remnant Church Is Led Completely By the Holy Spirit!

The Lord has a people in these confusing times who are not confused. They are so given to Jesus — so in love with Him, so open to the reproof of His Spirit, so separated from the wickedness of this age — that they know the ways and workings of the Holy Spirit. They know the difference between what is pure and holy, and what is fleshly and foolish. Wherever the cloud moves, they follow!

"...for upon all the glory shall be a defence" *(Isaiah 4:5)*. The original Hebrew here reads: "Over all shall be a covering of glory." This means, in essence, "Over each of these remnant people, and all of these holy remnant assemblies, there will be a hiding place, a blanket, a covering. And that covering is the glory of God!"

You may remember from Exodus 40 that a cloud of glory covered the tabernacle in the wilderness: "Then a cloud covered the tent of the congregation, and the glory of the Lord filled the tabernacle. And Moses was not able to enter into the tent of the congregation, because the cloud abode thereon, and the glory of the Lord filled the tabernacle" *(Exodus 40:34-35)*.

Read also what happened in Solomon's tabernacle, when he dedicated the temple: "Now when Solomon had made an end of praying, the fire came down from heaven, and consumed the burnt offering and the sacrifices; and the glory of the Lord filled the house. And the priests could not enter into the house of the Lord, because the glory of the Lord had filled the Lord's house" *(2 Chronicles 7:1-2)*.

Beloved, every time the tabernacle was in order — every time it was completed and prepared according to God's design — His glory came down and filled it. Now, here in Isaiah 4, we are promised that in the last days the Lord will create a glory that covers His remnant church. The very glory of God is going to fill every heart and cover every house. We will worship under the canopy of God's glory!

What is this glory? It is none other than the manifested presence of Jesus Christ, God's Son. Jesus is the fullness of the Father's glory. "In that day shall the branch of the Lord be beautiful and glorious..." *(Isaiah 4:2)*. "...his Son...being the brightness of his glory..." *(Hebrews 1:2-3)*. The glory can't get any brighter than Christ manifesting Himself to you!

The word manifested means "to lay hold of by the hand." In other words, when Jesus' presence fills a place, it is so real, so evident, that your spiritual hands can touch it, your spiritual eyes can see it. It is as real as the air you breathe! Likewise, the kind of revival I want to see is the kind where the presence of Jesus becomes so powerful and overwhelming — so beautiful and glorious — that the "fruit" (or conversions) will be excellent! *(see Isaiah 4:2)*. Already we've seen the beginnings of this in our services at Times Square Church — with people streaming forward, weeping and being broken before the Lord.

If people are going to fall down, I want to see them falling under the conviction of the Holy Ghost. And the vision I want them to receive is a renewed vision of Jesus. And the manifestation I want them to have is their rising from the floor as a new creature in Christ. That's when people ought to be able to laugh. When the consuming fire has done its purging work, and all sin is gone, and there has been a heartrending — then we should be able to laugh all night long. Let the joy of the Lord come then!

I would not want to attend a church where the glory of God has departed. The psalmist testifies that when the ark was captured by the Philistines, "(God) delivered his strength into captivity, and his glory into the enemy's hand" *(Psalm 78:61)*. When the priest Eli's daughter-in-law gave birth, her son was named Ichabod, meaning "...the glory [of the Lord] is departed..." *(1 Samuel 4:21)*. Our testimony should be, "If I can't have the presence of Jesus, I don't want to live. He has to be my guide, my cloud, my pillar of fire!"

Why Is the Glory of God So Important Today?
What Purpose Is the Glory of His Presence?

The answer is found in Isaiah 4: "And there shall be a tabernacle for a shadow in the daytime from the heat, and for a place of refuge, and for a covert from storm and from rain" *(Isaiah 4:6)*. First, the glory of God's presence will be our shelter from the heat. The Hebrew word for heat means "drought, desolation, barrenness." It is a type of God's judgment on an evil society.

In Revelation 16, the fourth angel of judgment is given power "...to scorch men with fire. And men were scorched with great heat, and blasphemed the name of God..." *(Revelation 16:8-9)*. Right now, God is turning up the heat. And it is going to get even hotter, with judgments on all sides. But the glory of God will be our cover: "And there shall be a tabernacle for a shadow in the daytime from the heat..." *(Isaiah 4:6)*. We won't feel the heat! Instead we'll rest in the cool shadow of Jesus' wings.

Second, the glory of God is our defense, our covering: "...and for a place of refuge, and for a covert from storm and from rain" *(verse 6)*. Already we are seeing the rain — not just of Holy Spirit outpourings, but of God's judgments. The storm clouds are gathering — but, thank God, there will be a covering over His holy remnant church!

Perhaps you are saying, "I have no 'glory church' I can attend. All I can find are man-centered churches. Where is my covering from the heat and storm?" Your dwelling place is the glory of God in your own heart! If Jesus is present in you, manifesting Himself to you, then you are covered in full. If you turn your heart and eyes on Him —allowing God's Word to reprove, convict and correct you — He will manifest Himself to you. He has promised it!

"He that hath my commandments, and keepeth them, he it is that loveth me: and he that loveth me shall be loved of my Father, and I will love him, and will manifest myself to him" *(John 14:21)*. God says, "I will be there with you. It doesn't matter how bad it gets. I'm going to see you through. I will never leave you nor forsake you!"

Trusting Fully in God, a nd Not in Self

I believe that justification by faith is the foundational truth of Christianity. You can't know true rest and peace until you are convinced you can never be made right in God's eyes by your own works of righteousness.

If you don't understand the perfect righteousness of Christ that is yours by faith, you'll lead a life of toil and sweat. You'll spend your days trying to please God through some kind of legalistic, hopeless attempt to establish your own righteousness. But the truth is, you'll never have any righteousness to bring to the Lord!

No doubt you're familiar with the passage in Isaiah that says all our righteousness is as filthy rags in God's sight. This doesn't mean God despises our good works — not at all. God does want our righteous acts, and we should do good works. But if you think your good works merit your salvation — that they allow you to stand holy before God — then they are nothing but filthy rags. And you are headed for shipwreck.

Of course, you may feel good because of the good works you do. You probably enjoy a moment of victory whenever you resist temptation. And there probably are days when you think you have overcome one of your pet passions. You feel righteous, and that God's favor is on you.

But the next day you fail — you fall back into a sin — and suddenly you lose all your joy. You think the Lord is angry with you. You wonder if you have lost your salvation. You think, "I'll never make it" — and you end up hiding from God.

It is a roller-coaster ride of emotional highs and lows — of up-and-down, hot-and-cold, sin-and-confess-and-sin-and-confess — according to how good or bad you think you have been on any particular day. It's a life of misery — because you're trying to please God in your flesh.

Beloved, no righteousness of the flesh will ever stand before God. Even the best people among us — the most moral, godly saints — have all failed miserably and fallen short of God's glory. None of us can ever be accepted in the Father's eyes by our good works. We are accepted by Him only as we are in Christ!

"...for ye are all one in Christ Jesus" *(Galatians 3:28)*. When we turn to Jesus with saving, self-emptying faith, we become one in Christ. Being "in Christ" means God credits Jesus' righteousness to us. All our sins are washed away because of His work, not ours.

Furthermore, we not only are one in Him, but we are complete in Him as well. At the Cross our old man — with all its fleshly lusts and desires, all its self-righteousness, all its strivings — was done away with in God's eyes. God said, "I am finished with the old man. He is nailed to the Cross. From now on, only one Man can stand before Me — a perfectly righteous Man — Jesus Christ. And all who are one in Him are forgiven, accepted — counted as righteous in My sight."

Unless You Grasp This Foundational Truth, You Cannot Overcome in These Last Days!

We are justified, made right in God's sight, by our faith in the work Jesus did on the Cross. You see, God accepts nothing less than perfect righteousness. And there is only one perfect righteousness — the righteousness of Jesus Christ. Only He perfectly fulfilled all the demands of the law. Only He satisfied the justice of God regarding sin.

I thank God for all good, clean, moral, faithful people in the body of Christ — folks who don't cheat, lie, steal, drink, smoke, use drugs, gamble, ogle pornography, or gossip. All Christians ought to live this way. But none of these things will stand on Judgment Day! We can't count on any of them to obtain favor or acceptance with God. Yet, sadly, millions of people think they'll stand before God on the goodness of their lives. No! We all have to understand this truth: We can be justified only by faith in the work Jesus has done on the Cross!

Having said that, however, let me tell you the rest of the story. If you go no further than justification by faith — if your doctrine ends at saying, "I am made the righteousness of Christ by faith" — then you are in grave danger! Here is where many Christians fail. They say, "I am the righteousness of Christ." No — we are not the righteousness of Christ. We have had the righteousness of Christ reckoned to us! We have no righteousness in ourselves; there is no good thing in us.

The perfect righteousness of Christ is not infused or poured into us.

Rather, we are accounted righteous in God's eyes because of Jesus. Christ's righteousness is credited to our account. God imputes Christ's righteousness to us. This righteousness is not something that is in us. Rather, it is only in Christ. Yet when God looks at us, He sees us only as being in Christ — as perfectly righteous!

When Paul First Preached Justification by Faith, He Was Falsely Accused of Preaching A Permissive Gospel.

As the apostle Paul preached this revelation of being justified by the perfect righteousness of Christ, it was said he was preaching a permissive lifestyle. People pointed out that if they were saved, forgiven, accepted and accounted righteous all by faith in Christ, then they all should go out and sin more. The reasoning was, "God can show forth even more grace — and He will get even more glory."

Paul cried, "That's slander! It's not what I'm saying at all." In later years, the truth he preached became further perverted by many who used it as an excuse to continue in sin. Out of this came a doctrine called antinomianism. This word means, literally, "anti-law," or, "without restraint." It is a doctrine with no restrictions. Exponents of antinomianism value being free in Christ. They say, "I have complete liberty in Christ. I have no bondage, no guilt, no condemnation — because Jesus paid it all for me. He is my satisfaction with God, so that now the Father sees only Jesus when He looks at me. I am safe, eternally saved — so I can do as I please!"

One of the leading theologians of the doctrine of antinomianism was a man named Dr. Crisp. Following are some passages from the heart of his doctrine:

"God's love is not at all dependent upon anything in me, so that love will never vary on account of my sinning; and for this reason, when I sin, suppose by adultery or murder, God ever considers me as one with His own Son, who has fulfilled all righteousness for me. And as He is 'always well pleased' with Him, so with me, for I am 'bone of His bone and flesh of His flesh.' There are no lengths, then, I may not run, nor any depths I may not fall into, without displeasing Him; as David did, who in spite of his repeated backslidings did not lose his character as a man after God's heart. I may murder with him, I may worship Ashtaroth with Solomon, deny Christ with Peter, rob with Onesimus, commit incest with the Corinthians, without forfeiting either the divine favor or the kingdom of God....

"Jesus Christ by one offering 'perfected' me — who am 'sanctified' in all my sins. In Him I am complete in all my iniquities.... I believe God will overrule my sin, whether it be adultery, murder, or incest, for His glory and my good...."

The doctrine of antinomianism sounds abhorrent to any true believer. Yet Christianity today is rife with people living in this very kind of "fool's paradise." They claim they are made the righteousness of Christ. They boast they are eternally redeemed. Yet they have never forsaken their sins. They drink, smoke, carouse, sleep around — and all the while they say, "I'm saved, because Jesus is my righteousness! It's all settled by faith. So it doesn't matter what I do." Such people are enslaved to their old corruptions. They are still "of the world" — living in pleasure, polluted by the spirit of this age, blinded and deceived by sin.

Indeed, many Christians hear grace preaching — sermons on the perfect righteousness of Christ that is available by faith — and yet it gives them a false sense of comfort. They continue in their sin, telling themselves, "Maybe my sin is not so bad. Maybe Jesus is my righteousness to the point that God will overlook it."

No! Such people have sinned despite the grace of God. Paul says they have abused the message of grace!

There Is Always a Risk in Preaching a Message of Grace.

The risk in preaching grace is that people will abuse it, as they did with Paul — slanderously reporting that the more we sin, the more God's grace can be manifested among us. Such a doctrine is dangerous, because it omits something vital — something central to the gospel!

Let me give you the heart of the true grace message: It is not a permissive gospel — but one that teaches holiness: "For that grace of God that bringeth salvation hath appeared to all men, teaching us that, denying ungodliness and worldly lusts, we should live soberly, righteously, and godly, in this present world; looking for that blessed hope, and the glorious appearing of the great God and our Savior Jesus Christ" *(Titus 2:11-13)*.

According to Paul, we are not walking in grace until we have broken from wordly corruptions. Unless we are endeavoring through the power of the Holy Spirit to lead godly and righteous lives, looking for the Lord's coming in our every waking moment, then we do not know God's grace.

The majority of Christians want forgiveness — but that's all. They don't want to be delivered from this present world, because they love it. They are attached to their sins, not wanting to give up the pleasures of this earth. So they cling to a doctrine that says, "I can live as I please — as long as I say, 'I believe!'"

They don't want to hear about obedience, repentance, self-denial, picking up their cross, taking on the yoke or burden of Christ. They would rather live in this world without restraint, thinking they have a Savior who will forgive them in the end. They want simply to be excused on Judgment Day — to have all their iniquities overlooked. They expect Jesus to open up the pearly gates, put His arms around them and lead them down a golden street to their reserved mansion — even though they've never broken from the spirit of this world!

Paul writes, "And be not conformed to this world: but be ye transformed by the renewing of your mind, that ye may prove what is that good, and acceptable, and perfect will of God" *(Romans 12:2)*. We are to break from this world completely — and be conformed to Christ alone!

Jesus justifies us through faith for a purpose: It is to embolden and empower us to resist the devil and overcome the world, in the power of God's Spirit. Yes, Jesus died for us so that we could have eternal life; that is truly wonderful. But He also died so we could enjoy deliverance in and from this present evil world!

"...Jesus Christ, who gave himself for our sins, that he might deliver us from this present evil world, according to the will of God and our Father" *(Galatians 1:3-4)*. "Who gave himself for us, that he might redeem us from all iniquity, and purify unto himself a peculiar people, zealous of good works" *(Titus 2:14)*.

There Is a Complex Theological Problem That Has Divided Christianity for Centuries.

A centuries-old theological question still rages today. That is: "What is God's part in our salvation, and what is our part?" It is a question of faith versus works.

One school of thought, called Calvinism, says Christ has done a finished work, so that no further work is required. The other camp, called Arminianism, says we are justified so that we may do good works through the power of the Holy Spirit. One camp quotes Galatians, stating, "Paul says the gospel is by faith alone, without works." The other camp points to James, saying, "James states that faith without works is dead. We're to give evidence of our faith in our actions."

In truth, both of these positions are right. There is no contradiction between them. Here is what is really being said:

1. Works will not justify or earn salvation for anyone.

2. Those who are zealous to do good works prove they have the kind of faith that justifies.

These are both wonderful, life-giving, scriptural truths about the nature of faith. Yet, the fact is, not all faith justifies. Not all faith is a faith that saves. Let me explain:

Since Times Square Church was founded nine years ago, thousands have walked down the aisles here, stood at the altar, prayed a sinner's prayer and said, "Lord, I believe. Save me!" But the majority of them went back to their seats and back to their homes unsaved. They returned in the same condition in which they came.

Many Christians say they believe in justification by faith. Yet merely saying the words, "I believe," does not justify them. After all, the Bible says the demons believe and tremble. Such people have not brought to the Lord a saving, genuine faith.

If you were to go into the streets and ask people at random, "Do you believe Jesus was the Son of God — that He came to this earth to minister — that He was crucified and resurrected?", the vast majority of people would answer, "Yes — I believe all of that." But they are not saved! Merely giving mental assent to those things does not constitute a saving faith. It is not a faith that justifies!

The church of Jesus Christ desperately needs some plain talk about faith. We simply are too glib about it. We offer faith to people who are not ready for it. We present it as if it were a first installment on a new car. In doing this, we downgrade faith to something no more valuable than a prize in a box of Cracker Jack!®

The church's concept of faith has been corrupted by our American culture. People in this country have been feeding on a demonic gospel of self-esteem, self-worth, self-help. We've been told, "Believe in yourself." Then add to that our obsession with "instant everything" — instant meals, instant drinks, instant information, instant gratification. Now, in turn, churches offer a demonic diet of self-will and self-trust. Preachers say, "Just give mental assent to God's promises. You'll get instant heaven, instant holiness, instant happiness!"

This has produced a temporary, false faith. People today are running to God's altar with no real conviction, saying, "Jesus saved me. I believe!" But they don't have true faith. What they have is presumption!

You Cannot Trust in God Until You Quit Trusting in Yourself.

Paul did not speak of having faith until he had lost all confidence in his flesh. He took all that he knew — all his education, self-confidence, abilities, doctrines and zeal — and cast them aside as dung. He spoke of faith only after he had said, "I have no confidence in my flesh!"

The same is true for us. We don't have saving faith until we come to the end of believing that someone or something other than Jesus can save us. Before anyone is capable of true faith, he must come to a sense of how lost, helpless and utterly hopeless he is.

You may object, saying, "Almost every time Jesus performed a miracle, He told people, 'Only believe!'" Yet in each instance, He said this to people who had come to the end of all hope — who had lost faith in everything else. This includes the father whose son was cast into the fire by demons. It also includes Jairus, whose twelve-year-old daughter had died. Their faith was born out of the knowledge that nothing else in the world was of any use. They had committed everything to Christ, crying out in faith, "Jesus, You are my only hope. If You don't do it, it can't be done!"

Yet saving, justifying faith involves more than giving up all confidence in the flesh. It also involves submitting your whole life to Christ with all your heart. It includes a repentance that says, "Jesus, I've got nothing to offer You. I am nothing and I have nothing. I come to submit to Your Lordship!"

In Romans 10:9, Paul characterizes saving faith as believing with your heart and confessing with your mouth. He's saying that faith is more than merely giving mental assent. Rather, it is submitting your whole life to Him — with all your heart!

In Acts 8:37, Philip said to the eunuch, "...If thou believest with all thine heart..." The eunuch replied, "...I believe..." — and he was saved! This was not simply a mental "yes" to Jesus by the eunuch. It was a full surrendering of his will — a committing of his very life and future into the Lord's hands. He believed with all his heart!

In contrast, Simon Magus believed Paul's preaching. Yet he had only a temporary faith, because his heart was not in it. Scripture says he still clung to bitterness *(see Acts 8)*. Indeed, multitudes of people in Jesus' day believed temporarily in the name of Christ. But Jesus would not commit Himself to them because He knew their hearts were not committed to Him *(see John 2:23-24)*.

So, you ask, who is truly justified by faith? Who has Christ's perfect righteousness credited to him? Who is seen as holy before God? It is the one who has come to the end of all human help — who knows he is lost and helpless. This person has tried everything and failed. And now he has committed his whole life into the Lord's hands — with all his heart, mind, soul and strength. He cries out, "Lord, I am Yours — take all of me! I want to be delivered from all my sins. I want to live the Christ-life. Lord, You are my only hope!"

There Is One Other Important Aspect of Saving, Justifying Faith.

The strongest feature of true, saving faith is a desire to draw closer to Him who loves you. "For Christ also hath once suffered for sins, the just for the unjust, that he might bring us to God..." *(1 Peter 3:18)*.

Why did Jesus suffer and die? Why did He provide justification for us? Why is His perfect righteousness accounted to us?

It was that He might bring us to God! It's all about intimate fellowship with the Father. You see, saving faith has in it a heart-cry: "Oh God, draw me nearer to You!" And unless you have this as a part of your faith, it cannot be saving faith. When you come to Jesus, it has to be about something more than just wanting happiness in life. Something in your heart — put there by the Spirit — must say, "I want to know Him who loves me. I want to know the One who gave His Son to die for me. I want to be drawn closer to the Lord!" There is a drawing power in saving faith.

When Adam sinned, he lost the most precious thing any man or woman could possess: intimacy with God. Sin drove Adam away from closeness with the Father — and he actually hid from His presence. And ever since then, whenever man sins, he has a tendency to run and hide like his forefather, Adam.

This is why God so hates sin — because it robs us of His fellowship! He created us for this very reason — for intimacy with Him. And He so yearned for our fellowship that He sent His own Son to die on a cross, to justify us and tear down the walls that blocked that intimacy from taking place. That is the power of justification — the glory of Christ's perfect righteousness imputed: It made a way back to God's original purpose in creating man — for fellowship with the Father!

This present world is full of evil, slander, satanic lies, seductions, guilt, fear, condemnation — all of it designed by Satan to keep us feeling unholy, unworthy to come into God's presence. The devil would have us hide as Adam did — to keep us from intimacy with God!

But we have been delivered from all that. We have a right to God's presence — an invitation to His throne — because we stand with a perfect righteousness before Him. Our heavenly Father is not willing that anything stand between us and Him. Because we wear the cloak of Jesus' righteousness, nothing can keep us from the Father's saving grace!

Yet not only has God invited us to the throne of grace, but He accepts us as being holy in Christ. Our sin is under the blood, forgiven — and now we have a right into His holiness. Moreover, if we have come to Jesus with saving faith, then we have yielded all to Him. And something in our hearts constantly yearns after Him.

Beloved, Jesus didn't die just to take you to paradise. He died so that every day you could live in beautiful, close fellowship with the Father. You can talk to Him, listen to Him, ask Him to lead you, guide you, tell you where you're wrong, convict you of sin — because He abides in you by His Spirit!

To be delivered from this present evil world means simply this:

• He delivered us from the power, guilt and condemnation of sin.

• He delivered us from the condemnation of an accusing conscience.

• He atoned for our every sin, robbing Satan of all accusations against us.

• He buried our sins in a sea of forgetfulness, nailing everything against us to the Cross.

• He rent the veil in two — opening up to us the Holy of holies, a way for us to come in to Him and for Him to come out to us.

You don't need to understand deep theology — Calvinism, Arminianism, antinomianism or any other theological concept to accept this truth. You don't need a four-year Bible college education. All you need is a faith that yearns to know Him in whom you have believed — and a hunger in your heart for Him!

The Church Isn't Ready for Revival

23

Are You Overwhelmed by the Darkness, or Full of Bright Faith?

There are two kinds of churches in the world today. First, there is the dead, formal church, which has a form of godliness but no power. Its ministers are hirelings, most of whom are unconverted. God calls such shepherds "...twice dead..." *(Jude 12)*. And He promises to pluck up such churches by the roots and burn them!

I have preached in several of these lifeless mausoleums over the years. A pastor would invite me because he had read *The Cross and the Switchblade*. Yet whenever I preached in such a church, and the Holy Spirit fell upon me, the pastor grew nervous, slumping in his seat. People would be weeping under Holy Ghost conviction. But as soon as I gave an invitation, the pastor stepped in quickly and dismissed the meeting.

Oh, how that bothered me! Those pastors dreaded the very thought of anyone having an emotional response to my preaching. All they wanted was to get the people up off their knees and out the door before the Holy Ghost could do something "out of control."

We know God cannot bless such churches with revival, because He doesn't pour out His Spirit where He is not welcome. And the dead, formal church has rejected the Holy Ghost outright. It simply does not want to be raised from the dead. But there is another kind of church in the world today. And that is a holy remnant church — a praying, God-fearing, uncompromising, righteous body of believers. It is comprised of people wholly given to Christ — people who pray, fast and seek the face of God regularly.

My concern here is primarily with this righteous, Holy Ghost church. Why? **It is the only church in a position to receive a great outpouring of the Holy Spirit!** You see, God pours out His Spirit only on those who ask Him to come, and who prepare themselves to receive Him.

Yet I do not believe the true church is ready for revival — for God's last, great, promised outpouring of His Spirit. A church can be engrossed for months in prayer, fasting, weeping, supplications, begging and beseeching

216

the Holy Ghost to fall — and yet still may not be ready for revival!

(Let me explain the terms I'm using here: The word "revival" literally means "the resurrection of that which threatens to become a corpse." So, if you revive someone, it means he has already passed out. Yet I do not believe God's holy, remnant church has fainted. And when I use the word "revival," I'm actually talking about an outpouring of God's Spirit.)

It is necessary to search God's Word to find out how His people prepared themselves. God has given us many biblical promises that are "on call" — that is, ready to be fulfilled. And I believe He is simply waiting on a people who will prepare themselves to lay hold of these promises.

Of course, God is sovereign and can pour out His Spirit on anyone He chooses. There are reports of the Holy Ghost falling on various peoples around the world, bringing resurrection life to those who neither expected it nor were prepared for it. Yet God also gives us a biblical pattern that shows us His standard and way. And His way is this: He works through a prepared people! He digs up fallow ground before He sets things in divine order.

I want to give you three reasons why I believe the church is not ready for revival. I pray that as we look at these, we will line up with God's Word in preparation to receive what He has promised:

1. We Are Not Ready for Revival If We Are Convinced This Society Has Sinned Away Its Day of Grace.

America has so grieved God — its intensity of sin is so horrible — that many are convinced there is no hope left! In recent years I too have been nearly convinced by America's terrible moral landslide that God has no option left but judgment. So I have preached His impending judgments intensely, especially over the past ten years. And I still believe that message with all my heart — and will continue preaching it with all authority.

You see, God may wait patiently for repentance, sending many prophets to warn of judgment. But a day finally comes when He says, "Enough!" — and prayer is useless at that point. I call this "the dread release" — when God releases a society to destructive judgments. We see several examples of this in church history:

• It happened to Noah's generation. God strove with wicked mankind for 120 years, with mercy, warnings and visible signs such as the ark. But finally He said, "No more!" — and He wiped out all of humanity, except for those who entered the ark.

● It happened also to Lot's generation, in Sodom and Gomorrah. God counted the days of wickedness in that society, was so saturated with homosexuality, lust and violence. Finally, He could endure no more and said, "Your cup of iniquity is full. Your sins have ascended to heaven!" And He wiped out those cities and all the surrounding towns. They were given over to "the dread release"!

● It happened as well in Jerusalem. Christ walked the streets of that city and wept, warning of the coming judgment. Seventy years later, God said, "That's enough!" And Jerusalem fell, razed to the ground. Thousands were murdered in a horrible holocaust.

God put this same message in the heart of Jeremiah. He sent the prophet to the gates of the temple with this solemn cry: "But go ye now unto my place which was in Shiloh, where I set my name at the first, and see what I did to it for the wickedness of my people Israel.... Therefore will I do unto this house, which is called by my name, wherein ye trust, and unto the place which I gave to you and to your fathers, as I have done to Shiloh.... Therefore pray not thou for this people, neither lift up cry nor prayer for them, neither make intercession to me: for I will not hear thee" *(Jeremiah 7:12-16)*.

God told the righteous, "You can stop praying now! My patience is gone, and I have determined judgment. I'm going to take My Spirit from the east gate and lift it from My house completely. It's going to be just like Shiloh!"

Shiloh stands as a testimony to all generations that judgment begins in God's house. God's people had become so backslidden and wicked that the Lord moved in with sudden and awesome judgments. Shiloh was where the Spirit of God departed, and "Ichabod" was written above the door. The Lord removed all His glory, shut the doors and departed — leaving it in ruin!

The Word of the Lord also came to Ezekiel with the same kind of warning: "Son of man, when the land sinneth against me by trespassing grievously, then will I stretch out mine hand upon it, and will break the staff of the bread thereof, and will send famine upon it, and will cut off man and beast from it: Though these three men — Noah, Daniel and Job — were in it, they should deliver but their own souls by their righteousness, saith the Lord God...they shall deliver neither son nor daughter; they shall but deliver their owns souls by their righteousness" *(Ezekiel 14:13-14, 20)*.

God was saying, "Even these three men — Noah, Daniel and Job — couldn't pray down a revival. Even their righteous prayers couldn't buy more time. You see, I determine judgment. And all the praying people in the world can't change My mind!"

When I See What God Did to Noah's Generation, Sodom and Jerusalem, I Can't Help But Deduct That America Is Ripe for Destruction!

Think about it for a moment: None of those societies killed 25 million babies, as we have through abortion. Their inhabitants didn't commit random acts of murder in their streets in such aggregate numbers as we do today. And Sodom's entire population didn't equal the number of gays who march in one parade in New York City. Beloved, we are a million times worse than those generations — and God judged and destroyed them all!

I often pray, "Oh, God — if You destroyed them, how can You spare us? Why have Your fierce judgments been held back from America?" Experts say the ecomony is booming. Our gross national product is increasing. Automobile factories are producing cars at a record-breaking pace. Inflation is holding steadily. Indeed, everything looks good ahead. Yet, why doesn't all this good news bring any sense of security to people? All across the country, people feel that something is hanging in the air, about to happen. Even the worst sinner doesn't feel secure. Why? It is because, deep down, this nation knows it deserves judgment! We all know we're living on borrowed time.

How can we be ready for revival if we believe that all hope is gone — that we have sinned away our day of grace and there is nothing left but judgment? We can't have faith for a revival until we're convinced God still wants to pour out His Spirit on us!

Why hasn't America been judged? Why hasn't Jesus come yet? It is because there is still a great harvest ahead! And God is "…not willing that any should perish, but that all should come to repentance" *(2 Peter 3:9)*.

We see this great mercy of the Lord in a passage in Isaiah. God instructed the prophet to tell Judah: "Thus saith the Lord, Where is the bill of your mother's divorcement, whom I have put away? Or which of my creditors is it to whom I have sold you? Behold, for your iniquities have ye sold yourselves, and for your transgressions is your mother put away. Wherefore, when I came, was there no man? When I called, was there none to answer? Is my hand shortened at all, that it cannot redeem? Or have I no power to deliver?…" *(Isaiah 50:1-2)*.

God had already divorced Israel, giving them "…a bill of divorce…"

(Jeremiah 3:8). But now His attention was on Judah, a people who had cheated on Him and walked away from Him. God still had a heart for Judah, and He came to them crying, "Where is the bill of...divorcement..." *(Isaiah 50:1)*. He was saying, "Show Me your divorce papers! Prove to me I ever put you away. It was you who walked away from Me! I did nothing to grieve or hurt you. I loved you the whole time. I came to you and I called you!"

Try to picture it: There was the Lord, going into the very dens of Judah's harlotry to look for her, calling, "I'm coming after you. You're telling everyone that there's no hope, that there can never again be a love between us. But I'm coming back for you!"

Beloved, that is exactly what I see God doing with America right now. He is saying to us, "Show Me your divorce papers! Show Me I walked away from you! I have not yet removed My Holy Spirit. Rather, I am still at work all over this nation — still wooing, calling, coming to you!"

The Lord is speaking this through Times Square Church and many other pulpits across this nation. And He is speaking it through godly men and women who spend precious time seeking Him. He is calling America back to repentance — back to His own heart!

Yet, when He comes, He asks, "Where are those who will answer My call? Where are those who will return to Me?" This is what our weeks of prayer at Times Square Church have been about. It all has to do with His last call!

Many who sit in our church are proof of the Lord's wooing. At one time He stirred their hearts and shook them out of apostasy and compromise. He called out, "I love you!" — and they responded. And now the same Spirit who roused them wants to gather in a whole multitude.

Our part is to pray with faith that, as the Spirit woos backsliders, a multitude will answer and return. We have to be fully persuaded that there is still time (though short), still hope — and that while we are praying, the Spirit is at work in all levels of society, calling and wooing people to Himself.

2. We Are Not Ready for Revival When We Are Overwhelmed by the Darkness That Has Settled Over the Nation and by the Fury of the Enemy.

I see a fury and an intensity in sinners today as in no other generation. When I was a boy, the church referred to Africa as "the dark continent" because of its spiritual darkness. But today, a spiritual darkness is hovering over America that is almost tangible. America is now "the dark continent"!

"For, behold, the darkness shall cover the earth, and gross darkness the people..." *(Isaiah 60:2)*. "Gross darkness" signifies a darkness you can feel. And the darkness over America right now is intense, widespread, thickening every moment.

When you fly into New York, you're dazzled by all the city's bright lights. Yet, once you get off the plane, take a cab into Manhattan and get out at Broadway, you instantly feel the darkness. It's heavy, demonic, blinding people's hearts and minds — and it's getting worse! Yet, the Bible says God has a part in that darkness: "Give glory to the Lord your God, before he causes darkness, and before your feet stumble upon the dark mountains, and, while ye look for light, he turns it into the shadow of death, and make it gross darkness" *(Jeremiah 13:16)*.

God makes the gross darkness! When people are so set on their sin that they reject the Lord, they are driven to darkness. David said of the wicked, "Let their eyes be darkened, that they see not..." *(Psalm 69:23)*. The Spirit of God allows a darkness to fall over their hearts and minds.

"And they shall look unto the earth; and behold trouble and darkness, dimness of anguish; and they shall be driven to darkness" *(Isaiah 8:22)*. Sinners are actually driven to their dark acts. Satan has come down upon the earth with an army of demonic powers who are whipping godless people into a frenzy of evil!

The fury and intensity of this present vileness is a thousand times darker than when I first came to New York a generation ago. Today I look at people's eyes as they're on their way to make a drug connection, stumbling out of a bar, running to and fro looking for pleasure — and there is no mistaking they are driven.

When I first began this ministry some thirty-five years ago, I spoke in churches all over America, warning of the moral landslide to come. I told people in Iowa, Oklahoma and all the Southern states that drugs would strike even the smallest hamlet. Pushers would appear in schools and on playgrounds. I warned of blatant homosexuality, with nude parades taking place in our cities. And I prophesied that nudity and sexual acts would air on prime-time TV.

Most of the people who heard me thought I'd come from Mars. Pastors berated me. And sincere Christians came to me afterward, saying, "No way! God will never let that happen to America."

Today, some of those people who ridiculed me are grandparents. They sit before their TV watching the R-rated, perverted movies I prophesied about. And their children and grandchildren are addicted to drugs and alcohol. The darkness I warned about has now come into their very souls!

Can you imagine how dark it's going to be ten years from now, should the Lord tarry? Yet, I ask you: As you see the darkness thickening and growing on all sides, do you believe it will exceed the light of the gospel? Are you afraid the darkness is going to squash it, quell it, snuff it out?

No — never! God's people must never be intimidated by the darkness and fury of the enemy in these last days. It doesn't matter how dark the world becomes. The Bible says Jesus is going to rise and shine in the darkness!

● "I, even I, am he that comforteth you: who art thou, that thou shouldest be afraid of a man that shall die, and of the son of man which shall be made as grass; and forgettest the Lord thy maker, that hath stretched forth the heavens, and laid the foundations of the earth; and hast feared continually every day because of the fury of the oppressor, as if he were ready to destroy? And where is the fury of the oppressor?" *(Isaiah 51:12-13).*

● "Yea, the darkness hideth not from thee; but the night shineth as the day: the darkness and the light are both alike to thee" *(Psalm 139:12).*

● "...he knoweth what is in the darkness, and the light dwelleth with him" *(Daniel 2:22).*

● "The people that walked in darkness have seen a great light: they that dwell in the land of the shadow of death, upon them hath the light shined" *(Isaiah 9:2).*

We live in a time of widespread death and darkness. But God says that in such times He will shine His light the brightest: "And I will bring the blind by a way that they knew not; I will lead them in paths that they have not known: I will make darkness light before them, and crooked things straight. These things will I do unto them, and not forsake them" *(Isaiah 42:16).*

It doesn't matter how wild it gets in the streets, or how many homosexuals curse Christ in gay parades. We are not to be overwhelmed by any darkness! When gross darkness covers the earth, we must expect the Lord to shine in all His glory and to deliver multitudes: "Arise, shine; for thy light is come, and the glory of the Lord is risen upon thee. For, behold, the darkness shall cover the earth, and gross darkness the people: but the

Lord shall arise upon thee, and his glory shall be seen upon thee. And the Gentiles shall come to thy light, and kings to the brightness of thy rising" *(Isaiah 60:1-3).*

No darkness will ever stop God's light! So get your eyes off the darkness, off the sin, off the fury of violent people. And believe the Lord for the bursting forth of His shining, effusing light!

3. The Church Is Not Ready for Revival Because of Its Weak Faith in God's Willingness and Power to Save Wicked, Hardened Sinners.

God put His finger on Judah's problem: They doubted His willingness and power to redeem a people entrenched in apostasy and idolatry. "And they said, There is no hope: but we will walk after our own devices, and we will every one do the imagination of his evil heart" *(Jeremiah 18:12).*

Judah had given up hope, thinking, "We've gone too far — and now there's no going back. We have left the Lord, mocked Him, abused Him, cast Him aside. We are so deep into our sins, it's hopeless. Not even God can bring us back!"

Beloved, after all my years in ministry, I still have to fight this kind of thinking. You may feel the same way. Your husband may be an atheist, mean and godless. And you have convinced yourself, "All around me, people are getting saved. But my husband is different. He's so hard!"

The Lord said to Judah, "...Is my hand shortened at all, that it cannot redeem?..." *(Isaiah 50:2).* To shorten means to "chop off." God was saying, "Tell me — has the enemy chopped off My mighty arm? Have I lost My power to save? No! My mighty arm dried up the Red Sea. It clothed the heavens with blackness. It opened blind eyes. You have seen that I save to the uttermost. Why do you think I have lost My power to redeem you?"

Dear saint, when did God lose His power to save the vilest sinner on earth? When did He lose His willingness to deliver drug addicts, drunkards and prostitutes, when nobody was praying for them? Would God then somehow decide not to save your family members, for whom you have fasted and prayed faithfully? Absolutely not! We must cry out to Him in faith, "Oh Lord, You can save Wall Street. You can deliver the worst homosexual in New York. You can redeem any Muslim in any foreign land. And you can save any member of my family. Your arm is not too short. You can save anybody!"

We will never be ready for revival until we stop limiting God. Don't believe His hand has been chopped off; instead, believe Him for the impossible. Get a vision of His mercy and love — of His mighty, outstretched arm, all-powerful to save!

If Jesus prophesied a great harvest, then we are going to witness supernatural outpourings of God's Spirit on vast multitudes. When the Spirit was poured out the first time in Jerusalem, thousands were saved at once. And, likewise today, we ought to pray with faith for the Spirit to fall on entire nations — even those with incredible strongholds. In recent years, the Holy Spirit has moved in China, and great multitudes there have been saved. Isaiah prophesies of many people being gathered in from Sinim, which represents China: "Behold, these shall come from far: and, lo, these from the north and from the west; and these from the land of Sinim" *(Isaiah 49:12)*.

That same Holy-Ghost fire is also falling in Russia and in parts of India. God's Spirit is moving, wooing, calling people all over the world. Yet God is asking His remnant church to begin with our own families, one person at a time: "Turn, O backsliding children, saith the Lord; for I am married unto you: and I will take you one of a city, and two of a family, and I will bring you to Zion" *(Jeremiah 3:14)*. We are to pray and be patient — and He will gather in our loved ones, one at a time!

Here at Times Square Church, we are praying that God will sweep many into His kingdom through outpourings of His Spirit. But the Lord also wants us to focus on our own families. We must have an urgency in us to pray, "Lord, send conviction on my family. Save my son, my daughter, my wife."

Several years ago there was a popular song, "Raindrops Keep Fallin' on My Head." I believe that song tells us the way we ought to pray — for God to literally rain down His Holy Spirit! Scripture promises that in the last days the Holy Ghost will fall as rain. And you can pray Holy-Ghost raindrops down upon the heads of your loved ones: "Ask ye of the Lord rain in the time of the latter rain; so the Lord shall make bright clouds, and give them showers of rain, to every one grass in the field" *(Zechariah 10:1)*.

God is waiting and anxious to pour out His Holy Ghost. Are you ready to pray down His rain? We are to pray not for the fire of judgment, but for rain!

Yes, God's judgment is coming; it is at the door even now. But while we still have time, we are to believe God to pour out His Spirit. So lay hold of His divine, "on call" promises — and you will see a Holy-Ghost revival poured out all around you!

24 Falling Away to the Antichrist

Who Is On the Throne of Your Heart?

The apostle Paul speaks of two frightful things that will strike the church just prior to Jesus' return. The Lord will not come back until these two awful things happen. I want to show you that both things are taking place right now — before our very eyes!

First, Paul tells us that in the last days there will be a great falling away. And second, he warns that an evil spirit of antichrist will overtake many believers who are turning aside!

Of course, the church has been preaching and teaching for years about the coming antichrist. We have been expecting the appearance of the man of sin, the son of perdition. Some speculate that he will be revealed in our time — that, in fact, he already has been born and is living somewhere on the earth.

Is there such a man? Yes, I believe there is — and he is totally possessed of Satan. Yet when he appears, he will be well-received. He will demand the devotion of all mankind — setting himself up as God before the world. The only reason the antichrist hasn't been revealed yet is because his time hasn't come. But one day the Holy Spirit will lift His restraining hand, and the man of sin will be revealed in full power. The Bible assures us, however, that when this evil man's time is finished, he will be consumed by God: "...whom the Lord shall consume with the spirit of his mouth, and shall destroy with the brightness of his coming" *(2 Thessalonians 2:8)*.

There Is an Antichrist — And There Is Also a Spirit of Antichrist!

We have a Savior who exists right now in glory as a man. He is a living person — with flesh, bone, hair, eyes — even though He is God. And though we are here on earth, His Spirit dwells within us: "And because ye are sons, God hath sent forth the Spirit of his Son into your hearts, crying, Abba, Father" *(Galatians 4:6)*.

Yet, there is another spirit at work in the world — the antichrist spirit. Just as surely as Christ has given us His Spirit, there is an antichrist spirit possessing many apostate Christians. And that spirit is at work, preparing hearts for the coming of the man of sin! "...this is that spirit of antichrist, whereof ye have heard that it should come; and even now already is it in the world" *(1 John 4:3)*. John is saying here, "You've heard about the coming of the Antichrist. It has been preached and taught, and you expect his arrival. But, beloved, wake up — because the spirit of antichrist is already at work!"

You must understand — the Antichrist is not suddenly going to appear on the scene and overwhelm humankind. Rather, his spirit is mysteriously at work now, setting up his kingdom in cold, compromising hearts. And when the man of sin finally appears, he will publicly be revealed to a world that is already prepared for him — to hearts his spirit already possesses. Right now we see a growing antichrist sentiment and conduct. But soon this will turn into a flowing stream, and, eventually, a vast ocean. And when the Antichrist finally appears, even many former Christians will welcome him — because their hearts will be of a kindred spirit!

Paul warned of this. He said that in the last days false prophets would infiltrate the church, preaching another gospel and another Jesus. Many such false prophets have already appeared, preaching the gospel of the Antichrist: "For the mystery of iniquity doth already work: only he who now letteth will let, until he be taken out of the way" *(2 Thessalonians 2:7)*.

The antichrist spirit is invading the hearts of many apostate Christians even now. They are being absolutely possessed of evil. "But how?" you ask. "Why would certain apostate Christians ever turn to the Antichrist?" It is because they are like-minded with him! John writes: "Love not the world, neither the things that are in the world. If any man love the world, the love of the Father is not in him. For all that is in the world, the lust of the flesh, and the lust of the eyes, and the pride of life, is not of the Father, but is of the world.... Little children, it is the last time: and as ye have heard that antichrist shall come, even now are there many antichrists; whereby we know that it is the last time" *(1 John 2:15-18)*.

John is warning us that those who still love the things of this world have opened themselves to the spirit of antichrist. He's saying, "You know these are the last days — because so many are full of the covetous antichrist spirit!"

"Who is a liar but he that denieth that Jesus is the Christ? He is antichrist, that denieth the Father and the Son" *(verse 22)*. The apostle adds, "If you have not come under the total Lordship of Jesus — if you do not acknowledge Him in all your ways — then you have opened yourself up to this spirit of evil!"

Beloved, if you are serving Jesus only 50 percent — or even 90 percent — then you are denying His full salvation. You aren't serving Him with all your heart, mind, soul and body. And you have opened up an inroad for the antichrist spirit to come in. It's not enough to say, "I believe Jesus was God in flesh." Rather, we must say, "Jesus, You are God in flesh in me. You have all power and authority over lust and sin. And I yield to You completely!"

Those Who Are Righteous —
Who Worship God in Spirit and in Truth —
Are Prime Targets of the Antichrist!

"Who opposeth and exalteth himself above all that is called God, or that is worshipped..." *(2 Thessalonians 2:4)*. The spirit of antichrist is opposed to all who walk closely with God. He goes after true worshipers — because he wants their worship for himself!

Satan wants nothing more than to destroy pure worship. He wants to rob God of all praise. And if you walk in intimacy with Jesus, the antichrist spirit will come against you with everything he has. He will attack you with fear, doubt, lust — anything to give him an inroad to hinder your worship.

Yet his spirit of lawlessness is being restrained by the Holy Ghost: "And now ye know what withholdeth that he might be revealed in his time" *(verse 6)*. It is the power of God's Spirit in His church — that is, in you and me — that holds back Satan's anarchy. Indeed, if God were to lift His Spirit from on-fire churches and godly believers, our nation would be a raging hell.

Yet careless, lazy Christians — those who have never forsaken their sin, who are still engrossed in the things of the world — will not be able to stand in these last days. They will be overtaken by evil! The apostle Peter wrote: "These are wells without water, clouds that are carried with a tempest; to whom the mist of darkness is reserved for ever....For if after they have escaped the pollutions of the world through the knowledge of the Lord and Saviour Jesus Christ, they are again entangled therein, and overcome, the latter end is worse with them than the beginning. For it had been better for them not to have known the way of righteousness, than, after they have known it, to turn from the holy commandment delivered unto them. But it is happened unto them according to the true proverb, The dog is turned to his own vomit again; and the sow that was washed to her wallowing in the mire" *(2 Peter 2:17, 20-22)*.

The people whom Peter describes here claimed to be saved. They once had escaped the pollutions of the world, delivered by the power of God. They had known the way of righteousness. And yet they became entangled again in sin. They were overcome by the spirit of antichrist!

Peter couldn't have been speaking of nonbelievers here. After all, the unsaved have no faith to fall away from. Rather, those who fall have something to fall away from. Obviously, Peter is talking about apostate Christians. Such half-hearted believers do more than fall away from the Lord. They also fall into something — into the hands of the antichrist spirit! Peter says such people have been "…overcome…" *(verse 20)*.

The apostle Paul makes an astounding statement. He says that even now the antichrist spirit has taken his place in the temple: "…so that he as God sitteth in the temple of God, shewing himself that he is God" *(2 Thessalonians 2:4)*. It's time to stop looking to Jerusalem — to the rebuilding of the temple — because the spirit of antichrist is already ascending his throne!

"What?" you ask. "What is this temple where the antichrist spirit now sits, showing his power and reign?" It is the temple of people's hearts! "Know ye not that ye are the temple of God, and that the Spirit of God dwelleth in you?" *(1 Corinthians 3:16)*. "What? Know ye not that your body is the temple of the Holy Ghost which is in you, which ye have of God, and ye are not your own?" *(6:19)*. "…for ye are the temple of the living God; as God hath said, I will dwell in them, and walk in them; and I will be their God, and they shall be my people" *(2 Corinthians 6:16)*.

Yes, we are God's temple. But for some, another spirit has invaded that temple. The Spirit of God is gone — and lust, pride, covetousness and slander all reign supreme. There is no longer anything pure, holy or divine. A mysterious spirit of lawlessness is in control!

How could such a terrible, frightful thing happen? At one time the living God possessed this temple, ruling and reigning. He was once enthroned here. This happens because so many Christians have grown careless. They no longer walk in righteousness or holiness. And they end up giving an inroad to the spirit of antichrist. Now he sits in the temple of their heart — showing himself to be absolutely in control!

There Will Always Be a Christ on the Throne of Every Heart — Either Jesus Christ the Lamb of God, Or the Antichrist!

Every person reading this message has a Christ on the throne of his or her heart — either the Spirit of Christ, or the spirit of antichrist.

I am totally convinced that the antichrist spirit's most effective means of preparing hearts are cable TV and filthy movies. He knows that the eye is the gateway to the heart. And he marches straight through the corrupted, jaded eye of a Christian and takes over the throne of his heart.

This is why the antichrist spirit has taken control of the secular media — TV networks, movie production, Broadway theater, the press. Who but the antichrist spirit could so bias the media that abortion is now considered a right rather than a sin? Who but this spirit could justify euthanasia, the killing off of the elderly or infirm? Who but the spirit of antichrist could mock everything that is sacred and holy, through wicked movies and vile TV programs? I believe the antichrist spirit is actually producing the programs on MTV and the Fox Network. From what I read of their shows, it's all absolute filth. Who but the antichrist spirit could be responsible for it?

The spirit of lawlessness is growing bolder and bolder, and our society is on the brink of becoming a raging hell. The antichrist spirit now pervades our schools, our courts, our streets, our businesses, even our homes. And, sadly, this evil is rapidly moving into the church. I believe the spirit of antichrist is actually establishing churches all over the United States. This spirit is the motivating force behind "outsider friendly" churches. Who but the antichrist spirit would call for the ungodly to set the spiritual agenda — sending church founders door to door, surveying people: "What would you prefer church to be like? We want to tailor it so that you'll come."

These megachurches are being built on skits and dramas, because people don't want to hear reproof. They want no conviction — so they hear a gospel that is almost totally devoid of repentance, judgment, the Cross. They are told all about God's grace and mercy, how to cope with problems — but nothing of God's judgment and hell. They're being lulled to sleep in their sinful lifestyle.

I ask you: What would happen if I went into the streets, rounded up all the kids who were skipping school, and asked them, "What kind of school would you like? I'll build one that you'll enjoy, just so you'll want to come." Those kids would answer: "We want a school that lasts only three days a week — and just two hours a day! We want no algebra, no calculus and no science. And we want lunch from noon to two, with nothing but pizza and snacks. There won't be any lectures, rules or grades. And we'll be able to come and go as we please."

If I followed through on that, I would have the biggest school in New York, with every dropout in sight. But what would happen to those kids ten years down the road, without any real preparation for living? That's what preachers in "outsider friendly" churches should be asking themselves! What will they do when they stand before God's holy throne and watch helplessly as, one by one, many of their sheep are condemned because they were never confronted about their sins? Their people never heard a word of reproof that would lead them to true righteousness. There was no convicting message to shake people out of their sins, to prepare them to face the judgment seat of Christ.

This is exactly what the Bible warns of — churches with forms of godliness, but without power. I ask you: Who brought the music of the world into the church? Who turned weekly prayer meetings into "entertainment night" at the church? Who made Christians more concerned whether their team wins the Super Bowl than whether lost, dying people are saved? The spirit of antichrist is telling Christians they can drink from two cups — the Lord's cup, and the cup of demons!

"But I say, that the things which the Gentiles sacrifice, they sacrifice to devils, and not to God: and I would not that ye should have fellowship with devils. Ye cannot drink the cup of the Lord, and the cup of devils: ye cannot be partakers of the Lord's table, and of the table of devils" *(1 Corinthians 10:20-21)*.

You may be thinking, "This is really frightening. How does a Christian get to the point of being overcome by the antichrist spirit?" There are two causes by which the spirit of antichrist can overcome a Christian:

The First Cause by Which the Antichrist Spirit Can Take Over an Apostate Believer Is a Loss of Love for the Truth.

"...they received not the love of the truth..." *(2 Thessalonians 2:10)*. The spirit of antichrist moves in when God's truth is no longer loved or appropriated: "...all might be damned who believed not the truth..." *(verse 12)*.

The prophet Jeremiah wrote: "Run ye to and fro through the streets of Jerusalem, and see now, and know, and seek in the broad places thereof, if ye can find a man, if there be any that executeth judgment, that seeketh the truth; and I will pardon it. And though they say, The Lord liveth; surely they swear it falsely. O Lord, are not thine eyes upon the truth? Thou hast stricken them, but they have not grieved; thou hast consumed them, but they have refused to receive correction: they have made their faces harder than a rock; they have refused to return" *(Jeremiah 5:1-3).*

This passage is not speaking of heathen, but of Israel, God's people. God is saying to Jeremiah, "Go find me just one person who has a heart for the truth — anyone — and I'll pardon him. But you won't find one, Jeremiah! These people say they love Me, but they don't receive My correction. They don't grieve when I reprove them. They no longer tremble at My Word!"

You may think, "I'm glad I'm not like Israel. I love God's Word. I haven't lost my love for truth." Yet I urge you to test yourself! Let me give you three ways to determine whether you have the love of truth in your heart:

1. The first sign of a loss of love for the truth is when you forsake assembling with other believers.

If it's a task for you to make it to church, then you've lost your love for God's truth: "Not forsaking the assembling of ourselves together, as the manner of some is; but exhorting one another: and so much the more, as ye see the day approaching" *(Hebrews 10:25).*

When you no longer look forward to being in God's house with His people — when the preaching seems boring, and worship no longer matters — you have opened yourself up to the spirit of antichrist. And the Lord admonishes you: "The closer you get to My coming, the more perilous the times will be. And the more imporant it is that you gather with My people!"

Yet something tragic is happening all across America and Canada. Pastors are calling our ministry and telling us, "We have to shut down our midweek service because so few show up. We've already had to stop holding Sunday night meetings, because people won't come unless we show a movie or put on a concert. And people don't want to come on Sunday mornings anymore if they think the service will last more than an hour."

Where are God's children if they aren't in the Lord's house? They are at restaurants, parties, socials, sporting events. Most of all, they are parked in front of their TVs — watching programs of ever-increasing evil!

2. A second sign of a loss of love for the truth is when reproving

messages make you think of someone else's sin and not your own.

Whenever you hear a prophetic sermon, do you sit smugly by, thinking, "Wow, does that ever describe brother so-and-so. Thank God, he's finally being reached. Lord, pour it on!"

I ask you — how much, if any, of this message are you applying to yourself? How much stirring and conviction are going on in your heart? Are you praying, "God, turn Your Word on my heart"? I urge you to heed David's words: "Thy word have I hid in mine heart, that I might not sin against thee" *(Psalm 119:11)*.

3. A third sign of loss of love for the truth is when reproof angers you rather than humbles you.

God says hatred of reproof reveals a forsaking of the path of holiness: "Correction is grievous unto him that forsaketh the way: and he that hateth reproof shall die" *(Proverbs 15:10)*.

Perhaps you often walk away from a reproving sermon, saying, "That word was just too hard. And that preacher is just too angry!" Beloved, any godly shepherd will preach with holy anger. That's because he is angry at the devil, angry at the antichrist spirit — angry at anything that draws your soul away from true worship of the Father!

The Second Cause by Which the Antichrist Spirit Can Take Over a Compromised Christian Is the Love of Pleasure.

"That they all might be damned who believed not the truth, but had pleasure in unrighteousness" *(2 Thessalonians 2:12)*.

Paul is speaking here of "pleasure madness." Yet he is not talking about the jet set, the wild crowd, gamblers, prostitutes, drug addicts. No — the last-day pleasure-seekers referred to are found inside the church! Paul warns: "This know also, that in the last days perilous times shall come. For men shall be lovers of their own selves, covetous, boasters, proud, blasphemers, disobedient to parents, unthankful, unholy, without natural affection, trucebreakers, false accusers, incontinent, fierce, despisers of those that are good, traitors, heady, highminded, lovers of pleasures more than lovers of God" *(2 Timothy 3:1-4)*.

"Blasphemers in God's house?" you ask. "Trucebreakers? False accusers? Traitors? Surely not!" Oh, yes — absolutely! When Paul uses the phrase, "...lovers of pleasures more than lovers of God...", he is intimating that these people have a measure of love for God. But that love is overcome and polluted by a love for the pleasures of the world. Paul is talking about those who pursue the pleasures of unrighteousness!

You can pluck down five dollars for a movie if you want, and sit through two hours of violence, bloodshed and blasphemy in which God's name is freely taken in vain. But be warned: You will be drinking from the cup of devils — fellowshiping with demons! When you pay for that kind of thing, you show your allegiance to the antichrist spirit who rules the media. God calls it a sacrifice to demons *(see 1 Corinthians 10:20)*. Worst of all, you are inviting the antichrist spirit into your heart. And if you keep drinking from the cup of devils — if you keep letting that filthy antichrist spirit seep into your soul — it won't be long before nothing bothers or convicts you!

A Holy Remnant Will Love the Truth.

Paul gives thanks to God for a holy people who remain steadfast in perilous times. This holy remnant will rise up against the spirit of antichrist and stand strong. They will never be overcome. On the contrary — they will overcome the world, the flesh and the wicked one.

"But we are bound to give thanks always to God for you, brethren beloved of the Lord, because God hath from the beginning chosen you to salvation through sanctification of the Spirit and belief of the truth: Whereunto he called you by our gospel, to the obtaining of the glory of our Lord Jesus Christ. Therefore, brethren, stand fast, and hold the traditions which ye have been taught, whether by word, or our epistle.

"Now our Lord Jesus Christ himself, and God, even our Father, which hath loved us, and hath given us everlasting consolation and good hope through grace, comfort your hearts, and stablish you in every good word and work" *(2 Thessalonians 2:16-17)*.

This holy remnant loves the truth. They aren't afraid to be reproved. So they examine themselves in light of God's Word, letting it pierce them to the very marrow — and God is able to sanctify their mind and spirit.

Beloved, if you keep your heart open to the truth — if you continue to love God's Word — the Lord will establish you. And when the evil spirit of this world comes in like a flood, Satan will be unable to make any inroad to your heart: "They that trust in the Lord shall be as mount Zion, which cannot be removed, but abideth for ever. As the mountains are round about Jerusalem, so the Lord is round about his people from henceforth even for ever. For the rod of the wicked shall not rest upon the lot of the righteous; lest the righteous put forth their hands to iniquity" *(Psalm 125:1-3)*.

The antichrist spirit has a rod, signifying authority. But his power and reign will not be over you. On the contrary — you will overcome him! "I have written unto you...because ye are strong, and the word of God abideth in you, and ye have overcome the wicked one" *(1 John 2:14)*. "...and this is the victory that overcometh the world, even our faith" *(5:4)*.

Let the spirit of antichrist come. You won't be moved, because you'll be firmly established on the truth of God's Word. You'll be found in God's house, worshiping from a pure heart. And your faith will overcome all that the enemy brings against you — because Jesus sits enthroned in the temple of your heart.

I want to give you a great defense against the antichrist spirit. It's found in Psalm 139: "Search me, O God, and know my heart: try me, and know my thoughts: and see if there be any wicked way in me, and lead me in the way everlasting" *(Psalm 139:23-24)*.

25 Prayer That Is Pleasing To the Lord

Coming to the Lord in Delight

I want to talk to you now about a kind of prayer that is most pleasing to the Lord. Not all of our praying blesses the heart of God. Yet, with the help of the Holy Spirit, I trust that what I share with you here will change the way you pray — from now until Jesus comes!

I have no intention of complicating prayer. It has been made too complicated already by well-intentioned teachers who have turned it into formulas, strategies and theatrics. Some Christians literally put on combat boots and uniforms to dress the part of "prayer warriors." Others attend prayer meetings where they are given "prayer guides," booklets that tell them how to fill up the hours they'll be there.

I am not condemning any of this. But I would like to show you the kind of praying I believe most pleases the Lord. Actually, it is very simple and easy to understand. It is so simple, in fact, a little child can pray in a way that pleases Him.

Let me begin by saying, I believe most Christians want to pray. At one time in our walk with the Lord, we all prayed with some consistency. But after a while, many believers quit. And now they are convicted by their prayerlessness.

The disciples said to Jesus, "…Lord, teach us to pray…" *(Luke 11:1)*. They would not have asked unless they had wanted to learn. And I believe that most who are reading this message would love to be faithful in prayer — but they don't know how. The problem is, they simply don't understand the purpose of prayer. And until they grasp this vital purpose, they will never be able to maintain a fulfilled, meaningful life of prayer.

Many Christians pray only out of a sense of obligation. They think of prayer as something they are "supposed" to do. They tell themselves, "Others around me are always praying. And the pastor is always provoking us to pray. Besides that, the Bible calls for prayer. So, I have to pray. It's just the Christian thing to do."

Others pray only when tragedy strikes or when a crisis befalls them. And they do not pray again until the next difficulty comes along.

The church will never understand the importance of prayer until we grasp this foundational truth:

Prayer Is Not Just for Our Own Welfare or Relief — But For the Delight of the Lord!

Unless these two elements go together, we do not have a foundation upon which to build a prayer life. Prayer is not just for our benefit — but for the delight of our God! We are not just to intercede for things we need, but to ask for the things He desires.

Christians can be very self-centered and selfish when it comes to prayer. Often we go to the Lord only to unload our troubles and sorrows to Him — to seek a supply of strength for the next battle. Of course, that is Scriptural; we are invited to come boldly to God's throne of grace, to find mercy and help in our times of need. He has told us to cast all our cares upon Him. But our praying is not complete — it is not prayer that is most pleasing to the Lord — if we do not understand God's need! Whereas we seek relief and help from the Lord, He desires fellowship with us — intimacy and communion.

Our primary purpose in praying ought always to be fellowship with the Lord. After all, He already has made every provision for our daily needs: "…Take no thought for your life, what ye shall eat, or what ye shall drink; nor yet for your body, what ye shall put on.…Behold the fowls of the air…your heavenly Father feedeth them. Are ye not much better than they? …your heavenly Father knoweth that ye have need of all these things. But seek ye first the kingdom of God, and his righteousness; and all these things shall be added unto you. Take no thought for the morrow …" *(Matthew 6:25-26, 32-34)*. "…for your Father knoweth what things ye have need of, before ye ask him" *(verse 8)*.

God is saying to us: "When you come into My presence, focus your attention on fellowship with Me — on getting to know Me. Don't let your focus be on material things. I know what your needs are. You don't even have to ask — I'll take care of them all! Just seek Me. Let us enjoy sweet communion."

Yet, how much of our prayer time is spent asking God for a better job, a better home, food, clothes and other necessities? If most Christians subtracted such petitions from their prayer time, there would be little or no prayer left!

Perhaps prayer is a burden to you. Do you pray mostly out of a sense of obligation? Is prayer boring to you? Is it more of a duty than a pleasure? So few Christians enter God's presence with delight, simply for the pleasure of His company. Some think of it only as "work" — labor, exertion, effort. Yet, when we commune with a dearly loved one here on earth, do we think of it as work? No — that is a pleasure to us! If you are happily married, you don't think of your times of intimacy with your spouse as "work."

How many marriages have been ruined by a mate who thought of intimacy only as duty? There is a generation of older Christian women who taught their daughters that intimacy with a husband was only a difficult, burdensome duty. They considered it to be work, an obligation, with no delight at all.

Christ likens His relationship with His people to that of a husband and wife — and the Bible says Jesus delights in us! The fact is, a husband's pleasure in enjoying intimacy is not simply the satisfaction of his own needs. No — his real pleasure is in the joy of knowing his wife shares his delight. He says in his heart, "She really wants to be with me. I'm first in her heart — I'm everything to her!" She is not reluctant to enjoy intimacy with him. She doesn't see it as a duty or obligation. Rather, she delights in him. And when he reaches out to her, she reciprocates by reaching out to him. They delight equally in each other.

We know the Lord delights in His people. The Bible tells us: "How fair and how pleasant art thou, O love, for delights!" *(Song of Solomon 7:6)*. And David said, "…he delivered me, because he delighteth in me" *(Psalm 18:19)*. Can you imagine the Lord being exuberant with delight over His children? That is the picture Scripture gives us. Our God delights in us!

Yet, do we delight in Him? The Bible tells us the Lord should be our delight: "Delight thyself also in the Lord; and he shall give thee the desires of thine heart" *(Psalm 37:4)*. "…I sat down under his shadow with great delight, and his fruit was sweet to my taste" *(Song of Solomon 2:3)*.

Delighting in the Lord doesn't mean simply being gleeful or happy in His presence. I asked the Lord what the expression "delighting" means. He answered:

"David, delighting in Me means simply being able to say: 'I would rather be with Jesus than with anyone else on earth! I prefer His company even over that of my spouse, my family, my friends. I prefer Him over all celebrities, world leaders, famous people, even great men and women of God. I would rather spend time with Him than with anybody else. He is my delight!'

"It also means being able to say, 'I long to be shut in with Him — because He is the only One who can satisfy me. All others leave me empty and unfulfilled. No one but Jesus can touch my deepest needs. And I rush to Him as often as I can!'"

Indeed, Jesus is waiting for us with every resource — everything we need for comfort, strength and power. Yet, often we either sit and brood in His presence, or we rush off to phone a friend to try to find help. Can you imagine what that must do to His heart?

Our "delighting" is something the Lord recognizes in us. He knows when we are drawn to His presence. If we truly delight in Him, everything that hinders us from coming to Him will bother us. We'll grow lonely, heartsick for Him, knowing that nothing else can touch or fill that deep spot in our hearts. No prayer can be wholly pleasing to Him until He is assured we come to Him because we prefer Him. He wants to know that above all else!

Coming to the Lord With Delight Does Not Mean We Cannot Come to Him With Sadness and Grief.

Keep in mind my definition of "delighting in the Lord" — that is, preferring to be with Him above all others. This gives new meaning to our times of being sad, downcast, heavy-hearted, confused. To whom do we run in such times? Whose company do we prefer then?

Hannah is an example of a woman who came daily into the Lord's presence. She came to the temple sad of heart — weeping, with a sorrowful spirit. "And she was in bitterness of soul, and prayed unto the Lord, and wept sore" *(1 Samuel 1:10).* Hannah shared her husband with another wife, Peninnah, who had borne several children. Hannah had remained barren, and Peninnah harassed her about it day and night. Scripture says this woman "…provoked (Hannah) sore…" *(verse 6),* making her life miserable.

Now, Hannah was dearly loved by her husband. But even he could not comfort her nor abate her sorrow. He said to her, "…am I not better to thee than ten sons?" *(verse 8).* Yet Hannah must have thought, "You don't understand. I have a need you can't meet!" So Hannah stood before the altar weeping, sorrowful, with a deep groaning in her spirit. She testified to

Eli, the priest: "…I am a woman of a sorrowful spirit: I…have poured out my soul before the Lord.…out of the abundance of my complaint and grief have I spoken hitherto" *(verses 15-16)*.

Hannah was not afraid to come into the Lord's presence with her sadness. In fact, in her sorrow she preferred His company. Yet many believers today simply will not come into God's presence because they are sad, downcast, weeping, broken, going through trials. They say, in essence, "I don't want to offend God by coming to Him this way. I'll wait till I'm happy and joyful before I come into His presence."

We're accustomed to going before the Lord corporately with hand-clapping, praises, joyful worship. But this account of Hannah makes it clear we're to come to Him even in our saddest moments. And, as Hannah was in intimate prayer with the Lord, He spoke peace to her heart: "…So (she) went her way, and did eat, and her countenance was no more sad" *(verse 18)*.

This passage tells me: "Don't hide from the Lord. Don't run anywhere else. Run straight into His presence, and weep it all out before Him! Tell Him everything you're going through. Let Him have all your sadness."

We all tend to shy away from the Lord during our sad times. I recently had a time of unexplained sadness. There was no real reason for it; it was just one of those heavy times I couldn't understand. I hesitated to go to prayer that morning, thinking, "I'll wait till this evening. Then I'll be okay. I can have my time with the Lord then." But the Holy Spirit prompted me to turn to the book of Nehemiah. As I read chapter 2, I saw something I hadn't seen before. This chapter contains an encouraging story for all who come to the Lord with a heavy heart.

Nehemiah was a cupbearer to King Artaxerxes. He tasted the wines before they were brought to the king's table, making sure they weren't poisoned. Over time, Nehemiah became a trusted servant to the king.

Now, Nehemiah had received a report from his brother Hanani that Jerusalem was in ruins. The population had been decimated, the people were in terrible straits, and conditions were worsening daily. This tore at Nehemiah's heart. He loved Judah and Jerusalem — and a sorrow and sadness began to grip him. Scripture says: "And it came to pass…I took up the wine, and gave it unto the king. Now I had not been beforetime sad in his presence. Wherefore the king said unto me, Why is thy countenance sad, seeing thou art not sick? This is nothing else but sorrow of heart. Then I was very sore afraid" *(Nehemiah 2:1-2)*.

You must understand — people were forbidden to come into the king's presence with sadness, especially if they were court employees. Nehemiah knew this could have cost him his head, and he was terribly fearful. But the king was moved with compassion when he saw the grief of Nehemiah. Scripture tells us he gave his downcast servant a leave of absence. He also gave him a letter of credit, opening the royal treasury to him. Nehemiah then received from the king the desire of his heart — permission to go to Jerusalem to rebuild the temple and city walls!

Here is my point: If it were possible for Nehemiah to go into the presence of a pagan king with a sad, heavy countenance, and yet find favor, compassion and blessings beyond imagination — how much more will King Jesus show compassion to each of His children in our sadness, lifting our burden and supplying our need? Would a pagan king show more mercy to a downcast servant than our all-merciful Savior and King would?

Perhaps at this point you are confident you love the Lord and delight in Him. You have learned to run to Him just for the pleasure of His company. And in your wonderful times of intimacy with Him, He lifts all your burdens and floods your soul with peace, joy, assurance of His love. But is that the end-purpose of prayer? Is it to give us ecstasy — to provide us with rest and peace? No! There is much more to this matter of praying in a way that's pleasing to God:

If We Are Going to Pray in a Manner Pleasing to the Lord, We Must Learn to Pray Through!

"Praying through" is a term coined by the early Pentecostals. To some it meant simply staying on your knees until you were assured you had an answer from God. To others it meant continually coming back to the Lord until you had the answer in hand. (This was also called "persevering in prayer.")

As a young boy in those early camp meetings, I heard people testify, "I'm going to lay hold of the horns of the altar — and I won't let go until God answers!" Yet I don't believe that is the truest meaning of "praying through." You can be shut in with the Lord on the Mount of Transfiguration, delighting in His presence. You can spend quality hours, even days, with Him, glorying in sweet communion. You can have all your needs met. Your heart can be totally satisfied. His presence can heal you, lift you, empower you, strengthen you. But what happens when you leave that hallowed place of intimate communion? You may rise up from your knees only to go back to a crushing situation that has not changed. You can see the devil waiting there for you, ready to throw the same problems and emptiness at you. I ask you: What good is it to get the glory on the mountain if it won't see you through your battle?

Let me explain what I believe is meant by "praying through." The phrase means simply this: The strength, power and encouragement you receive from the Lord while shut in with Him must see you through the trials ahead! The victory you get in the secret closet has to give you victory on the battlefield.

Think about it: What exactly did you get from your time of prayer, if it wasn't something that could see you through the battle? Was yours a "completed" prayer? You see, "praying through" means waiting for the completion of your prayer — that is, for total completion. Many Christians see only half-answered prayers — because they don't allow what they received from the Lord in prayer to carry them through their trial. Indeed, many sincere prayers have been wasted, aborted, lost — because they were not "carried through" in this way.

How many of us have gone to the Lord in prayer, giving the burdens of our hearts to Him — and afterward were lifted out of a pit, our joy restored, our faith rising up? The first thing He tells us in our time with Him is, "Don't be afraid. I am with you." He settles our spirit, bringing us rest and peace. And we go out of His presence feeling strong, ready to fight the good fight.

But what happens the next day, when a trial arises? How do you react when your circumstances begin to fall in on you? Do you collapse after only a short while? Many of us get discouraged when our circumstances don't change after much prayer. We believe God for a change — and, indeed, many times He does bring one about. But in the times when He doesn't, we often go from a wonderful mountaintop experience straight into a battle — and we fail miserably!

Prayer is not finished — it is not "completed prayer" — until it sees you through to the other side of your trial. We have not "prayed it through" until we have "lived it through" — that is, lived through our trials by the strength we received in God's presence. God fully intends that what He gives us in prayer will fully supply us with everything we need for our battle. He wants to give us something powerful enough to see us through any situation — to place us above the battle!

I must confess, this is where I fail most in prayer. I have known and enjoyed the ecstasy of intimacy with my Lord; He has become my delight.

I know what it is like to run to Him with heaviness, sorrow, tears flowing — and to experience His awesome touch, filling me with peace and relief. But when I face the next trial or crisis that comes along, all of my peace and joy seem to evaporate. I discover I have not yet prayed through!

Has this ever happened to you? Perhaps you went to church and were blessed, coming out of the sanctuary with a sense of power and anointing. Yet, when you got home, you got into an argument with your spouse. Then you went to work on Monday, and everything went wrong. Where, at that moment, was the joy, peace and rest you got from being in the Lord's presence not long before? Your prayer has not been prayed through!

Somewhere between the glory and the crisis, we lose everything we gained during our intimacy with the Lord. So, how can we keep it? What can we do to see our prayer through to a triumphant conclusion? I have prayed about this continually because of the many Christians everywhere who are hurting so badly. Our ministry receives between 30,000 and 40,000 letters a month from our readers — and I have never heard of such pain as I now read in these letters.

Many Christians are suffocating from a loneliness that is so bad, they can hardly see themselves through a day. Others are suffering through all kinds of marital and family problems. Pastors are grief-stricken over all the hurting people in their congregations. As I read of such grief, I have to cry out to God, "Father, I can't write a message that will add to their burden. Please, Lord — what am I to say?"

The answer I received is the message I am writing to you now: The Lord wants you to receive something from your intimate time with Him — to have a power and authority that will carry you through your trials. He wants you to pray through them completely!

"But how?" you ask. "How can I maintain the victory I receive in my prayer time with Him? How can I take it through to the other side of the battle?"

There are two things we must do to pray through our trial:

The First Way We Learn to Pray
Through Is by Listening.

Most Christians don't listen to God. They go to Him only to talk! Yet the Scriptures reveal that any person who was ever used of God learned to remain in His presence until hearing from Him. Scripture makes it clear the

Lord wants to talk to every one of us: "And thine ears shall hear a word behind thee, saying, This is the way, walk ye in it, when ye turn to the right hand, and when ye turn to the left" *(Isaiah 30:21)*.

I heard of a little girl who was dying of leukemia. As she neared death's door, she struggled with the thought of dying. Yet one morning, when her mother came into her room, the girl was all aglow and happy. "What has happened to you?" her mother asked. The little girl answered, "An angel came to me and said I was going on a trip. God came and took my hand and walked with me through a beautiful garden. He told me, 'You're coming here tomorrow, to be with Me.'" God spoke to that little child — and took all the pain and fear from her heart! When she left to be with Him the next day, she had total peace.

Tell me — when you are intimate with Jesus, do you receive such direction from Him? Does He tell you what to do — and when and how to do it? Some Christians don't believe God does this. But Jesus says, "My sheep hear my voice...and they follow me" *(John 10:27)*.

There is no way through your trial, except to get alone with Jesus and cry, "Lord, You're the only One on this earth who can help me. Only You know the way through this trial. So I'm going to stay here till You tell me what to do. I'm not going anywhere until You speak to my heart!" This is the kind of "praying through" that is pleasing to God. It means stopping everything, all activity, until you hear His voice. Only then will you hear Him speak clearly to your heart: "You've got to make things right with this person..." Or, "You've got to make restitution here..." Or, "Just stand still till next week. Don't get in a hurry. Sit in My presence and trust Me...." He will give you clear directions!

Yet, something even more is needed for us to see our prayers through the coming trials — to make our prayers complete:

The Second Thing Needed to Pray Through Is to Add to Our Intimacy Total Confidence in God's Word.

Christ is the living Word of God. And when you are shut in with Him in prayer, the Holy Spirit will always lead you to God's revealed Word. He will build up your faith by feeding you from the Bible — even while you're in the secret closet! We are commanded: "Put on the whole armour of God, that ye may be able to stand against the wiles of the devil.... Wherefore take unto you the whole armour of God, that ye may be able to stand in the evil day...And take...the sword of the Spirit, which is the word of God" *(Ephesians 6:11, 13, 17)*.

Often when you receive specific instructions from the Lord, His Spirit will whisper, "Now turn to…", directing you to a passage of Scripture. God's Word will speak to you directly — telling you how to get through your crisis!

Right now, there are many Christians reading this message who simply have to hear a word from the Lord. Nobody on earth can help them. There is but one way for them to get through their trial — and that is by staying in Christ's presence until He gives them direction! He must tell them the way through — what to do, and when and how to act. His exclusive direction to them won't come one minute too early or too late. It will all be in the Holy Ghost's timing!

Dear saint, there is no need for you to worry about your trial. God is faithful to respond to your every need and request. So, as you go to prayer now, simply pray, "Lord, I come now not just to have my needs met — needs You have foreseen and are eager to supply. No — I come also to meet Your need!"

We were made for fellowship with Him — even in our heaviest times. I ask you: Do you love to be with Him? Do you prefer Him above all others? Does your heart cry out, "Jesus, You're my everything. You are my soul's great pleasure — and I love Your company!"

God, put in all of us a heart that is easily wooed to Your presence. Help us to pray through all our trials to completion…to listen closely to Your Spirit in our secret time of communion with You…and to put all our confidence in Your revealed Word. In these ways, we can know our prayers are pleasing to You.

26

God Wants You to Know His Voice

Laying Aside All Hindrances to Intimacy

The devil does everything in his power to make his voice heard in this world. At one point, he even had the audacity to interrupt Jesus while the Lord was speaking in the synagogue:

"And they went into Capernaum; and straightway on the sabbath day he entered into the synagogue, and taught....And there was in their synagogue a man with an unclean spirit; and he cried out, saying, Let us alone; what have we to do with thee, thou Jesus of Nazareth? Art thou come to destroy us? I know thee who thou art, the Holy One of God. And Jesus rebuked him, saying, Hold thy peace, and come out of him" *(Mark 1:21-26)*.

Using the voice of the man, Satan cried out loudly, having one purpose in mind — to send fear throughout the entire congregation! He wanted every person within the sound of his voice to cower in fear — to believe he had power and authority, even as he was being cast out. Indeed, Peter warns last-day believers that Satan will come to them with a loud voice, trying to bring fear: "Be sober, be vigilant; because your adversary the devil, as a roaring lion, walketh about, seeking whom he may devour" *(1 Peter 5:8)*.

Here is my point: If Satan is making his voice known in these last days, showing his power to the masses of lost souls, how much more important is it for God's people to know their Father's voice? Do you think the Lord would sit by as Satan roars at the world — and yet remain silent Himself? Never! Isaiah said: "And the Lord shall cause his glorious voice to be heard..." *(Isaiah 30:30)*.

Since Adam and Eve, God has been speaking to man. Scripture says that from the very beginning, "They heard the voice of the Lord God..." *(Genesis 3:8)*. Adam said, "I heard thy voice in the garden..." *(verse 10)*. From Genesis onward through the New Testament, God made His voice known to His people — to Abraham, Moses, Caleb, Joshua, Samuel and David, to righteous kings and judges. In the books of the prophets we see this phrase repeated time after time: "And God said..." God's voice was known and understood. He always made His voice to be heard!

Jesus confirmed this in the New Testament, using the example of the Good Shepherd: "...the sheep hear his voice: and he calleth his own sheep by name, and leadeth them out. And when he putteth forth his own sheep, he goeth before them, and the sheep follow him: for they know his voice. And a stranger they will not follow, but will flee from him: for they know not the voice of strangers" *(John 10:3-5)*.

Jesus stated to Pilate: "...Every one that is of the truth heareth my voice" *(18:37)*. The message to us is clear: If you have God's Spirit in you, then you will hear and know His voice! Yet we live in a day when many voices clamor for our attention. Paul warned: "There are...so many kinds of voices in the world, and none of them is without signification [meaning]" *(1 Corinthians 14:10)*.

Perhaps you have had the experience of many other Christians: When you pray, seeking to hear and know God's voice, your mind is flooded with all kinds of voices. You may wonder, "How can I distinguish the voice of God from my own flesh? How can I be sure it is God speaking, and not the voice of a tempting spirit?"

Let me share with you a few insights I believe God has given me on this matter of hearing and knowing His voice:

If You Are Living in Sin, You Will Never Hear God's Voice!

If you are coddling some secret sin, you can be sure you really don't want to hear God's voice. That is because you already know what He will say to you — and you don't want to hear it!

When Adam and Eve sinned, it brought shame. And with that shame came guilt, fear and condemnation. This shame is called "nakedness" in the Old Testament — and being naked meant standing in God's presence clothed only with guilt. "And the Lord called unto Adam, and said unto him, Where art thou? And he said, I heard thy voice in the garden, and I was afraid, because I was naked; and I hid myself" *(Genesis 3:9-10)*. Adam hid from God's voice, because of the guilt and shame of his sin. And that is exactly where many of God's people are today — hiding, afraid to hear God speak!

You may have lukewarm Christian friends who don't like to go to church with you. When you first met them they were living carelessly. Indeed, they were burdened with guilt and shame — but they weren't ready to give up their secret sin.

When you brought them to church with you, God's Word pierced their conscience. They knew they were hearing the voice of God, calling out to them, "Where are you — what are you doing?" And fear struck their heart. The holy presence of Jesus made their sin seem vile — and they could not wait to run out of church and hide!

Beloved, if you want to hear God's voice, you have to be ready for a total cleansing. You must be willing to have every sin exposed and cast away!

The prophet Isaiah had an awesome vision of the Lord sitting on a throne, high and lifted up. Seraphim covered themselves with their wings because of the holy presence of God. They cried out: "...Holy, holy, holy, is the Lord of hosts: the whole earth is full of his glory" *(Isaiah 6:3)*.

God's voice was so mighty it shook the temple. And at the sound of it, the righteous prophet Isaiah fell on his face, crying: "...Woe is me! for I am undone; because I am a man of unclean lips: for mine eyes have seen the King, the Lord of hosts" *(verse 5)*. Isaiah was stricken with a sense of sin and uncleanness — because God's voice is a purging voice!

"Then flew one of the seraphims unto me, having a live coal in his hand, which he had taken with the tongs from off the altar: and he laid it upon my mouth, and said, Lo, this hath touched thy lips; and thine iniquity is taken away, and thy sin purged" *(verses 6-7)*. Isaiah could not hear God's "directing voice" until he had first heard His "purging voice." You see, direction and guidance come only after purging — because if you haven't been purged, you can't go any farther with the Lord.

Yet thousands upon thousands of God's people today flock to meetings to get a quick, "cure-all" word from God. They want a prophet to lay hands on them — to tell them what to do and what the future holds. Most of what they hear, however, is flattery: "Thou shalt be mightily used of God!" "Thou shalt be a witness to the nations!" "Thou shalt be blessed and prosperous!"

How many of these people do you think would flock to meetings if the "star preacher" pointed a finger at their heart and gave them the purging Word of God? "You're still unclean — you never have let go of your secret sin. You have no vision of Jesus' holiness. Hear His voice — repent!"

If you want to hear God's voice of direction, you must first be ready to have your soul purged and cleansed. His Word comes to pierce our conscience and expose wickedness — so He can use us!

It Was Only After Isaiah Heard the Voice of Purging That He Heard the Voice of Direction.

Once he had received purging, Isaiah received direction from God: "I heard the voice of the Lord, saying, Whom shall I send, and who will go for us? Then said I, Here am I; send me. And he said, Go..." *(Isaiah 6:8-9)*.

How excited we become after the purging! Once we have repented and become broken, we pray, "Lord, You know that I've been cleansed, that all sins have been purged. Now I'm ready to hear Your voice of direction. Speak to Thy servant — for I'm ready to obey!"

Yet if you want direction — if you think you're ready to do what He asks — then let me ask you: Are you ready for an unsettling word — a mission of hardship and rejection — a life of faith with no guaranteed comforts except those of the Holy Ghost? That is exactly what happened to Isaiah! The prophet volunteered, "Send me, Lord." And God sent him on a hard, difficult mission!

"And he said, Go, and tell this people, Hear ye indeed, but understand not; and see ye indeed, but perceive not. Make the heart of this people fat, and make their ears heavy, and shut their eyes; lest they see with their eyes, and hear with their ears, and understand with their heart" (verses 9-10).

The word Isaiah heard was not flattering! On the contrary, it would make him hated, unpopular. The Lord told him, "Go, harden those who refuse to hear Me speak. Close their eyes and ears. Finish the hardening of their hearts!"

If you want to know God's voice, then you have to be willing to hear anything He says. God will never say, "Go!" until He first asks, "Who will go?" He comes to you, asking, "Are you willing to do anything I tell you — to do it My way? Are you willing to lay down your life?"

When I prayed for direction a few short years ago, the Lord told me clearly, "Go back to New York." That was a most uncomfortable word for me! I had been ready to retire. I had planned to write books and preach at a few selected places. I thought, "Lord, I've already spent my best years there. Give me a break!"

Yes, we want to hear the voice of God — but we want to hear it comfortably! We don't want it to shake us. Yet, why should God give us His voice of direction if He is not sure we will obey Him?

Abraham learned to hear God's voice by first obeying what he heard — at the time he heard it. God's word to him was a hard word: "Sacrifice your son, Isaac!" Abraham acted on that word — and his obedience became a sweet-smelling aroma that touched the whole world: "And in thy seed shall all nations of the earth be blessed; because thou hast obeyed my voice" *(Genesis 22:18)*.

There Is One Major Cause Why So Many Believers Cannot Know or Understand the Voice of God.

The leaders of Israel came to Moses and said: "Now therefore why should we die? For...if we hear the voice of the Lord our God any more, then we shall die. For who is there of all flesh, that hath heard the voice of the living God speaking out of the midst of the fire, as we have, and lived? Go thou near, and hear all that the Lord our God shall say: and speak thou unto us all that the Lord our God shall speak unto thee; and we will hear it, and do it" *(Deuteronomy 5:25-27)*.

These men were saying to Moses, "You go to God! You hear His voice and tell us what He says, and we will do it." But Moses reminded these leaders that at one time they had heard the Lord's voice for themselves: "The Lord talked with you face to face in the mount out of the midst of the fire" *(verse 4)*. God had talked to them personally — and they had lived! In fact, that very night, before retiring, they had agreed: "...We have heard his voice out of the midst of the fire: we have seen this day that God doth talk with man, and he liveth" *(verse 24)*.

No, these Israelites were not afraid of hearing God's voice — they were afraid of what He was going to tell them! It was because they still clung to idols — golden mice they had carried with them from Egpyt. God already had commanded them: "Thou shalt have no other gods before me. Thou shalt not make unto thee any graven image....Thou shalt not bow down thyself to them..." *(Exodus 20:3-5)*. And now He was saying to them, "I want all of your heart. Lay down your idols!"

Amos spoke for God, saying: "Have ye offered unto me sacrifices and offerings in the wilderness forty years, O house of Israel? But ye have borne the tabernacle of your Moloch and Chiun your images, the star of your god, which ye made to yourselves" *(Amos 5:25-26)*.

The writer of Hebrews says Israel begged "...that the word should not be spoken to them any more: (For they could not endure that which was commanded...)" *(Hebrews 12:19-20)*. Here is the key: The Israelites could not endure what God had commanded of them — because they could not bear the thought of giving up their hidden idols and secret sins! They thought, "Moses is meek. We'll let him talk to God, and then we'll listen to him. He's led us all these years, and he still hasn't caught onto our hidden idols. He won't be as hard on us as God!"

No! God is not an entertainer who plays parlor games with idolatrous Christians. He seeks intimacy — He wants to speak to the smallest details of our lives. And He speaks with one purpose in mind — to possess all of our heart! He wants to destroy all idols and purge all sin so He can bless, favor and reward. The Lord said of Israel: "O that there were such an heart in them, that they would fear me, and keep all my commandments always, that it might be well with them, and with their children for ever!" *(Deuteronomy 5:29)*.

God's Voice Cannot Be Heard When You Are Depending on a Man's Voice.

Israel could not hear God's voice because they preferred hearing the voice of a man. I ask you: Could this be the reason you are not able to hear His voice? Perhaps you have an idol — a certain minister, teacher or evangelist. He speaks to you of good things — of healing, prosperity, faith and blessings. But he does not dig into your heart about sin! You don't want to be searched; you want only to be blessed — so you listen to his tapes for hours, devouring his messages. But you are feeding on a man instead of on Christ!

The reason many Christians today cannot hear the voice of God is because they have been indoctrinated by a man. The Bible speaks of this as the worst idolatry of these last days — addiction to false doctrine, false teachers, indoctrination by men who do not speak for God. I do not speak against these men, but against heresy and error — against false doctrines that are coming forth and ruining men's souls. Those who run to such doctrines end up half-hearted, confused, shipwrecked. And they miss the true blessing and favor of God.

It is time for every believer to go directly to the Lord and hear His voice — without a man in the middle! You have to learn to hear God's voice for yourself. Yes, His Spirit will be digging, searching, convicting, dealing. But you will never know His voice until He has all your heart.

I want to speak now to those repentant, remnant believers who truly want to hear and know their Lord's voice:

God's Desire Is for His Holy People to Enjoy a Daily, Consistent, Conversational Hearing of His Voice!

God desires to speak to you as if you were sitting down to dinner with

Him. He wants to converse with you, heart to heart, on any and all matters. The Bible says: "Behold, I stand at the door, and knock: if any man hear my voice, and open the door, I will come in to him, and will sup with him, and he with me" *(Revelation 3:20)*.

This verse often has been misapplied to the unsaved. We speak of Jesus standing at the door of the sinner's heart, seeking entrance. No — it is to the believer that Christ is speaking! The context shows that Christ is talking to those who are clothed in white raiment (righteousness), who have bought gold tried in the fire, whose eyes are anointed ("having revelation"), are loved, reproved and chastened *(see verses 18-19)*. These are repentant, holy people who want to know the voice of God!

As I read and reread verse 20 in this passage, three words kept leaping out at me: "Open the door! Open the door!" And the Spirit of God spoke clearly to my heart: "David, the reason you have not heard Me as I want to be heard is because you are not wholly open in your spirit to hear!"

Now, we know theologically that Jesus abides in our heart. Yet most of us keep a little place in our heart that we never open up to the Lord. This is the seat of our soul, the very core of our being; it makes us the person we are. And out of it springs all of our emotions.

This is the room Jesus comes to, knocking, calling. He is saying there is a closed door between you and Himself — something that is blocking Him from coming in. This door, as I see it, represents a commitment — one that many Christians have not yet fully made. Most believers pray: "Lord, all I need is a little advice, a few words of direction — a reminder that You love me. Just let me know whether I'm doing right or wrong. Go before me and open the doors!"

But Jesus answers us: "If all you want from Me is direction, I can send a prophet to give it to you. If you only want to know where to go and what to do, I can send someone and you can filter it all through him. But you're missing Me!" The fact is, Jesus wants more. He wants your closeness, your deepest emotions — your locked-up room. He wants to sit down with you and share all that is in His heart — to talk to you face to face. He wants to be intimate with you. He is calling for "dinner for two"!

Revelation 3 is a wonderful picture of this. It speaks of love and intimacy, of sharing secrets, of tender voices. Christ is saying here, "I want to share My heart with you. I want you to know My ways, so that the very thoughts you think are My thoughts. I want My voice to emerge more and more in your heart — until your very mind is the mind of Christ!" He stands at the door, knocking, asking for a commitment — a step of faith that says you will open up your heart, soul and mind to Him. This can't happen through emotions or feelings. Rather, it must be through a commitment of faith that says, "Jesus, I commit to You — not to answers, not to direction. I open the door of my all to You!"

And when Jesus comes in, He brings food, bread — in other words, Himself. And when you feed on Him, you will be satisfied completely!

The Song of Solomon Offers a Beautiful Picture of Christ Wanting to Come in the Door!

The bride portrayed in the Song of Solomon says: "I sleep, but my heart waketh: it is the voice of my beloved that knocketh, saying, Open to me, my sister, my love, my dove, my undefiled: for my head is filled with dew, and my locks with the drops of the night" (Song of Solomon 5:2).

The bridegroom in this scene represents Jesus. He is knocking on his bride's door, saying, "Open to Me, My beloved. My head is filled with dew [meaning, I have suffered for our love]." The bride hears Him knock, but she is in bed. She loves the bridegroom, but she is too tired to get up and open the door to him.

Then something happens. She says, "My beloved put his hand in the hole of the door, and my bowels were moved for him" *(verse 4)*. In oriental times, doors were built with an opening in them. Here, the bridegroom wants so badly to be with his bride that he puts his hand in the opening and tries to undo the lock from inside. But for some reason he is hindered. So he looks through the opening at his bride — and he sees her sleepy-eyed and half-awake. He wonders: "Does she truly love me? Why does she not open to me with anxious jubilation? Why am I so anxious to be with her — and yet she is so unconcerned about being with me?"

This is exactly what the Lord is wanting from His church! He wants us waiting at the door, full of love — not slighting Him as if He were not the altogether lovely One of our hearts! After all, people who are in love want to be alone together. And this picture shows Christ's heart toward us: He wants intimacy with us so badly that He literally reaches inside and tries to unlock the door. Yet, I ask you — how many times has Jesus wanted intimacy with you, but you've shut Him out?

At this point, the bride rouses herself and smells her beloved's fragrance (the myrrh) on the lock of the door: "I rose up to open to my beloved; and my hands dropped with myrrh, and my fingers with sweet smelling myrrh, upon the handles of the lock" *(verse 5)*. Finally, she says: "I opened to my beloved; but my beloved had withdrawn himself, and was gone: my soul failed when he spake: I sought him, but I could not find him; I called him, but he gave me no answer" *(verse 6)*. The bridegroom was gone! He still loved her — but his actions said, "She has no intense love for me — she's taking me for granted! I've got to withdraw until she learns to appreciate who I am."

Sometimes the Lord has to withdraw from us for the same reason. When He does so, He is saying to us, "I want you to come to Me with all your heart. I want you to love Me — to yearn after Me with everything that's in you!"

Suddenly, the bride realizes she has slighted her bridegroom. So she runs into the streets, crying, "I charge you, O daughters of Jerusalem, if ye find my beloved, that ye tell him, that I am (faint with desire)" *(verse 8)*. She tells everyone, "…He is altogether lovely…" *(verse 16)*.

This is a picture of an awakened church — awakened to her need for Christ! Those who hunger for the Bridegroom are already standing at the door when Jesus knocks. They're ready, with their hand on the door, to open up to intimacy with Him!

Like the bride in this passage, we must wake up to who Jesus is to us. We have to say, as the bride does, "That's my love, my life. I can't do without Him!" Have you not yet opened up to loving intimacy with Jesus? Have you not yet let the Bridegroom in? Open up your soul and spirit to Christ, and trust He will enter. Let Him be your source, your everything. And believe what He said: "I will come in — I will dine with you!" *(see Revelation 3:20)*.

In His presence, shut in with Him alone, you will get to know Him — His fragrance, His ways, His heart. And you will learn to know His voice — the voice of the One who loves you enough to keep knocking and begging for your intimacy. Get close to Him — and you will know His voice!

The Devil Can't
Have You!

27

Trusting God's Miraculous Deliverance

Every story recorded in the Old Testament was written for our benefit and instruction in the ways of the Lord. If you want to know who God is, His methods and His ways, then study the books of the Old Testament. They aren't just ancient war stories or accounts of God's miracle-working power in bygone days. Paul said they were recorded to teach believers in these last days great lessons about how God operates on our behalf: "Now all these things happened unto them for ensamples: and they are written for our admonition, upon whom the ends of the world are come" *(1 Corinthians 10:11)*.

I want to take you into Isaiah 36 and 37 to glean some important lessons about God's keeping, delivering power. In these two chapters we will see how God turned an impossible situation into a glorious salvation of His people. Let me give you a brief outline of this unusual story:

Sennacherib, king of Assyria, came against Judah and their king, Hezekiah. The Assyrian army had already captured forty-six cities of Judah, and Jerusalem was to be their last conquest. Samaria and Israel had already fallen. And now the Assyrians wanted Judah because it stood in their pathway to Egypt, their next battlefield.

King Hezekiah, knowing the Assyrians were coming, had been preparing for almost two years. He had stockpiled great stores of food and water to help Jerusalem endure the siege. He also had built an outer wall around the city, some twelve to fifteen feet wide. Jerusalem's gates had been closed and locked, probably encased with iron. And crowded within the city were many surviving soldiers and refugees from other Judean cities.

Now Hezekiah and the people peered down from the wall and onto the fields below. Everywhere they looked, the landscape was covered by the surrounding army — thousands of soldiers, chariots, horses, war machines. The Assyrians had pitched their tents, preparing for a long siege. They were bent on Jerusalem's total destruction!

The captain of the Assyrian army was an evil man named Rabshakeh, who spoke three languages, including Hebrew. He came forward and stood in an open field before the city, calling out to Hezekiah's envoys on top of the wall. So Hezekiah sent out three of his envoys to hear him. Rabshakeh spoke to them in Hebrew, mocking the God of Israel — his words full of sarcasm, mockery, pride. He boldly predicted their fall, saying, "You know that no army, god or people has been able to withstand us. We have already captured forty-six of your cities. Your nation is gone — Israel and Samaria are gone. We know how weak you are. Tell your king I'll give him 2,000 horses if he can supply 2,000 trained men to ride them! There is no way you're going to withstand this siege. Why not give up now?"

Rabshakeh came back day after day, with a new round of ridicule and sarcasm. "You are finished! We are all-powerful — nobody has resisted us yet. Your God cannot save you from destruction!"

Beloved, this message is about how God saved Jerusalem — and how He does the same for us today! No matter what your problem is — finances, health, marriage, a trial or temptation you can't seem to get victory over — you are going to see how God still delivers His people from the clutches of the devil!

This story holds great significance for us today. You see, Sennacherib in Hebrew means "lord of hosts." He represents the devil and his demonic army — king of a proud, arrogant, evil host. And Rabshakeh represents destructive principalities and powers. His name means "to quaff down" or "to swallow greedily." Hezekiah, on the other hand, means "one who is dependent upon the Lord." And Jerusalem represents God's holy remnant. Think of it: The holy city Jerusalem is surrounded by the devil himself and all the powers of hell!

Let's consider the lessons we can glean from this Old Testament example:

1. Satan is Hell-Bent on Bringing Down Every Righteous Man or Woman!

You can be sure the devil has determined to destroy you if you have set your heart on seeking God. Satan hated King Hezekiah with a passion. His demonic siege on Jerusalem was more than a political battle; it was an all-out attack upon a righteous man who had brought holiness back to God's people.

Hezekiah's father, King Ahaz, had devastated Judah with wickedness. He had reigned for sixteen years — a period filled with vileness, evil and bloodshed. During that time, Ahaz made alliances with heathen nations. He sacrificed to idols. He stripped the temple of all its gold and chopped up all the holy vessels. He went up to Assyria to worship their god. And he set up idol worship in Jerusalem and shut the doors of God's house, closing down all worship of Jehovah. He even offered one of his sons as a sacrifice to Molech!

The glory of the Lord had departed Judah during Ahaz' reign. And Satan had to be well-pleased that the seed of David had fallen into such corruption; how he must have gloated over the apostasy. Yet it was in the midst of all this spiritual darkness and demonic activity that Hezekiah came to the throne. Scripture says he was unlike his father — for Hezekiah "did that which was right in the sight of the Lord, according to all that David his father did" *(2 Kings 18:3)*. He was a holy, righteous man, doing what was right in God's eyes.

The first thing Hezekiah did was to destroy all the icons in the land. He tore down the high places, burned all the images, smashed the idols. He went to the valley of Molech and chopped to pieces the hideous god that the people offered their infants to. He dealt severely with homosexuality and sodomy. He cut to pieces the brass serpent Moses had made, which the Israelites had kept and now idolized. Hezekiah called it "Nehushtan," which means "just a piece of brass" — and he publicly cut it into shreds, crying out, "You'll not worship this piece of brass. We're going to worship Jehovah!"

Finally, he went down to the house of God, and he totally restored it. He took eight days to cleanse it, hauling out all the filth and garbage piled up inside. Then he renovated it, putting back all the proper instruments. He also sanctified and restored the Levitical order. And he sent word everywhere that God had returned to Zion: "Come, return to the Lord!"

Hezekiah had brought back true worship — true joy and reverence for Jehovah. He was a humble, praying man, and soon prayer was heard throughout Jerusalem. A revival broke out in the land, and the people had one of the greatest Passover celebrations ever. It went on for fourteen days: "So there was great joy in Jerusalem: for since the time of Solomon the son of David king of Israel there was not the like in Jerusalem" *(2 Chronicles 30:26)*.

How enraged hell must have been! Up until now, Satan's will had been performed; the devil had thought the seed of David would die. But now there was a revival of righteousness — a holy remnant rising in Judah, ready to lead all of Israel back to God. So, Satan decided to go after Hezekiah and the righteous. That is why the army of Assyrians now filled the hills and valleys surrounding Jerusalem. The principalities and powers of darkness had gathered to bring down God's holy people!

As Hezekiah stood on the wall, looking down at that awesome army and hearing their arrogant threats, what thoughts entered his mind? He probably wondered, "Lord, what have I done to deserve a test like this? I've only done what is right through You! I've cast down every icon. I've dealt with every perversion in the land. I've brought back true worship and praise. Why are we being surrounded, besieged? Everything seems hopeless!"

This is exactly where many sold-out Christians stand today. Perhaps you have set your heart on Jesus, and He has become Lord of all. You are cleaving to Him, doing only His will, walking in holiness, consumed with His eternal purposes. Yet suddenly you have found yourself surrounded by temptations and fiery trials. The devil has come against you to bring you down — to bring shame and evil on the name of the Lord!

You must understand, beloved: If you walk close to Jesus, you will have many afflictions. You will be tried with fiery trials. You will face the fury of hell. The devil will besiege you, taunt you, ridicule you. And few of your brothers or sisters will understand or believe you. You will be attacked on all sides!

King Hezekiah could have wasted time trying to figure it all out — searching for what he'd done wrong, examining himself, thinking he was under judgment. But none of that was the case. The devil simply was mad at him and Judah for their devotion to Jehovah! It had stirred up hell!

Likewise, you have to stop asking yourself "why" in the midst of your trial. Stop the constant self-examination. It's all very plain: The devil is mad at you for your devotion and work for Jesus! If your heart is set on Him, all hell will come to attention. You will be marked. So prepare to suffer — to be attacked!

2. The Devil's Tactics Have Never Changed. He Still Uses the Same Weapons of Warfare!

Satan's big weapon is lies. He is the father of all lies, and he plants them in our minds to rob us of our faith and trust in God's faithfulness. Consider the lies he told Hezekiah:

1. Lie Number One: "God has ordered all your present troubles. He is angry with you — and you're under judgment!"

Rabshakeh, an agent of hell, was there to taunt Hezekiah. He said: "And am I now come up without the Lord against this land to destroy it? The Lord said unto me, go up against this land, and destroy it" *(Isaiah 36:10)*. He was saying, "Your God told me to attack and destroy you. I've been sent by God to do this!"

No — that was a hellish lie! God did not send this evil army; He was not angry with Hezekiah. Yet Rabshakeh's implication was, "God has left you to do battle all alone — and you know you are too weak and helpless to fight. You might as well give up!"

If Satan can make you believe God is not with you, he has already won the battle without shooting a single arrow. He wants you to think God has stepped aside and abandoned you — that He has put you into this situation because you can't learn any other way. Yet you see how weak and helpless you are — and it all seems hopeless!

No — that is a lie! Don't you see? You are not alone — God has never failed you, nor has He ever left you. And He is not putting you into the hands of the devil to fight him alone. He knows you're no match for Satan. No — this is God's battle!

2. Lie Number Two: "All your self-denial, your diligence, your good works have been in vain. You have somehow displeased God!"

"But if thou say to me, We trust in the Lord our God: is it not he, whose high places and whose altars Hezekiah hath taken away...?" *(verse 7)*. Rabshakeh again was lying to Hezekiah and his people! His implication was, "All those supposedly holy things you have done — all your sacrificing, your worship, your ministry to the Lord — have all been in vain! Your motives have been wrong, and God hasn't heard you. What you tore down were really His holy places. If God is pleased with you, then why are you surrounded by trouble? Look at you — you're helpless, weak, tempted. Where is God if your praises have been acceptable? Why are we at your gate if He is pleased with you?"

Beloved, don't believe this vicious lie! God's Word says to you: "For God is not unrighteous to forget your work and labour of love, which ye have shewed toward his name, in that ye have ministered to the saints, and do minister" *(Hebrews 6:10)*.

God has not forgotten a single thing you have done for His glory! He has bottled every tear you've ever shed. He rejoices in your love and repentance. He has such wonderful thoughts about you: "For I know the thoughts I think toward you, saith the Lord, thoughts of peace, and not of evil, to give you an expected end" *(Jeremiah 29:11)*.

3. Lie Number Three: "Others stronger and better than you have fallen to my power. How do you expect to make it?"

Rabshakeh said, "Beware lest Hezekiah persuade you, saying, The Lord will deliver us. Hath any of the gods of the nations delivered his land out of the hand of the king of Assyria?" *(Isaiah 36:18)*. In other words, "Look at who has fallen — all so great and mighty! Hamath, Arphed, Samaria..."

Several years ago, our church was in a prayer meeting on the night the story broke that a well-known TV evangelist had fallen. I remember the gloom that fell over the whole congregation as the news was announced. Fear entered many, because not long before this another well-known evangelist had been exposed. After the service people came to me, distraught. One man said to me, with tears in his eyes, "Brother Dave, if he couldn't make it, what chance do I have? He knew the Lord — he preached holiness, and against sin. I mortgaged my house to give him money. He seemed so in love with Jesus, so much stronger than I. If the devil could bring him down, how can I hope to make it?"

Satan uses the failures of other apparently holy, strong believers to rattle your spine with fear. I'm sure Hezekiah, standing on the city wall, could have said, "Rabshakeh is right! The strong are falling left and right. Who ever would have thought Israel or Samaria would fall? Why do I think I can stand, when these others are going down all around me?"

No! That's the biggest lie the devil could ever tell! It's true that when that TV evangelist fell, many turned their backs on the Lord. But they wouldn't have turned away if they hadn't had the same mixture in their own lives. If you have your eyes on men or women, God is going to let them fall in front of you, one after another — until you finally get focused on Him!

Why did Samaria and Israel fall, while Judah still stood strong for the Lord? They fell for the same reason that many seemingly holy people fall today: "They feared the Lord, and served their own gods, after the manner of the nations whom they carried away from thence" *(2 Kings 17:33)*.

There was a mixture in them all along! Something of the world had their hearts. Outwardly they feared the Lord and did all that looked right and holy — but their hearts were given over to an idol that had never been cast down. While they had been going up to the mountain to worship Jehovah, all along they had an idol before their eyes!

For most Christians today, that idol is pride and ambition. These always bring a person down. I've talked to many well-known people who have fallen, and asked them, "The sin you were exposed for was not your real problem, was it?" Almost every time they acknowledged, "No — it was pride. An ego trip."

Beloved, it doesn't matter how much you worship the Lord; if you allow pride a place in your heart, that's an idol. And you're going to take a fall — because pride is the one thing God will not allow!

3. It Is Absolutely Impossible to Deliver Yourself From Temptations and Snares.

What do you do when the enemy comes in like a flood — when you seem trapped, the battle seems hopeless, and you feel on the verge of falling?

Behold Hezekiah on the wall, pacing. To the human eye, everything looked hopeless. What could he have been thinking? He might have wondered if he should try to escape by himself — to get a horse and flee to some quiet desert place. David had similar thoughts: "...Oh that I had wings like a dove! for then would I fly away, and be at rest. Lo, then would I wander far off, and remain in the wilderness....I would hasten my escape from the windy storm and tempest" *(Psalm 55:6-8)*.

Yet Scripture tells us what happened when King Zedekiah had tried to run: "...then they fled, and went forth out of the city by night...but the Chaldeans' army pursued after them, and overtook Zedekiah" *(Jeremiah 39:4-5)*. Running away from your battles solves nothing. Your problems will always follow you!

What about the option of standing on the wall and rebuking those nasty Assyrians: "Rabshakeh, I bind you! Devil army, I rebuke you!" Most Christians who "rebuke the devil" don't know that the word "rebuke" means simply to scold or reprimand. Thousands of believers today are going around scolding the devil! Try to picture Hezekiah rebuking the surrounding army: "I command you Assyrians to depart! You don't belong here — this is God's city. Get out of here!"

Do you think the Assyrians would have fled? No way! Yet we are always looking for a shortcut, an easy deliverance. We think we can stand on the wall and yell at the devil with no heart preparation, no cost. Please don't mistake me: I believe in casting out demons and binding the powers of darkness. But such power is reserved for those who have a holy life corresponding to the work — who walk in righteousness and have paid a price!

Put yourself on that city wall, and look at that devilish host all around you. You will see how helpless and powerless you are to deliver yourself. You can come to only one conclusion: "Unless God delivers me miraculously, there is no way out!"

Maybe you have tried hard to fight singlehandedly. You want to please the Lord, and you don't want to fall. So you grit your teeth and try, try, try — and fail, fail, fail! Dear saint, you've got to understand: This is not your battle — it is God's! He alone has the power to overcome. David said: "And all this assembly shall know that the Lord saveth not with sword and spear: for the battle is the Lord's, and he will give you into our hands" *(1 Samuel 17:47)*.

"And Moses said unto the people, Fear ye not, stand still, and see the salvation of the Lord, which he will shew to you to day...The Lord shall fight for you, and ye shall hold your peace" *(Exodus 14:13-14)*. No matter what problem you're having, neither you nor anyone else can get you out of it. It takes a miracle of God!

4. God Miraculously Delivered Hezekiah and Jerusalem!

God wants to deliver us in the same supernatural manner He delivered King Hezekiah and Jerusalem. But there are some things we must do — and they are the very things Hezekiah did:

1. He humbled himself: "And it came to pass, when king Hezekiah heard it, that he rent his clothes, and covered himself with sackcloth..." *(Isaiah 37:1)*. Tearing off the outer garment and putting on sackcloth was a sign of humbling oneself.

What is humility? It's not feeling unworthy or putting on some long face. True humility is casting oneself wholly on the Lord for everything! It is knowing you can do nothing in your own strength and power; it is admitting your helplessness and turning to God in utter trust. It is saying, "God, You have to do it, or it can't be done!"

As Hezekiah walked along the wall in sackcloth, he was testifying to the people, "I am only a weak man! I can't help anyone in my own strength. I can't even deliver myself. I am turning to the Lord as my only hope!"

Do you recognize this about your family problem? Your marriage? Your financial problem? Your temptation? You can't conquer it yourself — so don't even try. Only God can do it!

2. Hezekiah turned to prayer: "...and [he] went into the house of the Lord" *(verse 1)*.

Rabshakeh had written a letter to Hezekiah demanding full surrender, or the Assyrians would attack. "And Hezekiah received the letter...and read it: and Hezekiah went up into the house of the Lord, and spread it before the Lord. And Hezekiah prayed before the Lord...Lord, bow down thine ear and hear...save thou us out of his hand..." *(2 Kings 19:14-19)*. The way out of Satan's snare is prayer! Hezekiah took the letter from Rabshakeh and laid it out before the Lord!

Perhaps the devil has sent word to you that you're going to fall. Beloved, take it to the Lord! Lay everything out honestly before Him, even if you got yourself into your mess. Tell Him the truth; He knows all about it, anyway. Call on Him as Hezekiah did: "Lord, you know all about my problems and the trouble I'm in. Save me — deliver me!"

3. After humility and diligent prayer, the Word of the Lord came to Hezekiah. God always speaks to the praying ones!

"...Thus saith the Lord, Be not afraid of the words that thou hast heard...Behold, I will send a blast upon him...and I will cause him to fall by the sword in his own land" *(Isaiah 37:6-7)*. God said to Hezekiah, "You're not going to fall — your enemy is! I'm going to send him right back to where he came from. Just seek My face — and I'll deal with your enemy!"

"Be not afraid..." Beloved, those three words have kept me through every battle throughout the years. Whenever I shut myself in with the Lord and pour out my heart before Him, the first thing He whispers to me is, "Don't be afraid — fear not. I have not given you a spirit of fear, but of power, love and a sound mind."

How can you face such a strong enemy on all sides and not be afraid? Only by trusting fully in the Word of the Lord! You can look death straight in the eye when you've been shut in with God.

"Because thy rage against me...is come up into mine ears, therefore ...I will turn thee back by the way which thou camest" *(verse 29)*. God says the devil's rage against you is actually against Him. And He will turn the enemy back by the way he came! "...He shall not come into this city, nor shoot an arrow there, nor come before it with shields...[but] by the way that he came, by the same shall he return...For I will defend this city to save it for my own sake, and for my servant David's sake" *(verses 33-35)*. The city He's talking about is the holy remnant — us! God is going to save us and deliver us for His own glory. He wants a holy remnant in these last days to be a testimony to His saving power!

The Lord sent an angel to the Assryian camp — and in one night it was all over: "Then an angel of the Lord went forth, and smote in the camp of the Assyrians a hundred and fourscore and five thousand [185,000]: and when they arose early in the morning, behold, they were all dead corpses. So Sennacherib king of Assyria departed, and went and returned..." *(verses 36-37)*.

Can you imagine it? Jerusalem awoke the next day, and 185,000 dead corpses were lying in the fields! Someone probably came running to Hezekiah, crying, "You won't believe it! The trumpets are blaring all over Jerusalem — thousands are on the walls praising the Lord. There's not a chariot in sight! All the tents are gone, Rabshakeh's gone — and there's nothing left but corpses!" All those principalities and powers of darkness were slain by the angel of the Lord. God sent them right back to where they came from — and He will send the devil back to the abyss for you!

Keep His word as your hope: "Be not afraid. I will deliver you. I will send your enemy back to where he came from." That is His promise — and your deliverance!

Christ Our High Priest

28

Part 1

God the Father appointed His Son Jesus to become a **High Priest for us in glory.** Indeed, Jesus is in glory right now — as both Man and God — on our behalf. He is arrayed in the garments of a High Priest — and He stands before the Father interceding for us, even as I write!

No doubt the Father takes great pleasure in having His Son at His right hand. But the Bible does not say Jesus ascended for the sake of His Father. Nor does it say He ascended to regain His glory. No — Scripture says Christ ascended to heaven on our behalf — as a High Priest: "Christ...entered into heaven...now to appear in the presence of God...for us..." *(Hebrews 9:24)*.

John caught a glimpse of Jesus in His ministry as our High Priest in glory. He writes that Jesus appeared in the midst of seven candlesticks (representing His church) and ministered among them wearing a particular garb: "...clothed with a garment down to the foot, and girt about the paps with a golden girdle" *(Revelation 1:13)*. This is the attire of a high priest! Jesus wore a robe down to His feet and a breastplate around His midsection. And that is the same attire He wears as He ministers on our behalf right now in glory!

You probably remember that the high priest in the Old Testament was a type and shadow of Christ. Two priesthoods are mentioned — an Aaronic priesthood and a Melchizedek priesthood. Aaron was most certainly a type of Christ. Indeed, God gave us an illustrated sermon in the Old Testament high priest. Everything the high priest did illustrated the work and ministry of Jesus in glory!

Everything in the Temple Focused on Jesus And His Ministry!

Every piece of furniture and every arrangement in the Old Testament tabernacle pointed to Jesus. If you want to know about Christ's ministry to us in glory in these last days, study the tabernacle and the high priest. Exodus 30 gives us a wonderful picture of this ministry:

Between the Holy Place and the Holy of Holies in the tabernacle was a veil. And just before the entrance to the Holy of Holies stood an altar made of gold, three feet high and eighteen inches square. Incense was placed on this altar and burned at all times. As high priest, Aaron was commanded to take care of the lamps and wicks. Every morning when he went into the Holy Place to light them, he put incense on the altar. The altar had to have coals of fire in it always, so the fire would never go out. Even at night Aaron was to go in and put sweet incense "beaten small" on the altar.

"And Aaron [the high priest] shall burn thereon sweet incense every morning: when he dresseth the lamps, he shall burn incense upon it. And when Aaron lighteth the lamps at even, he shall burn incense upon it, a perpetual incense before the Lord throughout your generations" *(Exodus 30:7-8)*. For years, throughout all of Israel's wilderness journeyings, the golden altar filled the Holy Place with a cloud of sweet incense. An incense was constantly rising to heaven!

Now, incense in the Bible represents prayer. And the ever-burning incense on that altar in the Holy Place represents the prayers of Jesus while He was on earth. There was not a day in His life on this planet that Jesus did not pray for His disciples. His prayers for them were a sweet incense wafting daily to the Father: "...I have given unto them the words which thou gavest me...I pray for them...keep through thine own name those whom thou hast given me..." *(John 17:8-11)*.

Jesus prayed constantly: He went to the mountains to pray. He sought solitude for prayer. He prayed in the morning and in the evening — at all times. In fact, Jesus said He did nothing without hearing it first from His Father — in prayer!

John 17 is all about Jesus' prayers for His disciples and His people — for those who followed Him and believed in Him. Yet, Jesus prayed not only for His followers, but "...for them also which shall believe on me through their [the disciples'] word" *(verse 20)*. What a powerful truth! Jesus' phrase, "them which shall believe on me," includes you and me. Jesus was praying for us when He walked this earth in the flesh! Centuries ago we were on His mind. He even recorded this prayer in His Word, knowing we would be reading it. He wants us to know He was interceding for us to the Father!

Beloved, this prayer which Jesus prayed for us did not vanish into thin air. It has been burning on God's altar all this time — and God has accepted His Son's prayer for each of us! Our conversion, our salvation, is the result of Jesus' prayers. That is why we are in Him today — because God answered His prayer for us!

"But this man, because he continueth ever, hath an unchangeable priesthood. Wherefore he is able also to save them to the uttermost that come unto God by him, seeing he ever liveth to make intercession for them" *(Hebrews 7:24-25)*. Right now Jesus is praying for transgressors who haven't yet turned to Him. Scripture says He can save to the uttermost — meaning, "to the end of time" — all who will ever come to Him.

Throughout my years in ministry I've seen many addicts and alcoholics get gloriously saved. Each time I would think to myself, "This one had to have a praying mother or interceding grandmother somewhere in the past. God is answering those holy warriors' prayers!" But now I see something better than that — something far more powerful and effective. It wasn't just a mother or grandparent who was praying for those who now believe. Jesus was praying for them all along! "...I pray...for them also which shall believe on me through (my disciples') word" *(John 17:9, 20)*.

If you've been running from the Lord, you'll never get away from His prayers! The Father answers His Son. And all who resist Him, continuing in their sinful ways, are hardening their hearts to the prayers of Christ — who prayed for them on earth, and is praying for them still!

The Praying of Jesus in Glory

Once a year, the high priest went into the Holy of Holies to make atonement for Israel's sins. After sanctifying himself — bathing himself thoroughly, to enter in purity — he took with him the blood of a bullock and a golden censer (or cup) held by three prongs or chains. The priest then removed some coals from the altar, put them in the censer, took a handful of incense and went into the Holy of Holies.

Inside was an ark, and atop it was the mercy seat — a lid or plate covering, with a little rib around it. On either side of the seat were two golden cherubim, whose wings spread over it. The mercy seat represented the very presence of God — where the Lord sat on His throne.

The high priest sprinkled the blood of the sacrifice seven times on this mercy seat. This was for the remission of all of Israel's sins. The blood sprinkling signified the satisfaction of every demand of God's justice and holiness, and every accusation of the devil. By this blood sprinkling, all were made clean. Then the high priest took the handful of incense and threw it on the fire in the censer. Suddenly, a beautiful aroma filled the tabernacle. The priest would swing the censer in front of the ark until the mercy seat was enshrouded in a cloud of aromatic, sweet incense.

Beloved, this is a perfect illustration of what Jesus has done for us — and is doing right now! First, it signifies Jesus' death and ascension to the heavenly Father as our High Priest. He went through the veil — splitting it in two — and straight into the Holy of Holies, taking with Him the blood of His own sacrifice. There, in a spiritual sense, He sprinkled the altar in glory, saying, "From this day forward, all who believe in Me — who follow Me and trust in Me, giving Me saving faith — are covered by My blood. I present this blood, O Father, as a sacrifice for the sins of the world!"

Second, this scene of atonement further signifies the time when Jesus began to pray for us, interceding to the Father on our behalf. Why? The sweet-smelling incense that filled the Holy of Holies represents the prayers and intercessions of Jesus now in glory! We have a friend in glory, an Advocate before the Father's throne, an intercessor at the right hand of God — for us: "Christ...entered into heaven...now to appear in the presence of God...for us..." *(Hebrews 9:24).*

This Advocate, or lawyer, isn't like an earthly lawyer. When you run out of money, He doesn't refuse to show up in court for you. No! He sticks closer to you than a brother. He will never leave you nor forsake you. He will always be there — interceding for you!

The initial work of Jesus' intercession was the sprinkling of His blood on every bond and debt we owed. A bond is "a sealed note of debt or obligation that is binding upon the debtor and his heirs." An example is a bank mortgage note. As long as you live, the law obligates you to pay that note — and when you die, your children are obligated to pay it.

Likewise, the devil once held the mortgage bond on your soul. He laid claim to you, because you were dead in trespasses and sins. Indeed, there are many in hell even now because the devil foreclosed on their unpaid note!

The Just Wrath of God Was Turned to Mercy — Through the Ministry of the High Priest!

God's justice demands that He be angry at sin. His holiness demands that His wrath go out against all rebellion. But God loves mercy! And now the blood of Jesus has satisfied God's justice and holiness — so that God can come out to us through the rent veil, showing mercy and grace!

The Old Testament includes a powerful foreshadowing of our merciful High Priest. In Numbers 16, we see the whole congregation of Israel rising up and murmuring against Moses and Aaron. Two-hundred-and-fifty princes had rebelled, and God was angry — so He destroyed them. Now the people were mad at Moses and Aaron over their deaths: "...all the congregation of the children of Israel murmured against Moses and against Aaron, saying, Ye have killed the people of the Lord" *(Numbers 16:41)*.

God appeared in a cloud, telling Moses and Aaron to stand apart from the rest: "Get away from them. I'm going to consume them instantly — right now!" *(see verse 26)*. Suddenly, a horrible plague broke out among the people. Moses was terrified — and he told Aaron, the high priest, "...Take a censer, and put fire therein from off the altar, and put on incense, and go quickly unto the congregation, and make an atonement for them: for there is wrath gone out from the Lord; the plague is begun...And he stood between the dead and the living; and the plague was stayed" *(verses 46, 48)*. Moses was saying, "Get the censer — and run through the camp waving the incense, covering the people!" Aaron did just that — and the incense went up throughout the camp.

Aaron is a type of Christ here — and the incense represents Jesus' prayers for a rebellious people. What an incredible picture of God showing mercy through the prayers of the High Priest! We see an image of Jesus running among rebellious sinners, sending up prayers to the Father on their behalf. With each person He sprinkles, He cries, "Lord, I have prayed for this one! I have sprinkled this heart with the blood. I've satisfied Your justice, Your holiness. So, Father, have mercy!"

An advocate is one who tells the court what is legal — what is right and should be done. In short, he describes the law. And our Advocate Jesus says, "I have fulfilled the law. I have paid the price to fully satisfy God's justice. The devil can never accuse God of being unjust!"

Though 14,700 Israelites died of the plague, 2 or 3 million others should have fallen. All of Israel should have been destroyed. But God showed mercy!

Likewise, you and I should have died long ago because of our sin. But the Father, through Jesus' prayers, has mercifully kept us by His power. He loves mercy!

The Book of Zechariah Also Reveals Something About Our High Priest in Glory!

Zechariah 3 describes a high priest named Joshua standing before the Lord, and Satan standing at his right hand to oppose him. Also present was an angel, who had to be Christ (or Jehovah of the Old Testament), because angels do not judge.

Now, this Joshua was a real man; he was not a type of Christ. Rather, he was the high priest during the time of Ezra and Nehemiah. Ezra 2:2 records that this Joshua came out of captivity along with the prophet Zechariah. In Ezra 10:18 it appears that Joshua and his sons had married heathen women and therefore were "clothed in filthy rags." At that time, the worst way a Jew could defile himself was by marrying a Gentile. Thus, Joshua defiled his priestly garments: "Now Joshua was clothed with filthy garments, and stood before the angel" *(Zechariah 3:3)*.

Consider the scene now: Joshua stands before the throne in his filthy garments, and the devil is at his side, accusing him. In Revelation 12:10, Satan is called "...the accuser of our brethren..." Think about it: The devil stood before the Lord to question Job's righteousness...he stood before the heavenly throne to oppose this high priest Joshua...and he stands before God right now to oppose you and me — to accuse us of sin and unfaithfulness!

Satan argued against Joshua: "God, You know all things. You know Your law — and this man has broken it! He has sinned against You, and now his heart is like filthy rags. He is unclean, evil, unworthy!" The devil's accusations were correct: Joshua had sinned. He was guilty, and his garments were spotted. And now Satan claimed Joshua for himself: "I claim this man as my own. He is filthy, living in darkness — and that is my kingdom!"

Beloved, this is exactly what happens with us! Many of the devil's accusations against us are accurate. When we fall into sin — when we fail in our Christian walk, and our garment is defiled — Satan comes before the throne to accuse, oppose and defame us. He points at us and says, "Look at him! You know all things, God. Don't You see the compromise in this one's life? If You are just, You must give me his soul!"

That is when our Advocate steps in. Jesus stands up and says, "It's true, Father — there is a blemish here. There has been failure, and his garment is defiled. But there is faith in his heart — faith in the power of My blood! You know I have made satisfaction for this man's sin. Indeed,

I have paid for every sin he has committed or will ever commit. So, by every law of justice, holiness and mercy, I hereby call for this man's pardon and freedom. He is a brand I have plucked from the fire. I have sprinkled his heart with My blood — and caused his iniquity to pass away!"

Jesus then turns to those standing by and says, "Take those filthy garments off of him, and put My robe of righteousness on his shoulders. Take that hat off his head and put on a crown!" This is just what happens with Joshua in Zechariah 3. Jesus pleads his case, interceding for him: "...I have caused thine iniquity to pass from thee, and I will clothe thee with change of raiment" *(verse 4)*. That is the passover — the sprinkled blood!

Jesus then says to Satan, "...The Lord rebuke thee, O Satan; even the Lord that hath chosen Jerusalem rebuke thee: is not this a brand plucked out of the fire?" *(verse 2)*. What a picture! The devil was forced to leave with a sound rebuke. And Joshua walked away with a pardon, a new garment and a crown of righteousness on his head!

"...if any man sin, we have an advocate with the Father, Jesus Christ the righteous..." *(1 John 2:1)*. Jesus has been in glory for these 2,000 years praying for us. When He was on earth, He said, "...men ought always to pray..." *(Luke 18:1)*. And that is how we know He is still praying for us: By His own testimony He said men ought always to pray — and He is still a Man Himself, even in glory!

You see, it is in His Manhood that Jesus prays for us. He prays as One who experienced all that we experience, who was tempted in all the ways we are tempted. And as our High Priest, He entered into the Holy of Holies understanding every human frailty, every human experience: "Wherefore in all things it behoved him to be made like unto his brethren, that he might be a merciful and faithful high priest in things pertaining to God, to make reconciliation for the sins of the people" *(Hebrews 2:16-17)*.

Our Greatest Comfort Ought to Be That Jesus Came Down and Lived in Our Shoes!

It was necessary for Jesus to take on human nature so He could go through everything we do on earth — rejection, pain, sorrow, temptation. Indeed, though He was God in flesh, He endured the whole human experience not as God, but as a human, with all our frailties. And that enables Him, our High Priest, to pray for us with tremendous sympathy:

"For in that he himself hath suffered being tempted, he is able to succour them that are tempted" *(verse 18)*.

Consider a dear sister in struggle. She is a lover of Jesus — but she is discouraged, cast down, feeling rejected. She stands in shame, thinking, "I've been so hurt. Nobody seems to understand me. Nobody knows what I'm going through. I have no one to talk to who really understands." Sometimes she wonders even if God can forgive her for having such weak faith. She is in total despair — on the brink of giving up. And now Satan stands beside her, accusing her: "Look at this one — she has virtually no faith. She lives in despair. What kind of a Christian is she, God? You have to condemn her!"

That is when her Advocate steps in! Jesus sees her hurt and feels her pain. He knows that her faith is weak — that she's on the verge of giving up, feeling too unworthy to go on. So He comes before the Father on her behalf and begins to intercede: "Father, I know how she feels. I've been there! I was rejected by My own brethren, My own flesh and blood. I was mocked by the religious crowd, spat upon by soldiers who put thorns on My head. In Gethsemane I cried in desperation, 'Why hast thou forsaken Me?' I know what it feels like to be misjudged, called names and ridiculed. I sympathize with this woman, Father — and I have washed away her sins. I know she still has a heart for Me — and I will not break a bruised reed!"

This is where Jesus' prayers for us come in: "Father, I would that she be forgiven for her discouragement. I would that she be given a new supply of grace from on High — that the Holy Spirit come upon her with a special renewing of encouragement. I would that she be given a spirit of peace and rest in the Holy Ghost. She is Mine, Father. Satan cannot have her!"

Suddenly, out of nowhere, the woman feels encouraged. Grace is given to her — through the prayers of our High Priest! He is touched by the feelings of our infirmities — and He acts in mercy.

Consider now a precious, worried man who stands accused because he has fallen into great temptation. He has sinned grievously against God, and he feels his heart growing cold. He thinks, "I can't make it! I'm too up-and-down, too hot-and-cold. Satan is throwing all of hell at me, and I'm tempted powerfully. I've been overtaken by my temptation many times. Yet, I love Jesus. Oh, Lord — I want to be free and clean!" This man is weary, worn out, discouraged. And the devil stands beside him, accusing: "He fell into sin, God. There is no question: He can't withstand temptation. His garment is spotted, filthy!"

But the Advocate steps in between this man and his accuser. He says, "Father, I know what this man is going through. The devil also drove Me into a wilderness and tempted Me severely. I was tempted to blaspheme — to fall down and worship Satan! I know what temptation is all about. And I know this man's heart. There is a spark of faith still in him — an ember of love in his heart for Me. Father, I would that You look upon him as righteous through My blood. I would that he be delivered from the power of darkness and the wicked one. I would that he be accepted, forgiven, restored — and given power from on high to resist the devil. I pray for his deliverance!"

The next day, this man picks up his Bible and reads a powerful truth he hasn't seen before. He falls to his knees, and God comes to him with deliverance — because the High Priest has prayed!

Dear saint, it doesn't matter what you're going through. Jesus has been there and walked in your shoes. And that is what makes Him a merciful High Priest! You don't have to tell Him all your pain. He knows all about it — because He's felt it all Himself! We haven't been through anything that He hasn't felt.

You may be thinking, "Wait a minute. How can Jesus be praying daily, simultaneously, for millions of believers at one time — and multiplied millions of transgressors?" That's a silly question — especially when you consider that a tiny computer chip is capable of storing and dispensing millions of pieces of data! A chip the size of a fingernail is capable of making billions of transactions. And if that is true of a tiny memory chip, how great must be the mind of God — capable of monitoring every human thought, every move?

Indeed, Jesus is capable of bringing all the needs, pain, cries and prayers of His people before the Father — at one time, at any time — and making intercession simultaneously for all of them. Your Advocate knows your address. He has counted every hair on your head. And He knows your every thought, feels your every pain, hears your every cry. Take heart, beloved: Jesus is praying for you!

29

Christ Our High Priest

Part 2

The Bible tells us that when Christ ascended to heaven, He took up the ministry of High Priest to all who come to Him by faith.** "This man [Jesus], because he continueth ever, hath an unchangeable priesthood" *(Hebrews 7:24)*.

Jesus is unchangeable! He is the same yesterday, today and forever. As long as you live, He will be your High Priest in heaven, interceding on your behalf. And He will remain your High Priest until you go home to be with Him. Our High Priest Jesus is seated at the right hand of the Father, in the seat of authority: "...We have such an high priest, who is set on the right hand of the throne of the Majesty..." *(8:1)*. Our High Priest has all power and authority at His command!

Jesus is in the Father's presence right now, interceding for us. He confronts our accuser, the devil, and says, "I rebuke you, Satan! This one is mine because he is sprinkled in My blood. He is secure, his debt fully paid. He is set free!"

Yet I believe there is even more for us to learn about our wonderful High Priest's ministry on our behalf:

Two Priesthoods Are Mentioned in the Old Testament — The Aaronic Priesthood and the Melchizedek Priesthood.

We know that Aaron, the high priest, was from the tribe of Levi. But Melchizedek — introduced to us in Genesis 14:18-19 — was a most mysterious figure. Biblical scholars know very little about him, and there has been a lot of conjecture about who he was. Here is the setting into which the high priest Melchizedek is introduced:

Genesis tells us that the cities of Sodom and Gomorrah, where Abram's nephew Lot lived, were attacked by a confederated army made up of several kingdoms. This army had plundered the cities' food and other supplies and taken captive many of the inhabitants, including Lot and his family.

Abram, directed by God, took a small army of 318 men and defeated this plundering confederation: "And he brought back all the goods, and also brought again his brother Lot, and his goods, and the women also, and the people" *(Genesis 14:16)*.

Here is the picture: Abram had just won an incredible victory, bringing down this whole confederated army. Now he was returning home from battle. On the way he met the high priest, Melchizedek, King of Salem, who came out to meet Abram "…(and) brought forth bread and wine…" *(verse 18)*.

Hebrews tells us this about the high priest: "For this Melchisedek, king of Salem, priest of the most high God, who met Abraham returning from the slaughter of the kings, and blessed him; to whom also Abraham gave a tenth part of all; first being by interpretation King of righteousness, and after that also King of Salem, which is, King of peace; without father, without mother, without descent, having neither beginning of days, nor end of life; but made like unto the Son of God; abideth a priest continually" *(Hebrews 7:1-3)*.

This sounds like some superhuman. He has no beginning or end — and that means he would have had to be God. Yet I believe Melchizedek is a flesh-and-blood man who serves as a type of Christ. As the writer of Hebrews tells us, Melchizedek's name means "King of Righteousness," and his title, "King of Salem," means "King of Peace." Now, we call Los Angeles the "City of Angels" and New York the "Big Apple." Apparently, God put His hand upon this man and anointed him to be high priest of Salem, a city affectionately referred to as the "City of Peace." The phrase "without father or mother" means simply that Melchizedek had no lineage of priesthood, as did the Levitical priesthood. "Without descent" means "without a priestly genealogy." He was not of a "generations of priests," as Aaron was. Rather, he was divinely appointed a priest by God. The writer of Hebrews also tells us that Melchizedek was "made like unto the Son of God" — meaning, he was like Jesus in that he had no priestly genealogy: "…our Lord sprang out of Judah; of which tribe Moses spake nothing concerning priesthood" *(verse 14)*.

Jesus' father, Joseph, was not a priest; he had no genealogical line out of Judah, from which the Levitical priests descended. So we see here that Melchizedek was a foreshadowing of Jesus' priesthood. This earthly high priest was meant as a type of our High Priest in glory — Jesus, King of righteousness and King of peace!

Abram paid tithes to Melchizedek from all the bounty he had taken from the defeated armies. Scripture tells us that, in turn, the high priest blessed him: "And he blessed him, and said, Blessed be Abram of the most high God..." *(Genesis 14:19)*.

Here is a beautiful picture of the very ministry of Jesus our High Priest. You see, it was the duty and privilege of the high priest to come forth from the Holy of Holies and bless the people. The Lord instructed Moses: "Speak unto Aaron and his sons, saying, On this wise ye shall bless the children of Israel, saying unto them, The Lord bless thee, and keep thee: The Lord make his face shine upon thee, and be gracious unto thee: The Lord lift up his countenance upon thee, and give thee peace" *(Numbers 6:23-26)*. In other words: After the high priest takes the blood into the Holy of Holies, sprinkles it on the mercy seat and waves the incense, then he is to come out, face the people and bless them.

This was the final act in the sequence of the high priest's ministry. He was to emerge from the Holy of Holies, raise his hands and bless the people with the blessing God gave him. And today, this is the unchanging ministry of our High Priest, by God's prescription. Our High Priest Jesus says, "I will cover you with My blood. I will intercede for you before the Father. And I will come forth and bless you!"

It is important to understand that these blessings Jesus bestows on us are not temporal but spiritual: "Blessed be the God and Father of our Lord Jesus Christ, who hath blessed us with all spiritual blessings in heavenly places in Christ" *(Ephesians 1:3)*. In the Old Testament, the high priest's blessings were temporal. God promised to bless crops, livestock, cities and all the people's activities. It was all physical, with no spiritual dimension, such as we have today — because the veil had not yet been rent in two. Yet because we walk in a spiritual realm today, the blessings we receive are spiritual in nature.

You may ask, "Doesn't God bless us with outward, physical blessings?" Yes, at times God does bless us with material things — but only as they produce a spiritual outcome! The Lord does take good care of His children. He told us to seek Him first, and that all our necessities for living would be provided. However, Christ's blessings to us are primarily spiritual!

When the Old Testament priest spoke this blessing to the people, it was not just a wish for them. He didn't say, "I wish you peace. I wish the Lord to shine His face upon you..." No — the blessing was backed by the full power of God: "And they shall put my name upon the children of

Israel; and I will bless them" *(Numbers 6:27)*. This means, "The priest will speak with the full authority of My name — and I will honor it. This blessing will have the power of My Godhead behind it!"

Likewise, when Jesus our High Priest blesses, He does not just wish us good. He pronounces His blessing with authority — and it is done!

Our Lord Jesus Delights in Blessing His People!

Many Christians think God delights only in chastising and correcting us. No! The Bible tells us He takes no pleasure in disciplining us. On the contrary, Jesus says, "Fear not, little flock; for it is your Father's good pleasure to give you the kingdom" *(Luke 12:32)*. He assures us, "I'll give you everything you need — because My heart is set on blessing!"

Nowhere in the Bible do we ever find Jesus cursing anyone. (The only thing He cursed was a fig tree.) No preacher, apostle, prophet or shepherd in history ever blessed people more than Jesus did. He pronounced blessings everywhere He turned. Consider the Sermon on the Mount in Matthew 5. Jesus said, "Blessed are the poor in spirit. Blessed are you who mourn. Blessed are the meek. Blessed are you if you hunger and thirst after righteousness. Blessed are the merciful, the peacemakers, the perse-cuted, the reviled." Everywhere Jesus turned He pronounced, "Blessed…blessed…blessed…"

He took children in His arms and blessed them. He blessed those who held feasts for the poor, crippled, lame and blind: "Thou shalt be blessed; for they cannot recompense thee: for thou shalt be recompensed at the resurrection of the just" *(14:14)*. …he lifted up his hands, and blessed them" *(24:50)*.

It touches my heart deeply that Jesus' last words before He left His disciples were words of blessing. Luke says Christ "…opened their understanding, that they might understand the scriptures" *(verse 45)* — and then "…he blessed them…" *(verse 51)*.

At this point you may be thinking, "I can understand how the Lord would bless children, or new converts, or even Christians in poor coun-tries who need miracles just to have food on their table. I can see how He would bless imprisoned believers in foreign countries, miraculously pro-viding them with glorious revelations of Himself. Yet, I can't understand those kinds of blessings for myself. I just don't think I ever live up to the light I have received. I feel God is mostly displeased with me. I don't feel worthy of His blessings."

I hope you understand by now — you'll never be worthy of God's blessings! No one earns His blessings. Rather, He comes out to us — strictly in His mercy and grace — and blesses us with spiritual blessings beyond our comprehension!

I am a father of four children, all of whom are married and have children of their own. Whenever my children face any kind of difficulty, I do not get angry at them. On the contrary — I am delighted when they call on me. Whether I can help them by providing prayer, counseling or financial blessings, I take great pleasure in reaching out to them and blessing them. How much more does our Lord Jesus delight in blessing His children in their time of need? He tells us, "You earthly fathers know how to give good gifts to your children. How much more does your heavenly Father want to bless you?" *(see Matthew 7:11)*.

Yet some of the most blessed people in God's house are blind to their blessings. They do not see or discern the great things the High Priest has given them — and thus they don't enjoy them. For example — you may look around in the body of Christ and see other Christians who seem more talented and blessed. Some can memorize and quote whole passages of Scripture. Others can can preach, teach or sing to God's glory. You say to yourself, "How blessed they are by God. But, poor me! I don't have the brainpower to memorize God's Word. I don't even have the ability to remember a sermon. I don't have any of the gifts my brothers and sisters have to serve God."

Beloved, you don't know how blessed you are! Are you poor in spirit? Is it difficult for you to rejoice or even to smile? Do you mourn over your weaknesses? Do you lament over seeing no spiritual growth in your life? Do you grieve because you feel inadequate, left out, unneeded? Jesus says, "You are blessed! You have nothing to be proud about. And in that way, you serve Me best — because My strength rests in your weakness! I can use you more readily than all others."

What a blessing this truly is. Jesus never said, "Blessed are the strong, the happy, the self-sufficient, the forceful." No! Our Lord blessed the weak, the reviled, the persecuted, the downcast — those who are considered nothing in the eyes of others. He is saying to you, "You know you have great need of Me — and therefore you are blessed!"

Our High Priest Has Blessed You With the Blessing of Abraham!

Paul writes: "So then they which be of faith are blessed with faithful

Abraham" *(Galatians 3:9)*. What is this blessing of Abraham?

James tells us, "…Abraham believed God, and it was imputed unto him for righteousness…" *(James 2:23)*. Abraham believed that he was in right standing with God, even though he was still being sanctified. And this is the blessing of Abraham — the knowledge that we are justified by faith! "That the blessing of Abraham might come on the Gentiles through Jesus Christ; that we might receive the promise of the Spirit through faith" *(Galatians 3:14)*.

This blessing is the knowledge that Jesus paid with His blood to blot out all our sins and iniquities. The Father credits Jesus' own righteousness to us, and we are made right in His eyes. We don't have to try to work to earn God's favor. Instead, we are to trust and believe in the complete work of Jesus on the Cross. And even though we still struggle — even though we sometimes fall and fail Him — we have right standing with Him as we continue in faith and repentance.

David understood this and was able to enjoy the blessing of Abraham: "Even as David also describeth the blessedness of the man, unto whom God imputed righteousness without works, saying, Blessed are they whose iniquities are forgiven, and whose sins are covered. Blessed is the man to whom the Lord will not impute sin" *(Romans 4:6-8)*.

As we are being blessed by God with the blessing of Abraham, our faith begins to expand. Soon we see and believe that the same Christ who justifies us gives us power to overcome sin. God says to us, "Now we're going to work on your holiness and sanctification. But you must understand that in the meantime, you are secure in Me. You are My child — and I'm going to keep you from falling!"

Has the blessing of Abraham fallen upon you yet? If you fully accept Christ's righteousness by faith, then you are blessed with faithful Abraham and David. Indeed, you are one of the most blessed people on earth! Yet millions of Christians have neither heard nor believed this. As a result, they live their whole lives in spiritual poverty and fear. They do not know what it is like to lay their head down at night with peace. They sin and confess, sin and confess, repeatedly. They have no security, no strength, no knowledge.

God wants such Christians to lie down in His arms, knowing they are completely justified in His presence. Having the blessing of Abraham means having absolute confidence that Jesus is continually sprinkling His blood on us. It also means giving Him a constant, saving faith. We are to come to Him saying, "Lord, I know I am Your child and that You will not cast me away. I know I've failed You and sinned against You. I've got dirt on my feet. But I come to You now to be cleansed. Cleanse me, Lord!"

There is yet another aspect to this blessing of Abraham. It includes trusting in the Lord to be our shield. You see, God made a covenant with Abram: "After these things the word of the Lord came unto Abram in a vision, saying, Fear not, Abram: I am thy shield, and thy exceeding great reward" *(Genesis 15:1)*. The Lord gave Abraham this blessing as he was on his way back from battle. Some biblical scholars believe Abraham was greatly fearful at this time. He may have thought the Asiatic kings would regroup and come against him while he had only 318 men. Or, he may have thought he would be attacked by the Canaanites, who had seen him grow strong while dwelling in their land.

We have to remember also that Abraham had been promised by God he would be the father of many nations. Here Abraham might have been thinking, "Look at all the time that has passed, and still I have no son. Now I am surrounded by mad armies and by people who feel no mercy toward me. My family, my heritage, is in jeopardy. I don't see any evidence of God's promise being fulfilled."

Have you ever been in this place? Perhaps you have been slandered on the job. Maybe your home life is miserable. Your prayers seem to go unanswered. Or perhaps a close friend has betrayed you. You've prayed about it for days, weeks, months — but nothing has happened. You say to yourself, "I don't see any evidence of God's blessing. On the contrary, I feel dejected and despairing. What can I do?"

Numerous times I've gone to prayer and had it out with the Lord! I've cried, "Father, You know there are some very important things I haven't seen come to pass. When are You going to answer my cries? Why are You waiting? Don't You hear my prayers at all? I have no more tears left. I believe Your Word — but I don't see any evidence of Your blessing. Lord, where are You?"

Abraham was in just such a fearful condition when the high priest Melchizedek came out to meet him. Scripture says: "After these things the word of the Lord came unto Abraham..." *(verse 1)*. This verse means, "After Abraham looked around fearfully at the enemies surrounding him... after he felt dejected, that he hadn't made any progress...the Word of the Lord came to him...."

The first thing God told Abraham was, "Fear not, Abraham: I am thy shield, and thy exceeding great reward" *(same verse)*. In this single verse, God has given us the secret to the greatest blessing any believer could ever have. You see, the first thing our High Priest Jesus says to us when He comes out to us from the Holy of Holies is, "Don't be afraid!" He sees our fearful condition and assures us, "No devil or demon in hell can touch you. You are under My blood — and you are not to fear!"

"...I am thy shield, and thy exceeding great reward" *(same verse)*. The actual meaning in Hebrew for shield here is "protector, defender." This verse means, "I will be your champion. I will fight for you!"

The Lord is saying to Abraham, "Go ahead and look at all those armies surrounding you. I will be your defense against them all! Nobody can touch you — because I am your shield. Entrust your life and future into My hands. If you will turn to Me as your source of fulfillment, I will reward you with more peace, more joy, more completeness than you have ever known!"

Indeed, this same verse tells us the Lord is much more than a shield to us. He is also our exceeding great reward! God says to Abraham here, "You will have your son, and he will be a joy to you. You will rejoice for a season that I have fulfilled My promise to you, and that your seed has come. But I want to be your heart's reward, Abraham. Even when you see My promises fulfilled, your son will not be your reward. No — I will be the One who fulfills your deepest needs!"

God knows all about human nature. He knew that Abraham would have a great measure of joy when he got his son. Abraham could then say, "God did it! He promised this to me, and He kept His Word." Yet God also knew that Abraham would not be totally fulfilled when the child came. He would still have an inner hunger, a restlessness, an unexplainable need that no human could touch.

Isn't this what happens to us when we finally get the thing we've wanted so badly? All along we think, "If only I can get this one thing, I'll be happy. It will make my life wonderful. It will end all of my problems." No, it won't! And you need to settle it once and for all: There is no man, no woman, no pastor or evangelist who can touch that deep need in you! We all have this same need: It's the need for total dependency on the Lord. And it can't be met by a mate, a child or a friend. Only the Lord Himself can fully satisfy our deepest need.

That is the spiritual blessing! Our High Priest says, "If you really want to know the secret of My blessing — it's that I'm what you're looking for. I am your reward — your answer, your blessing!"

The Surest Evidence That the Lord's Hand of Blessing Is On You Is That Others Are Being Blessed Through You!

God said to Abraham, "In blessing I will bless thee...in thy seed shall all the nations of the earth be blessed..." *(Genesis 22:17-18)*. He was saying, "The reason I'm blessing you, Abraham, is so that you can bless all the nations!"

Obviously, very few of us are called to bless entire nations. But each of us has a circle of family, friends, colleagues and coworkers. How many in your circle are being blessed by what the Lord is doing in you? Is Jesus' glory in your relationship with Him overflowing to those around you? Are your friends and family being blessed by Christ in you? Whom have you blessed lately?

When you start blessing others in the midst of your trials, you'll know that God's hand of blessing is on you. This is what happened with David. When his enemies showed him no mercy, he testified, "Let them curse, but bless thou: when they arise, let them be ashamed; but let thy servant rejoice" *(Psalm 109:28)*. David cried out to God for help and blessing as his enemies cursed him.

Jesus commands us: "But I say unto you, Love your enemies, bless them that curse you, do good to them that hate you, and pray for them which despitefully use you, and persecute you" *(Matthew 5:44)*. If you can keep this word, you are surely blessed of the Lord!

Finally, those who are being blessed are being drawn ever closer to the Lord. God never blesses without drawing that person closer to Himself, urging, "Come closer to Me." That is more of the blessing — increasing nearness to Him!

Perhaps you're still wondering, "I see no evidence of God's blessing in my life. My life isn't marked by any of these things you've mentioned. How can I have God's blessing?" I ask you: Do you love His Word? Do you love coming to His house with other believers? Does your mind keep running to Jesus throughout the day? Do you talk to Him? If you can answer "yes" to any of these questions, you can rest assured: He is drawing you, blessing you!

Rejoice, dear saint! If you find yourself lacking in the gifts you see in others...if you hunger and thirst for more of Him...if you are weak, broken, grief-stricken, mourning over your sin, you can rest assured — your High Priest is blessing you with all spiritual blessings. Come to Him in faith. He delights in blessing you!

It's Time to Weep For America!

30

A Prophetic Message

I have never claimed to be a prophet. But there comes a time when the Word of God becomes such a fire in my bones, I have to speak out what I see and hear. Call it a watchman's message, or whatever you will — but I have to tell you what God has put on my heart concerning this nation!

I do believe God has true prophets — those who are occasionally moved upon by the Holy Spirit to foretell future events and coming judgments. Indeed, on a few rare occasions, the Spirit has compelled me to warn of impending judgments. But the prophecy I bring to you now is not predictive. Rather, I want to take you straight into God's Word — to show you a few eternal principles of how the Lord works. Any Bible student can know how God intends to deal with America — or any other nation — by studying the history and patterns of God's workings in the Old Testament. We can know the future by studying the past!

The fact is, God's ways are absolutely unchangeable when it comes to His dealings with sinful nations. There is no shadow of turning in His ways; He works the same way in every generation — because He is just. In short, He will deal with our generation in the same way He has dealt with every other generation that sinned as we are sinning. And by learning these principles of His ways from Scripture, we can deduct exactly how He will deal with us today.

For example: The apostle Paul predicted to the Corinthian church what would happen to them if they continued to tempt Christ. Those Christians were murmuring and giving themselves over to unbridled lusts. So, Paul simply looked into history and saw what God did to Israel when they committed the very same sins. Paul told the Corinthians: "Neither let us tempt Christ, as some of them also tempted, and were destroyed of serpents. Neither murmur ye, as some of them also murmured, and were destroyed of the destroyer. Now all these things happened unto them for ensamples: and they are written for our admonition, upon whom the ends of the world are come" *(1 Corinthians 10:9-11)*. The apostle was saying, "This is a clear pattern in Scripture. It tells you what God will do to you if you continue to sin as Israel sinned!"

The apostle Peter also warned his readers by invoking an example from the Old Testament. He said God would judge them for their covetousness and unbridled lust, just as He had judged past generations: "And turning the cities of Sodom and Gomorrha into ashes [God] condemned them with an overthrow, making them an ensample unto those that after would live ungodly" *(2 Peter 2:6)*. Peter warned, "If you sin as Sodom and Gomorrha did, the Lord will destroy you just as He destroyed them!"

Like Paul and Peter, I bring you a warning based on my study of the Old Testament — specifically, the book of Isaiah. As I read through this book recently, the Spirit stopped me in chapter 22. Suddenly, I began to see how judgment came upon Jerusalem in Isaiah's day — in spite of all of the prophet's warnings!

Isaiah 22 contains a shocking account of a society that had sinned away its day of grace. Jerusalem and Judah had crossed a line, and there was no turning back. The people had backslidden completely and were living as though they were atheists. So God instructed Isaiah to prophesy to His people — to pronounce a "dread release" to judgment! God's call to repentance in Judah was over. There would no longer be a prophetic voice in the land, crying, "Return and be healed!" Now it was too late. This people had done something so brazen that God could not endure it one more day!

Tearfully, with a crushed heart, Isaiah brought this awful message: "And it was revealed in mine ears by the Lord of hosts, Surely this iniquity shall not be purged from you till ye die, saith the Lord God of hosts" *(Isaiah 22:14)*. He was saying, in essence, "You've committed a sin that God won't forgive. You've crossed a line — and it's too late to turn back!"

When You Fully Understand What This Society Did to Provoke God to Release Them to Judgment, You Will See How Their Actions Mirror American Society Today!

What Jerusalem and Judah did to bring judgment upon themselves is exactly what America is doing right now. And if the wicked behavior of God's people signaled the imminent destruction of that society, then our sinful behavior clearly signals the death throes of our nation! I believe that if the prophet Isaiah were living today, beholding the wickedness of our nation, he would cry out, "It's time to weep for your nation! History is repeating itself. Your cup of iniquity is full and overflowing!"

Chapter 22 of Isaiah is called "The Valley of Vision." And Isaiah's message here is so clear, so easy to understand, there can be no doubt about its meaning. According to commentators, Isaiah was evidently standing on a rooftop (or some other high elevation), looking down over Jerusalem and the surrounding valley. What he saw was so appalling, it broke him. He wept convulsively, saying to all who passed by, "…Look away from me; I will weep bitterly, labour not to comfort me, because of the spoiling of the daughter of my people" *(verse 4)*.

The prophet was saying, "Don't look at me. You won't like what you see! My heart is about to break, and my insides are about to pour out. I'm sorely pained, and I can't take it. My people are about to be destroyed!" "My heart panted, fearfulness affrighted me… my loins [are] filled with pain…I was bowed down…dismayed…" *(21:4, 3)*.

This clearly was not patriotism on Isaiah's part. It was the burden of the Lord! Here is a picture of a man broken over his society's sin — something we don't often see in the church today. There simply aren't many pastors or Christians in America who see judgment coming and who are broken over it.

Yet, for a long time, Isaiah had been speaking of a vision of judgment he had received from the Lord. He had foreseen a huge army — a contingent of chariots, cunning archers, powerful horsemen, men on camels — all coming against the city. And now Isaiah's prophetic vision was unfolding before his very eyes: Enemy armies had surrounded Jerusalem — and a siege was under way!

The noise of military movements echoed over the hills: The terrible, famed horsemen of Elam and hand-to-hand fighters of Kir were marching in the vanguard. War horses groaned and grunted, their hooves pounding the earth. Chariot wheels rumbled over the countryside, churning up great clouds of dust. Infantrymen had approached Jerusalem's wall and now were noisily picking away at it with their spears and crowbars. It must have been a fearful, awesome sight!

As Isaiah turned from this frightful scene, he looked upon the flat rooftops of the city — and he could not believe what he saw. The citizens of Jerusalem were on the rooftops — drinking and partying! The people had gathered to entertain themselves by gazing down on the Assyrian army as it prepared to attack.

Isaiah was incredulous at what he saw — and he cried out, "Thou that art full of stirs, a tumultuous city, a joyous city…" *(22:2)*. All this time the prophet had been walking up and down the land, warning God's people, "Your idols will be brought down. The city walls in which you trusted will be breached. Your glory shall fade. Time is running out!"

Yet, how did the people react? They jostled each other on the rooftops, trying to get the best view of the approaching enemy! The whole city was stirred up, full of excitement, joy and exuberance. The Bible uses a word here that means "boisterous, loud, excited."

People whose dwellings were closest to the wall had good views of the valley below, and they hosted their friends for "viewing parties." They cried, "Come on up — you've got to see this. Pack your lunch and bring the family!" Children screamed with delight: "Look at all the big white horses! Look at all the sleek chariots, and the mighty soldiers oiling their shields. What a sight!" They were all feasting, getting drunk, celebrating.

Isaiah could not contain himself. He cried out: "…What aileth thee now, that thou art wholly gone up to the housetops?" *(verse 1)*. I can see this prophet of God in my mind's eye — screaming from the rooftop: "Are you people crazy? What kind of spirit has possessed you? What kind of disease would drive you to your rooftops to party, while destruction sits at your gates? Judgment is at the door — and you're getting drunk!"

I have a question for you: What ails our American society? How can our whole nation party, dance, drink and be saturated with entertainment, while thousands of babies are being aborted? What kind of disease has so blinded our nation that the President could veto a bill outlawing doctors from sucking out the brains of babies just weeks before they're born? What horrible sickness allows our society to continue merrily in its sordid pleasure-seeking, while the elderly are being assisted in suicide?

America is under siege by an army of abortionists, pornographers, drug pushers, murderers of the elderly, coming at us from all corners of the earth. And yet, only a few prophetic voices can be heard! I am sure Isaiah's voice was drowned out by the partying crowds: "Oh, it's only that old man, Isaiah — the gloom-and-doom preacher. Don't pay any attention to him." And so it is today: Prophetic warnings are ridiculed and ignored!

I Ask You: Where Are Those Who Grieve for America — Who Are Broken Over the Sins of God's Church and Our Nation?

Consider that stupid, blind, stoned rooftop crowd in Jerusalem, celebrating on the brink of their own judgment. This is where you discover the flash point of destruction! What was their sin, which God would not forgive? It was much more than just shutting out God's warnings: They had hardened their hearts in the face of the predicted judgment!

Judgment was already taking place; it was evident all around them. And yet the people hardened themselves, knowing full well the hand of God had brought down this judgment upon them. Their hardness was the unforgivable sin!

Yet Isaiah was further incredulous: Not only were the people mocking judgment at the door, being entertained by it — but they were celebrating and feasting in the midst of a plague!

People were falling dead because a plague had swept the city: "…thy slain men are not slain with the sword, nor dead in battle" *(Isaiah 22:2)*. Historians confirm that Jerusalem was hit by a plague at this time. Refugees had fled there before the invading army, crowding into a city with little food and water. Health conditions were awful, resulting in the plague. People began dying left and right. The stench of death was horrible.

But the citizens of Jerusalem became accustomed to the plague. They became hardened to the death all around them — so much so that they could entertain themselves on rooftops while just below them people were dying. They carelessly wasted the city's scarce water, food and wine on their own pleasure!

I ask you: Doesn't this sound awfully familiar? It is a picture of America — in this generation. We have become like Germany just before that nation fell in World War II. I have a book at home with vivid photographs of the drunken parties that took place throughout Berlin. Hitler was in his bunker, close to suicide, as Allied forces made nightly bombing raids. Yet in between the waves of bombs, people rushed out to makeshift bars, to dance and drink the night away! Berlin became one massive party. And it all happened just before the city was annihilated — with the people staring into eternity.

Even now, here in New York City, fund-raising for AIDS research consists mainly of all-night dancing and drinking parties. I see posters all over Greenwich Village and Soho that read: "AIDS Research Party. Free drinks." Skeletal men, looking like death, dance the night away, racing from one party to another — all in the name of raising money for AIDS research. They're dying of the disease — but they go on partying!

Right now an AIDS plague is spreading throughout America. But I believe something even worse could happen to this nation — because of something I see in Isaiah 22!

Suppose the awful illness called ebola strikes with a fury in America. (This is the disease that can kill a person within a week.) Or perhaps one of the newly discovered, exotic diseases begins to snuff out life in mere days. Thousands of Americans would begin dying quickly. Our country would be as it was during the nineteenth century, when smallpox raged through the streets. During that awful plague, people fled the cities. But after a while, when the sight of funerals and hearses became common-place, the people grew enured to it all.

If such an outbreak were to decimate the United States today, do you think our nation would turn to God? Would we wake up and repent? Would the ungodly cry out for mercy and healing? No! On the contrary — America would be swamped with the most wild, unbelievable orgies and parties in the history of our nation. That has been the history of every nation that turned from God as we have!

As everything neared collapse in Jerusalem, the rich and influential made provisions to flee to safety: "All thy rulers are fled together...all that are found in thee are bound together, which have fled from afar" *(verse 3)*. Those seeking to flee were leaders, people "in the know." And they knew Isaiah was right — that society had reached a point of no return: "For it is a day of trouble, and of treading down, and of perplexity by the Lord God of hosts in the valley of vision, breaking down the walls, and of crying to the mountains" *(verse 5)*.

These people raced about, looking to make one last financial "kill" by which they could secure themselves against society's breakdown. Their attitude was, "I've got to make a bundle quickly. Then I'll find a safe, secure place to hide."

Yet Isaiah knew exactly what they were up to. He pointed out that the city treasurer, Shebna, had "...hewed him out a sepulchre on high, and that graveth an habitation for himself in a rock..." *(verse 16)*. The prophet was saying, "Look! Your city treasurer is up in the hills, building himself a rock shelter. He says it's a sepulchre — but he's going up there to hide!"

Beloved, that is the American dream for multitudes right now. The saying among Wall Streeters, businesspeople and politicians today is, "Get a golden parachute!" In other words: "Make a killing — and then head for the hills!"

Think about it: Why are so many wealthy people buying up isolated ranches and farms in Utah, Nevada, Wyoming, Montana? What do they know that the majority of Americans don't know? It is that they see the enemy gathering at the gate! They know America can no longer carry out its suicidal economic policies without crashing. This is not simply a gut feeling on their part; they know the end is near. They are not partying, but preparing!

Yet there is no safe place to hide! Isaiah said to the unscrupulous escapees in Jerusalem: "He will surely violently turn and toss thee like a ball into a large country: there shalt thou die, and there the chariots of thy glory shall be the shame of thy lord's house. And I will drive thee from thy station, and from thy state shall he pull thee down" *(verses 18-19)*. In other words: "God is going to kick you like a football, out into the open. There is no safe place outside of Jesus Christ the Lord!"

God, in His Mercy, Made One Last Attempt to Save Jerusalem.

The Lord sent His Spirit upon the people while they were partying. Suddenly, their eyes were opened to the danger they were in: "And he discovered the covering of Judah…" *(Isaiah 22:8)*.

We are not told exactly what happened when the Holy Spirit came down and interrupted the party. We don't know if anyone went to the temple to pray, or if anyone went to Isaiah and asked what to do. But there probably was a brief period when people at least thought of God and said a few prayers. Deep inside, they knew God's hand was in this judgment.

Perhaps you remember a similar scene in our nation a few years ago. When the war with Iraq broke out, it was reported that President Bush spent hours face down on the floor, praying with Billy Graham. Congress called for a national day of prayer. Churches were packed. Even the newspapers in New York City called for prayer.

Yet, this lasted all of one week! What happened? The same thing happened in our nation as had happened in Jerusalem: "…thou didst look in that day to the armour…" *(verse 8)*.

When the Lord exposed the people of Jerusalem to danger, they should have turned to Him. Instead, they turned to their own resources — the strength of their armor! They told themselves, "We have good, sturdy shields. And the city wall is strong. We have all the materials we need to fill the breaches. We can fortify ourselves." Simply put, they didn't need God!

And that is just how we reacted during the Gulf War. Television provided daily reports on the mighty exploits of our military. We watched as U.S. tanks rumbled swiftly through the desert, overwhelming the enemy. We watched in awe as our planes shot off laser-beam bombs, hitting pinpoint targets. One general boasted, "We're capable of putting a missile down any smokestack in Iraq!"

It all ended with a ticker-tape parade down Broadway. But was it to honor God, to whom we prayed? No — it was for our generals! God was pushed out of the picture completely!

I am not belittling our military. I thank God they were successful. And I thank God for the soldiers who served their country so well. But the fact remains that America trusts more in its military might than in Almighty God! "...but ye have not looked unto the maker thereof, neither had respect unto him that fashioned it long ago" *(verse 11)*.

This is why Isaiah wept so hard: A false security had gripped the people, and God was no longer even in their thoughts. Instead, everyone clung to a brazen self-confidence that said, "We will go it alone!"

America today is caught in the deception of a similar false security. The Russian empire has fallen. Iraq has been defeated. And now we think, "Who is strong enough to challenge our mighty army? There is no one left to bomb us. There is no longer a hydrogen scare." We have trusted in our armor!

But beware — Russia is not dead! The bear that the Bible said would be wounded will come back to life. And that Russian bear is stirring right now. I don't know whether it will happen by coup or by election — but the two or three men who are in line for leadership in Russia are all anti-Christian, anti-Semitic and anti-American. Communism is still very much alive!

These men who will come to power shortly will not be afraid to threaten America or the world. They will not take their finger off the hydrogen button. And right now, the Russian army is licking its wounds, itching to remove its shame before the world. Once it is finally released, it will conquer its former states — and then threaten Europe with a hydrogen holocaust!

A dictator is going to arise overnight — a man who threatens the whole world. Hitler rose up out of chaos, and so will a new, belligerent Russia. Just watch, as emissaries from all over the world start flocking to Moscow. Don't be deceived by the relative peace our nation now enjoys. It is merely the calm before the storm!

What Triggers God's Dread Release of a
Society to Judgment?

What final indignation, what brazen act, sets God's judgment into motion? What was Israel's iniquity that triggered judgment? What made God say, "That's enough. Now you've crossed the line!" Isaiah gives us the answer: "And in that day did the Lord God of hosts call to weeping, and to mourning, and to baldness, and to girding with sackcloth; And behold joy and gladness, slaying oxen, and killing sheep, eating flesh, and drinking wine: let us eat and drink; for to morrow we shall die" *(Isaiah 22:12-13)*.

Even in the midst of their brazen rebellion, God's Spirit was calling people to repentance. Up to the very end, the holy cry was heard in the streets: "Weep, mourn, put on sackcloth!" But instead of mourning, the people partied on! Instead of grieving and weeping, they reveled with food and wine. They reasoned, "By this time tomorrow we'll all be dead. Why should we save any of the livestock? Let's slay all the sheep and have one final, gluttonous feast. Quick — bring out the wine barrels. We'll go out stoned!"

So they danced and drank on the rooftops, watching as the enemy moved into place: Chariots lined up in row after row. Battering rams rolled into position. Legions of cavalrymen stood battle ready. Already, breaches were being made in the wall. In just a few more hours, it would all be over. The citizens of Jerusalem knew they were going to die — that they were facing eternity.

I would like to tell you that at the hour of the reality of death, people flocked to the temple to pray. I would like to tell you that they sought out Isaiah, begging him to tell them how to change God's mind and remove the enemy from their gates. But they didn't. Fatalism had already taken over — and the people preferred to face death as atheists!

Up to this point they could have been saved. The Spirit was still calling them to repentance. But now, no amount of mercy, fear or warnings could move them. It was as if they lifted their wine glasses in a toast to God and laughed in His face: "Here's to You, God. See you in hell!"

This was the final indignity against God — the trigger of judgment! And, beloved, the very same attitude is rampant in America today. Our nation is characterized by what has been called the "sensuality of despair." The thinking is, "I know I'm going to hell. But I don't want God in my face!" America has stuck its nose up at God!

Why Such a Message, When It Sounds So Gloomy?

You may be wondering: What is the purpose of a message like this? Why would God want me to share such a prophecy? I believe there are several reasons:

1. To keep us focused on things above, so that we don't become entangled with the world.

2. To remind us that God is always seeking out people who will stand in the gap, praying for the nation and their fellow human beings.

3. To awaken us to the shortness of time.

4. To remind us of Jesus' words to His disciples: "And now I have told you before it come to pass, that, when it is come to pass, ye might believe" *(John 14:29)*. "And take heed to yourselves, lest at any time your hearts be overcharged with surfeiting, and drunkenness, and cares of this life, and so that day come upon you unawares" *(Luke 21:34)*.

Perhaps you're thinking, "Brother Dave, I don't know how to react when I read this. I feel so downcast." No! That isn't the reaction of one who is prepared to go home to be with the Lord. Dying is a promotion. Jesus lovingly told us that when we see these things beginning to happen, we are to look up and rejoice — because our redemption is drawing close!

There is no need to be afraid. God hasn't given us a spirit of fear about such things, but a spirit of power, love and a sound mind. Look up — your Savior is drawing near!